THE
RUSSIANS
AT SEA

DAVID WOODWARD

THE
RUSSIANS
AT SEA

A History of the Russian Navy

FREDERICK A. PRAEGER, *Publishers*
New York · Washington

BOOKS THAT MATTER
Published in the United States of America in 1966
by Frederick A. Praeger, Inc., Publishers
111 Fourth Avenue, New York, N. Y. 10003

Library of Congress Catalog Card Number: 66-12477·

Printed in the United States of America

CONTENTS

Chapter   *page*

Maps 7–10

Introduction 11

I Into the Baltic (1703–1725) 20

II Into the Black Sea (1695–1738) 32

III The Battle for the Baltic (1725–1761) . . . 37

IV The First Russian Armada (1769–1774) . . 42

V Wars on Two Fronts: The Black Sea and the Baltic 57
(1787–1791) . . . .

VI War against—and for—Napoleon
Part 1: The Baltic (1795–1814) . . . 72

VII War against—and for—Napoleon
Part 2: The Mediterranean (1798–1808) . . 81

VIII Navarino (1827) 90

IX The Crimean War (1853–1856) 98

X The First Torpedo War (1876–1877) . . . 107

XI Course for Port Arthur (1904) 117

XII Course for Vladivostock (1905) 135

XIII Tsushima (1905) 146

XIV 'The Old Corruptive Influences' (1905–1914) . 156

XV The Baltic and the Black Sea (1914–1917) . . 165

XVI The Revolution (1917–1921) 180

XVII Launching the Red Fleet (1921–1941) . . . 197

XVIII Second World War (1941–1945) 209

XIX The Past Twenty Years (1945–1965) . . . 226

Acknowledgments 239

Index 243

TO
LIZ
WITH
LOVE

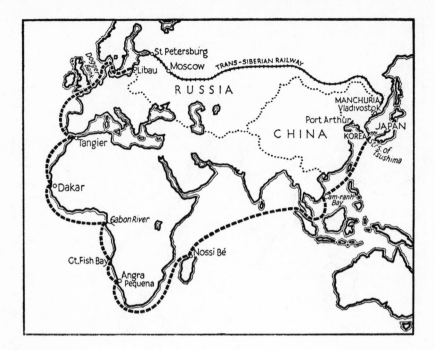

Page 7: Admiral Rozhestvensky's route
Pages 8 and 9: The Eastern Mediterranean
Page 10: The Baltic

7

E.G.Morton

INTRODUCTION

The Soviet navy which is now built round atomic submarines equipped with rockets with nuclear warheads and homing torpedoes is able to fight effectively against an enemy navy on the distant approaches to the Soviet shores.—*Marshal Rodion Malinovsky, the Soviet Minister of Defence*

Our navy is a modern fighting force, equipped with powerful rocket-nuclear weapons, capable of performing the duties entrusted to it far beyond our territorial waters. Ours is a fleet of modern, including nuclear-powered, submarines, a fleet of rocket-carrying strike planes and a fleet of surface rocket craft. The navy by the nature of its armament, its highly manoeuvrable forces and its combat facilities must be ready at any time and anywhere in the world to ensure the defence of the interests of our State. We consider that the main striking force in the struggle at sea is the submarine fleet.—*From an interview with Admiral of the Fleet S. G. Gorschkov, Soviet Navy, published October 31st, 1962*

Our atomic submarines are capable of reaching rapidly and undetected any point in the oceans of the world and destroying any target at sea or on the coast of any aggressors.—*Comment by Tass agency on the foregoing.*

TODAY the Russian navy is the second in the world. With its vast fleet of submarines, with its raiding cruisers, camouflaged auxiliaries, missiles, nuclear and otherwise, mines and torpedoes, it is a very formidable force. It is equipped to take part in any sort of war that Russia desires, from an all-out nuclear conflict to gun-running on behalf of local Communist parties or their friends anywhere in the world.

About forty years ago, in 1921, Lenin was on the verge of ordering the whole navy to be scrapped on the ground that keeping it in existence was a sheer waste of material and manpower.

Ten years later, despite Lenin's reprieve, the Russian navy was still only a collection of obsolete and semi-obsolete ships whose designs were pre-World War I, and which very rarely emerged from the Baltic or the Black Sea.

Ten years later still, by 1940, a beginning had been made with the construction of a new navy, with battleships, cruisers, submarines and

11

the rest. Work, however, had hardly been begun when Russia was attacked by Germany in the summer of 1941. Almost all construction stopped and the ships which did exist were unable to play any significant part in operations. This may in part have been due to the fact that the cadres of Russian naval officers had suffered a great deal from the Stalinist purges of the late 1930s.

Within a few years of the end of the Second World War the Russian navy was already second in size amongst the navies of the world, having overtaken the British navy during the run-down of British forces which took place immediately after 1945.

The last decade has seen the Russian navy consolidate its position. Brand-new ships have replaced those which have become obsolete, new weapons have been introduced, and the emphasis which, in the ten or fifteen years following 1945, had been divided between large cruisers and submarines shifted to submarines exclusively. In the background, a powerful mining force has always been a traditional element of Russian seapower since mines were first used against the British and French fleets in the Crimean War.

An indication of the extent to which the Russians felt that their position as a great naval power was at last consolidated came in 1955, when, for the first time, it was possible for Western observers to get a clear idea of the amount of naval construction which had been going on in the ten years following the end of the Second World War. The occasion for this was the visit of a British squadron to Leningrad as one of the manifestations of improved East-West relations which followed the post-Stalin thaw.

British naval officers and correspondents watched fascinated from the upperworks of the aircraft carrier *Triumph*, the British flagship, as their ship steamed past the harbour of Kronstadt, packed with modern warships, and up the River Neva to Leningrad itself, past berth after berth occupied by cruisers, destroyers and submarines building or completing. For years behind a smoke screen, half propaganda and half security, the Russians were believed to be building a great fleet, but there were few in the British ships or ashore in the West who were not surprised to find how much had been achieved, and how true were the reports which many had previously rejected as exaggerations.

In the background was the thought that this was only what the Russians wanted to show, just part of one of their fleets in one of their ports, albeit the most important. As a matter of fact, the British ships saw rather more than the Russians were prepared to show on the way out, and a real smoke screen was hastily deployed across some of the berths when *Triumph* came down the Neva at the end of her visit. However, the Russians, who have never had any aircraft carriers and were unfamiliar with their design, forgot to take into account their very great height out of the water, which provided on this occasion an excellent vantage-point from which it was possible to see over the top of the smoke screen. So the squadron left Kronstadt.

This British visit to Leningrad, and a reciprocal one by the Russian warships to Portsmouth at the same time, stimulated as much curiosity as it had satisfied so far as the Russian ships were concerned. A few months later the disappearance of Commander Crabbe, one of Britain's most famous diving experts, was linked with another call paid by a Russian warship to Portsmouth, when Marshal Bulganin and Mr. Khrushchev arrived for a visit in May 1956, on board the *Ordzhonikidze*. This ship handled so beautifully that there was a great deal of speculation ashore as to the arrangement of her screws and rudders and it is likely that curiosity on this score led to Crabbe's death.

Since those days of the first post-Stalin thaw we have had a number of thaws and freeze-ups of East-West relations, coupled with a steady trickle of information which shows that, thaw or freeze, the Russian navy increases every year in strength, both in numbers and in quality. No doubt this increase holds some nasty surprises for us in the future, but for the time being from a material point of view we can estimate pretty justly the strength of the Russian fleet.

What is much more obscure, however, is the professional quality of the officers and men of this fleet. Great courage and endurance, certainly the equal of that displayed by any other fighting service in the world, are clearly there. Technical skill, whether exhibited by the High Command or a radar mechanic, we know much less about; nor do we know much about the quality of material, though a nation which can make sputniks can be presumed to make good submarines, mines, torpedoes, anti-submarine detection equipment and the like. The fact still remains that the exercise of seapower in a war of any sort, great or small, is something which resembles nothing else in the world. The only guide that can be provided is the past, despite the fact that so much has changed, socially and technically throughout the world, and above all in Russia itself.

Of the lessons which are to be learnt there is, in the first place, the superhuman manner in which the Russians overcame difficulties in order to produce a navy at all. All the other navies in the world have grown from a sea coast, a merchant navy or fishing fleet and a sea-faring population. The Russian navy was instituted by Peter the

Great without a sea coast either on the Black Sea or the Baltic. Therefore there were no fishing or merchant fleets and no seamen to work the ships. In addition there was, of course, no shipbuilding industry. However, the first Baltic and Black Sea fleets were built, thanks to a lavish use of manpower, scores or hundreds of miles from the sea on the inland waterways of Russia. Crews were provided by professional soldiers, by foreigners, by conscripts or by the watermen of the rivers; almost none of these men, except the foreigners, had ever seen the sea.

In western Europe and on the Atlantic navies developed to protect merchant shipping. This did not happen in Russia, for there was no merchant shipping. The duty of the new fleets was to obtain the required outlets to the sea. All that existed when the building of the navy began was a limitless supply of poor-quality timber and a very nearly limitless supply of brave, hardy and quite untrained men. These two factors, in the hands of Peter the Great, were sufficient to form a navy. This navy consisted mostly of coastal vessels, but it was powerful enough to decide the struggle for the command of the Baltic and thus the outcome of the Great Northern War, which set Russia upon the path to world power.

How much the navy had been solely the work of Peter the Great was made clear when he died. His immediate successors as rulers of Russia, as well as the soldiers of whom he had made sailors, lost interest in his great creation and a long period of slackness followed, which lasted until the accession of Catherine the Great and later of her crazy son, Paul I. Both these rulers once again showed what fleets could do for Russia in her struggles with her two nearest enemies to north and south—Sweden and Turkey.

In addition, during the American War of Independence the influence of Russian seapower was felt for the first time outside the Baltic and the Black Sea, when the Armed Neutrality of the North came into being and Catherine threatened to turn off the tap of naval supplies from the Baltic when displeased by the interference with Russian trade provided by the British blockade. It must be underlined that, in the eighteenth and early nineteenth centuries, the Baltic with its supplies of hemp, tar and wood was akin to the Middle East oilfields of today as far as the maintenance of both naval and merchant fleets were concerned. When Catherine protested, the protest had to be heeded.

During the early part of the French Revolutionary wars a Russian squadron served in the North Sea under British orders. Later, tempted by Napoleon, Paul I resuscitated the Armed Neutrality with the co-operation of Denmark and Sweden, until Nelson's victory at Copenhagen in 1800 and Paul's murder broke up the combination.

Alexander I, who succeeded his father Paul as Tsar, took little interest in the navy, which once again suffered a decline. When, after a long and unsuccessful flirtation with Napoleon, Alexander found himself invaded by the French in 1812, plans were made for the Russian Baltic fleet to save itself by taking refuge in British ports.

The long period of peace between the Treaty of Vienna and the outbreak of the Crimean War was broken, for the Russians, by their participation in the Battle of Navarino, alongside the British and French fleets, and one more Russo-Turkish war which followed. By 1853, under Nicholas I, there were two strong Russian fleets in existence, one in the Baltic and one in the Black Sea. The Black Sea fleet opened the war by destroying the Turkish fleet at Sinope on the northern coast of Anatolia, thanks to the use of guns firing explosive shells, a huge novelty in naval warfare. Despite this excellent start, when the British and French fleets appeared before Sevastopol, the Russian fleet could find nothing better to do than scuttle itself. In the Baltic, the Russian battle fleet shut itself up in its home ports and made no effort to interfere with the combined operations of the Allies.

When the Crimean War was over, the Russians for the third time in their history signed as part of a peace treaty an agreement not to maintain a fleet in the Black Sea. This, however, like its two predecessors, was denounced by St. Petersburg at an opportune moment—in 1870, when the French were involved in the Franco-Prussian War. As the British were unwilling to act on their own, there was no obstacle to the rebuilding of the Black Sea fleet.

In the meantime in the Baltic a beginning had been made with the building of a fleet of ironclads, and thanks to Russian and foreign shipbuilders there followed, within less than a generation, a fleet which was second in size only to that of the United Kingdom. Geography and the demands of Russian foreign policy made it necessary that this navy should be kept in three widely separated seas, the Baltic, the Black Sea and the Pacific. When war with Japan came in 1904 the Black Sea fleet was neutralised and the Baltic and Pacific fleets were separately destroyed by a Japanese fleet which was hardly as strong as either one of them.

In the few years left to the Tsarist régime the construction of yet another fleet was begun. But in 1914 this was not strong enough to exercise a serious influence in the Baltic, although the Black Sea fleet, with a backbone of modern battleships, was able to exercise a large degree of command of the sea, despite raids by the two celebrated German warships *Goeben* and *Breslau*.

In 1917 the Russian navy in the Baltic collapsed in mutiny and the contagion in the following year spread to the Black Sea. Preliminary rumblings had been seen from the beginning of the Russo-Japanese War onwards, with the mutiny of the battleship *Kniaz Potemkin Tavricheski*—*Potemkin* for short—as the most notorious incident.

During the Revolution the sailors of the Baltic fleet were in the van of the Red forces, from the time when the cruiser *Avrora* brought down the last legitimate Government by firing blank ammunition against the Winter Palace on the Neva. But when the Russian civil war ended there was great disappointment as the nature of the Communist régime became clear. The crews of the ships immured in the ice at Kronstadt mutinied at the beginning of 1921 and were put down mercilessly. It was then that the exasperated Lenin proposed that the whole navy be scrapped and its personnel demobilised.

For about fifteen years after the Kronstadt mutiny the Russian navy might almost have been abolished, for it consisted of only a very scratch collection of warships, all of pre-1914 design, manned by crews whose only tradition of which boast could be made was a purely revolutionary one. Only much later was appeal made to the traditions of the Tsarist fleets. In the 1920s it was difficult to take the Russian navy seriously. On the one occasion when the Russians did, consciously or unconsciously, give a clear picture of the shape of things to come they seemed grotesque.

This occurred in 1924 at the Rome disarmament conference, when representatives of all the naval powers (except the big five—Britain, the United States, Japan, France and Italy, already limited by the Washington Treaty of 1922) met to discuss the reductions of their naval armaments. The Russians firmly claimed that in their case there should be no question of a reduction in naval armaments, but rather that they should have the right to build an entirely new fleet almost as large as that fixed as maximum by the Washington Treaty for the fleets of Britain and the United States, which were each permitted fifteen capital ships, while at that time Russia possessed only three.

After this conference Baltic mists once again descended on the principal Russian fleet and it was not until ten years later that the rebuilding of the Russian navy began on a large scale. This passed virtually unnoticed in the Western world, but a good deal more was known about it in Germany and Italy, for it was to Nazi and Fascist experts that the Communists turned for aid. German submarine designs and Italian plans for cruisers and destroyers were adopted and under German and Italian supervision work began. A year or so later, while this work still went on, the aid of German and Italian 'volunteers' at sea made it possible for General Franco's fleet to prevent Russian aid from reaching the legitimate Spanish Government during the decisive months of the Civil War.

At the same time that this clear example of the influence of sea-power on the history of the 1930s was being given, another series of events in Russia itself was undermining nearly all the work being done for the construction of a new navy. The great Stalinist purges of these years seem to have struck with especial force against the Red navy and almost all the officers qualified by experience for command of fleets, squadrons, flotillas or individual ships died or at least disappeared.

In August 1939 came the Russo-German agreement. This was the last phase in the story of the rebuilding of the Russian navy with German help. The Russians tendered an impressive list of demands; the Germans stone-walled in a masterly fashion to avoid doing anything important about them and this stone-walling was still going on when the Germans invaded Russia on Midsummer Day 1941.

The German attack took the Russians largely by surprise, but despite the great German victories of the early months it was impossible for them to destroy the Red army, which was able to carry out successfully a series of operations unparalleled in history by their extent and by the intensity of the fighting which took place. The Red navy was never strong enough to take a leading part in the war; there were, it was true, some 200 submarines divided between the Baltic, the Black Sea, the White Sea and the Pacific, but, apart from a sprinkling of medium-sized modern surface craft, that was all.

Nevertheless it was surprising that Russian naval forces in the Baltic and the Black Sea were unable to make any considerable showing against the enemy. In the Baltic the Germans used command of the air and laying of minefields across the Gulf of Finland to keep what there was of the Russian fleet pinned in its bases at Kronstadt and Leningrad, while the Russian submarines which emerged were able to achieve very little.

It was a disappointing performance, but what happened in the Black Sea was almost as disappointing, for there, opposed to a Russian fleet of a capital ship, cruisers, destroyers and submarines, was literally nothing except four obsolete Rumanian destroyers and later some small German submarines brought down the Danube. At first the Russians were able to use their superiority at sea to replenish

17

their garrisons in the beleaguered ports of Odessa and Sevastopol. Later, thanks to the Luftwaffe, the Germans were able to command most of the surface of the Black Sea and drive what was left of the Russian fleet—insufficiently supported by the Russian air force—back into the few ports which at the time of the greatest German success were left in Russian possession.

The Russian Pacific fleet was not engaged until the last few days of the war against Japan, when it carried out some well-planned combined operations after Japanese command of the air and the sea had been destroyed by the Americans.

When the Second World War was over the navies of Germany and Japan had entirely disappeared, the Italian navy was a shadow of its former self and the British navy had started a run-down which would reduce it by four-fifths of its total tonnage, while the United States navy was bigger than all the other navies of the world put together.

Russia had suffered enormously on land and it would seem that internal reconstruction would receive overwhelming priority in Russia's post-war planning, especially as she already possessed a huge army and air force. Nevertheless, despite the comparatively small amount that the navy had been able to contribute to Russia's war, it was decided that an all-out effort should be made to build it up on a scale which was to make it the second largest in the world, far exceeding in tonnage and manpower the British navy, and with the capability of challenging, in a non-nuclear war on shipping, the navy of the United States.

The Russian naval effort was for many years independent of the parallel Russian effort being made to catch up with the United States in nuclear weapons. Only within the last year or so has the Russian navy, with Polaris-type submarines, been in a position to contribute to the Soviet nuclear threat against targets anywhere in the world. Previously, the fleet of submarines coming off the ways at a rate of seventy or eighty boats a year would have been of value only in a 'limited' (i.e. non-nuclear) war. Now there is a comparatively small number of Polaris-type submarines, but the main body of Soviet nuclear strength still relies on land-based missiles. However this state of affairs may not continue for long.

Parallel with the threat of nuclear missiles is the threat of the conventional Russian submarine fleet which has the potential, in any non-nuclear war, of being able to starve out the United Kingdom and to cut the communications between the United States and the NATO powers of Western Europe. Faced by this threat without a sufficient conventional anti-submarine counterforce of fixed-wing aircraft, helicopters and ships, the only answer would be to use nuclear weapons.

The Soviet navy has three potentials: it could participate in a nuclear war with its Polaris-type missiles; it could be used in a non-nuclear war to command the Atlantic; or it could, by trying to command the Atlantic, cause NATO to start a nuclear war, even though it did not wish to do so. Thus the navy is to be reckoned as a vital part of the forces with which the Soviet Union backs its policy, and is therefore well worth study. A sufficiently clear idea of its numerical and technical strength can be gained from the pages of the current *Jane's Fighting Ships*, but further, and perhaps equally important to an understanding of Soviet seapower today, is the history of the Russian navy, which is a fleet now so large that it has approximately eight times as many men serving afloat as has the British navy.

CHAPTER I

INTO THE BALTIC

1703–1725

F OR twenty years at the beginning of the eighteenth century the Great Northern War involved the Baltic powers. It is a war almost without historians in our language; only occasionally did it touch the affairs of England, and then occasionally the English and later the British fleet intervened in it, first on one side and then on the other, though never to the extent of waging what came nearest, in those days, to 'total war'.

But total war of the time did go on for twenty years between Sweden and Russia; there the biggest issues were at stake, and in the course of the fighting the futures of Sweden and Russia were settled for good. Sweden, once the ruler of nearly all the Baltic coast and much more besides—a seemingly great power—was never again to be anything more than a power of the second rank. Russia, a dark land, unknown in quantity and quality, appeared at the end of the war as a power of the first rank and has never since ceased to be one.

The Russian success was the tangible outcome of the struggle between Peter the Great and Charles XII of Sweden, whose fantastic personalities and deeds throw almost the only light there is upon these battles of long ago.

Of the outbreak of this war perhaps all that needs to be said is that Peter the Great, at last firmly on the throne after uncertain years at home and abroad, and Charles XII, then only seventeen years old, were both looking for an opportunity to wage war for the expansion of their territories. The opportunity came in 1699 with a dispute between Sweden's enemy Denmark and the Duchy of Holstein. Sweden automatically became the Duchy's friend and espoused its cause in a quarrel over the violation of an agreement for frontier demilitarisation or disengagement. Russia was already engaged in a war with Turkey, endeavouring, not very successfully as we shall see later, to cut her way out of the heartland of eastern Europe to a port on the Black Sea. Despite this, however, and despite the dangers of a war on two fronts, Peter entered the war against Sweden with great enthusiasm and at once set to work to capture an outlet on the Baltic.

This took three years to accomplish, but by 1703 the Swedish fort of Nyenschantz was in Russian hands.

The first naval engagement in Baltic waters in which the Russian fleet took part and from which they gained their first seagoing ship took place just after the fall of Nyenschantz, when two Swedish vessels—one of twelve guns and one a longboat—sent to find out the fate of the garrison of that place, were trapped amongst the shallows at the mouth of the Neva and, after a fierce fight, taken by Russian small craft. The senior Swedish survivor was the mate of the twelve-gun ship, Charles van Werden, whose courage and ability so impressed the Tsar that he invited van Werden to join his own service, an offer which was accepted.

Upon the site of Nyenschantz, Peter began to build his new capital, St. Petersburg, which under that name, and as Petrograd and Leningrad, has been one of the key points of world history ever since. To protect the new city, which was built in a marsh at the cost of a quarter of a million lives of his own subjects, Peter built the fortress of Peter and Paul, the tall spire of which is still one of the features of the Leningrad skyline. On Kotlin island at the mouth of the River Neva, which links Leningrad with the sea, he constructed the fortress and naval base of Kronstadt. Foundations for the forts there were provided by great stone-filled wooden boxes measuring 30 feet × 15 feet × 10 feet, which were sunk in required places, Peter carrying out much of the surveying himself, lead line in hand.

But before Peter obtained his toehold on the sea and all this work could be completed, there had been considerable naval fighting, miles from the sea, on the waters of Lakes Ladoga and Peipus, between Swedish small craft and Russians brought from Voronezh on the Don, the Russians' old base in the fight against the Turks. The journey from Voronezh to the lakes meant a move of some 600 miles in a straight line, but in fact the distance travelled was much greater than that, mostly by the Don and the Volga. The journey ended, however, with the boats being pulled by men and beasts across plains and through forests where no roads ran.

This transport of a force of small vessels and of building materials overland—it took three years to move a given quantity of timber from the forest to the shipyard—as well as similar operations which had already been carried out in the war against the Turks, were early examples of the way in which the Russians were to bend events to their will by improvisation and the ruthless use of the lives of great numbers of men, women and children. The fighting that followed saw the beginnings of the traditional Russian way of warfare with the use of the great areas of their country and their vast population to defeat forces much smaller but generally much better trained and equipped.

In 1700 Charles XII, then eighteen years old, defeated Peter at the Battle of Narva and started off for the heart of Russia as Napoleon, Hindenburg and Hitler were to do after him. Charles shared the fate of the first and last of these at Poltava in 1709; had he had any idea of what St. Petersburg and Kronstadt were to mean in terms of the future of Russia and the Russian navy and concentrated on their recapture, much history would have been very different. Peter made no mistake about this matter.

Once the Swedish army had been destroyed at Poltava the way was open for Peter to concentrate on the vital area—the Baltic coast. Using his army to secure bases for his fleet during the year 1710, he occupied Reval (now Tallin), Riga and Elbing (now Elblag). Viborg (Viipuri) was taken in the same year by an assault from the sea, Peter leading his amphibious forces in a small boat burning a bright flare, which lit up for those who followed the way into the harbour through the shallows and past the enemy batteries. The credit for this action and for much else achieved by the fleet in these campaigns Peter gave to his naval commander-in-chief, the first Russian admiral, Feodor Apraxin, under whose orders Peter himself was serving with what was literally the *nom de guerre* of Mihailov, and the rank of rear-admiral.

The career of Apraxin had been as much of an improvisation as had been the building of his fleet which had taken place on the banks of a river 600 miles from the sea. He had started life as a soldier and had been transferred to high command in the navy in much the same way as Blake, Deane and Monk during the English Civil War in a similar emergency. It would seem that Apraxin was one of the few officers of Peter who could dispute with him on great matters and who could control and keep the goodwill of Peter's foreign naval mercenaries, English, Scottish, Dutch, Swiss, Norwegian, Greek, Italian and the rest. One of the English officers who served under him has thus described him:

> Frederick Count Apraxin . . . related at a distance to the Tsar is about 64 years of age, of a moderate height, well-made, fair, inclining to feed, curious [careful] of his hair, [which is] very long and now grey, and generally wears it tied up with a ribbon. A native cleanliness adds a lustre to the dignity of his magnificent mien, wherein he surpasses all the noblemen of his years in Russia . . . you observe an incomparable economy, order and decency in his house, gardens, domestics and dress and all . . . unanimously vote in behalf of his excellent temper; but he

22

loves to have men comport themselves according to their rank, and expects from all that approach him a due and adequate respect; nor dare the Court buffoons, even in the presence of the Tsar take their usual liberties in Count Apraxin's palace. Sobriety and early rising greatly recommend to his notice.[1]

Apraxin had the rare qualities which were needed in order to form and to command a new navy fighting a vital war, and by 1714 the offensive had passed to the Russians. This led to the first Russian naval victory, the Battle of Gangut, a name taken from the Russian transliteration of the scene of the fighting—Hangö Ud, or Hangö Head.

War in the Baltic was, of course, a seasonal matter because of the ice; with the coming of the spring thaw the Swedes that year had been first off the mark, sending squadrons to threaten Åbo, Helsingfors, Reval and Narva.

Peter countered by taking eighteen sailing vessels to Reval to act as a diversion, while Apraxin with ninety-nine galleys and transports carrying an expeditionary force of 24,000 men, moved westward along the northern shore of the Gulf of Finland, planning to seize the Aland Islands and threaten Stockholm. The galley fleet, mostly commanded by Greeks and Italians who had had experience of war under oars in the Mediterranean, was much looked down upon by the Russian sailing navy, but in this action it was to lay the foundations of Russian seapower.

On July 10th, after preliminary engagements between the two fleets, Apraxin found his way westward barred by a fleet of Swedish ships of the line. He summoned Peter from Reval and retired under the shelter of Hangö Head to await rescue. The Swedish commander-in-chief, Admiral Wattrang, on August 4th sent Rear-Admiral Ehrenskiold to destroy Apraxin before Peter arrived; the Tsar, leaving his big ships behind, arrived in a galley and set about rescuing his commander-in-chief. In order to attack the Swedes from two directions he ordered that some of the galleys be carried overland across the narrow spit of land leading out to Hangö Head and re-launched on the other side. In that way he hoped that, while the Swedes watched the Russians to the eastward of the Head, they would be taken from the westward in the rear by the galleys which would have come overland.

To deal with this double threat Wattrang had to split his fleet;

---

[1] Pp. 77–78, from *History of the Russian Fleet during the Reign of Peter the Great, by a contemporary Englishman* (1724). Navy Records Society, 1899. Edited by Vice-Admiral Sir Cyprian Bridge.

Ehrenskiold in his flagship *Stockholm* (sixty-eight guns), with some light craft, was sent to meet the Russians who were crossing the spit, while his second-in-command, Lillje, took eight ships of the line as close inshore as possible to deal with that part of the Russian force, to the eastward, who were not crossing over. Apraxin, seeing the force gathered to meet the boats which were crossing the spit, gave up the idea of the crossing, after one boat had been got over and another so badly damaged that she was out of action.

To Apraxin it seemed that the only solution was to send his galleys round Hangö Head by sea, through the Swedish fleet. Twenty of the galleys, each propelled by twenty-six oars, set out; it was growing dark and the Russians got past Lillje unseen. They were spotted at last light by Wattrang, who decided to wait until daylight to attack. It was a bad mistake, for next morning there was no wind. The big Swedish sailing ships were becalmed while the Russian galleys could move as they wished; to catch them some of the Swedish big ships got out their own small boats which, under oars, began to pull the ships of line into position, while others laid kedge anchors out ahead on which they pulled, advancing with painful slowness, while the Russians could be seen concentrating some sixty galleys between the forces of Wattrang and Ehrenskiold, but out of range.

Ehrenskiold then withdrew up a narrow fiord across the mouth of which he sank a blockship. The Russians followed and summoned him to surrender. He sent a rude answer and on the afternoon of August 6th Apraxin sent thirty-five galleys to destroy him; the attack failed. A second attack by eighty galleys also failed, but Apraxin collected everything that he had, and a third attack went in, against the line of Swedish ships lying head to stern across the fiord.

The Russians concentrated on the left of the line—on the Swedish galley *Trana*. The Russian boarding parties swept over the little vessel and literally sank her by the weight of their numbers as they clambered aboard. The Swedish line was now broken and the Russians, passing through the gap, moved along what remained of the line, taking ship after ship, one after another, for the Swedes were moored and could not come to each other's help, while the Russians could mass as many galleys as the fiord would hold to attack the individual Swedes from seaward and from inshore at the same time.

The Swedish casualties were 361 killed, while the rest of Ehrenskiold's force of over 900 men were prisoners. Of these only 200 seem to have survived their first six weeks in Russian hands. One of them, however, was Ehrenskiold, who was very chivalrously treated.

There is considerable dispute as to whether Peter personally took part in this action; the author of *The History of the Russian Fleet under Peter the Great* claims that the Tsar watched from the shore, but Russian legend has it that he took a leading part in the action. Whoever was responsible for the Russian success, it was a famous victory, the first major battle that the Russian navy had ever won; although what had been fought was not a fleet action, but only an engagement between the light oared craft of both sides.

The Swedish battle fleet withdrew. The Russians accordingly were able to seize the Åland Islands with a force of 16,000 men and Apraxin sent galleys to raid the Swedish ports on the coast of the Gulf of Bothnia. But winter was coming on, the Baltic was freezing, and the campaign ended in mid-November, the Swedes going to Karlskrona in the south of their country and the Russians to Nystadt, near Åbo in Finland.

Russia was now a first-class naval power. Every year, down to Soviet times, the anniversary of Gangut was celebrated by the Russian navy; neglected for a space, its glories were recalled during the war against Germany in 1941–5, when the victories of Tsarist days were refurbished and extolled as an aid to morale. Although in the last 250 years the Russian navy has been through great triumphs and even greater disasters, since that battle it has been a force which neither Russia's enemies nor Russia's friends could ignore. Gangut, following on Poltava, made Russia a great power.

Sweden was now vastly overextended—her population was a little more than a million—for her resources both on sea and on land were those of a power of the second rank, but the Great Northern War, that most untidy of European struggles, went on nevertheless. For years, Britain's first concern, and that of her allies, was to try and prevent the spread of the conflict. Intervention by the Prussians against the Swedes, for example, would have meant troops diverted to the Northern War which, according to Marlborough and his allies, would have been much better employed fighting the French.

But by 1715 the War of the Spanish Succession was over and George I was king of the United Kingdom and, as well, Elector of Hanover. His countries' war over he soon permitted himself the luxury of becoming embroiled with Charles XII, who after five years' internment by his allies the Turks after Poltava, was now back in his native land and prepared once more to become master of northern and eastern Europe.

The cause of the new embroilment was twofold; first, in his capacity as Elector of Hanover, George I had bought some loot—the towns of Bremen and Verden—which the Danes had taken from the Swedes; Charles demanded them back, George I refused. At the same time British interests were being damaged by the Swedes' claiming and exercising a right to interfere with neutral shipping in the Baltic. Accordingly a British fleet of eighteen ships of the line under Admiral Sir John Norris arrived in the Baltic early in July. With it was a Dutch force of twelve ships of the line, for the Dutch, too, were neutral in this war and had had their trade interfered with by the Swedes. Convoyed by the Anglo-Dutch fleet was a large number of merchantmen; the Anglo-Dutch command was simply under orders to see that these merchantmen were not interfered with; if they were not molested, they were not to take the offensive.

This is the first instance which we have met of the importance with which the maritime powers—and notably Britain and Holland—regarded freedom of access to the Baltic—the principal source of shipbuilding materials—timber, hemp, tar, flax. As we have seen, closing the Baltic in those days was like cutting off supplies of oil from the Middle East in our own times.

In the meantime the main body of the Swedish fleet was in the southern Baltic, near Bornholm, and the Russians were putting to sea from their base at Reval. Norris went to meet them, bringing some British warships purchased by the Russians. These and other former British ships in the Russian navy mostly retained their English names, the spelling of which, transliterated from Latin characters into Cyrillic and back again into Latin, sometimes look very odd: *Ritchmond, Britania, Viktoria, Straford, Lansdou* (Landsdowne), *Arondel, Oksford.*

A number of demonstrations of Anglo-Russian friendship took place and the combined British and Russian fleets put to sea under the command of Peter, together with Dutch and Danish forces.

The Swedish fleet defending Stockholm remained in harbour; whether by acting the role of 'the fleet in being' it prevented a Russian landing on the Swedish coast is not clear, but there is more than a suggestion that secret negotiations were in progress between Peter and Charles, arch-enemies though they were in public, for a joint attack on Copenhagen, despite the fact that the Danes were the allies of the Russians.

In any event, these reports of plotting between Charles and Peter were in part responsible for the failure of the Russian-British-Dutch-Danish alliance to carry out a landing on the coast of South Sweden which had been planned for 1716. To take part in this landing, ostensibly, Peter sent an expeditionary force of 40,000 men into

Danish waters, which caused the Danes such alarm that they spent the whole of the summer moving their fleet so that it was always between their Russian allies and Copenhagen. Eventually the landing in South Sweden was fixed for September 21st, but four days previously Peter cancelled the operation and a little later the Allied fleet broke up, the various ships returning to their home ports.

Operations continued in the southern Baltic and North Sea between the Swedish and Danish fleets without either side gaining a decisive advantage. During this lull the British and Russians continued to co-operate until 1718, when Charles was killed invading Norway, which was then a part of the Danish realm, as it remained until 1814.

In the next year Peter mounted another great amphibious expedition of thirty ships of the line and 150 galleys and transports, the latter carrying some 30,000 troops, to be used for raids on the Swedish coast. During the preparations for these operations three Russian ships captured a Swedish ship of the line, in an action which was the first success of the Russian sailing fleet, as distinct from the galleys.

In 1719 Sir John Norris and a British fleet returned to the Baltic, no longer as allies of the Danes and Russians, but as their enemies; the Russians' successes now gave them the same opportunity of disrupting Baltic trade that the Swedes had previously enjoyed, and to prevent this the British Government intervened to prevent the defeat of the Swedes. The fact that Admiral Norris had changed sides did not, however, affect the determination of Peter and Apraxin to attack Swedish soil. They themselves raided the skerries off Stockholm while other squadrons under their command attacked places along the coast; the Russians cruised down the coast as far south as Calmar, raiding and burning as they went, while to the north of Stockholm another force was operating in the same way. Finally, on July 26th a detachment of Cossacks landed on the mainland and attempted to raid Stockholm itself, but without success. A second attempt was made on August 14th, this time with 6,000 men, to take the Swedish capital; this also failed, the Russians being driven off by a single Swedish regiment.

Fred T. Jane, founder of *Jane's Fighting Ships* and author of *The Imperial Russian Navy*, points out that these Russian operations were carried out with complete disregard of the Swedish fleet, which might have appeared at any minute and, concentrated, attacked the isolated Russian squadrons scattered as they were along the coast. The Russian action completely violated the theory of the fleet in being, according to which the Russians should have kept their fleet

27

concentrated so long as the Swedish fleet was 'in being' and able to attack with overwhelming superiority smaller enemy groups.

How Peter and Apraxin were able to take this risk with impunity is not clear, but it must be remembered that Sweden with a tiny population had been at war for twenty years and was so short of men and money as to be on the verge of chaos. This may have been the explanation of the failure of the Swedish fleet to take advantage of the opportunities offered it.

The combined Anglo-Swedish fleet, consisting of twenty-two British ships of the line and eleven Swedish, continued to operate during 1720 with, it would seem, no specific plans, while Norris and Sparre, the Swedish admiral, quarrelled with each other.

At last, in the next year, 1721, after twenty-one years, the long confused Great Northern War came to an end with the Treaty of Nystadt, which confirmed Russia as a great power and as the first sea power in the Baltic as well. Russia ended the war with the provinces of Livonia, Estonia, Ingria, part of Courland, eastern Finland, including Viborg and an indemnity of 2,000,000 Riksdollars; thus she had a strip of coast reaching from Viborg down to Riga—twenty years before, all this had been Swedish.

Peter celebrated his victory with an enormous display in Moscow which included a full-size battleship dragged through the streets to show the inhabitants of the inland city what a big ship looked like; this ship was accompanied by smaller vessels on wheels or sleds with their crews rowing, taking soundings or aloft spreading canvas as they went through the town.

Together with the ships for his navy Peter had also built up the dockyards and training establishments which were necessary to create a force of professional naval officers and seamen to succeed the very brave amateurs and soldiers and the foreigners of greater or less skill who had been responsible for Russia's first victories at sea. The fact that Russia had had no coastline (except in the Far North) meant that she also had had no seamen; the lower deck appears to have been manned in about equal proportion by soldiers and boatmen from the inland waterways. The officers, as has been said, were a very mixed lot, either Russian soldiers or foreign mercenaries glad to leave their own countries for financial or political reasons (some at least of those from Great Britain were Jacobites in exile).

There is very little known about this seagoing foreign legion, apart from one source—a manuscript written in 1724 and entitled *History of the Russian Fleet during the Reign of Peter the Great, by a contemporary Englishman.* This was not published until 1897, when it appeared in

Russian; two years later it was published in English by the Navy Records Society and edited by Vice-Admiral Cyprian A. Bridge, as he then was.

The unknown writer of this manuscript is generally supposed to have been an Englishman who had served for some time in the Russian navy. Although there is no further clue to his identity, there are a good many, within the manuscript, as to his disposition. Like a good many others who have gone to Russia to work from the outside world, he was disgruntled by his experience, so much so, in fact, that much of his evidence is of doubtful value, both as regards the abilities of the Russians and as regards those of his foreign colleagues; as far as the former were concerned he was no doubt influenced by the fact that he seems to have received his pay at very irregular intervals, always in arrears and sometimes not at all, but this was the fate of everyone, it would seem, who ever worked for Peter the Great. Inflation of the rouble and various 'deductions and defalcations' reduced officers in the Russian service 'to very mean circumstances', according to the English writer.

Of shipbuilding the same writer said:

It is usual when an English master begins a ship, to order a Russian master to set up one near at hand, and the Russian must be indulged the liberty of observing and measuring the Englishman's work.

He added on manning problems:

It is very difficult for the Tsar to have any good warrant officers . . . because of the very ill usage they meet with from the lieutenants, generally Russians and men of little worth, upon the least provocation . . . Nor has he any great opportunities for forming seamen . . . for the Russians in general have an aversion to the sea.

Attempts to recruit young men of good family, it is claimed, also failed, though a number, in fact, did serve as volunteers with the British and Dutch fleets in the War of the Spanish Succession. Writing in 1724, the author says:

It being about twenty years since the Tsar began to build and rig his ships, he has a sufficient number of people tolerably skilled in fixing the rigging and going through all parts of a seaman's duty to be done ashore, or whilst the ship is in the haven, and yet are good for little at sea; and the great want he is in of able seamen outweighs all other difficulties he has to grapple with.

The reasons for this were in part, at least, geographical and to a considerable extent persist to this day. First, and most important, the long winters when the Baltic freezes and all shipping is sealed in harbour; in addition, and second, the fact that as the Baltic is not tidal 'some essentials in a seaman's duty are not to be learned by the ignorant'—at least in the eighteenth century.

An additional trouble was the fanaticism with which crews adhered to the rigorous discipline of their religious fasts; another complaint by the Englishman of 250 years ago was that they insisted on having a bath once a week, as otherwise they became 'verminous'. Whatever the dislike of many of the ratings for naval service some of the officers at least were anxious for plenty of sea time, urging Peter to undertake cruises to the Mediterranean and to send an expedition to secure the island of Tobago in the West Indies, to which he was said to have some claim by reason of his having seized the Duchy of Courland— but, says 'the contemporary Englishman', this was due to the fact that 'notwithstanding the glitter of their present state and outward appearance of satisfaction they [the naval officers] necessarily regard Russia no otherwise than as an unavoidable prison'.

Generally from this account we have a depressing picture of Russian seagoing efficiency and, although the author of it was un- doubtedly biased, his conclusions were borne out 200 years later by the French author Waliszewski, amongst others, who in his *Pierre le Grand* remarks, 'Peter strove with passion and complete lack of success to make the Russians a people of sailors'.

But even the sour author of *The Russian Fleet* ended on a slightly more encouraging note:

> During one or two summers on some few days, cruisers, continuing a good while at sea, took several prizes; and thereby the Russian common sailors permitted to taste of the sweets of success, were brought to a greater improvement than ordinary.

Certainly, whatever Peter's ambitions he rarely permitted himself excessive optimism as to the results which he had achieved, and even after his first successes at sea insisted that the Russian fleet should never attack unless it had a numerical superiority of at least one-third.

Summing up that which had been accomplished at sea during this reign, Dr. R. C. Anderson says in his *Naval Wars in the Baltic*:[1]

> The rise of the Russian navy was quite unparalleled. In a few years it had not only come into existence, but had risen to the foremost place in the Baltic . . . and this rise had taken place in spite of the active opposition of the Swedish fleet, which, up to the last few years of the war, was undoubtedly superior to the Russians in every way.

[1] C. Gilbert Wood, London, 1910.

During the Great Northern War itself attempts were made by both the Russians and the Swedes to carry hostilities to the very edge of the known world as it then was. The buccaneers of the West Indies had largely been expelled from that area and a number of them had moved to Madagascar, from bases on which island they hoped to resume their old profession. In order to obtain armed support against their enemies they appealed for help to both the Russians and the Swedes and both prepared expeditions to the island to seize it, but neither expedition succeeded in getting that far, and Madagascar was not directly involved in a major war until 1942.

However, one of the buccaneers, Narcross, expelled from the West Indies, instead of going to Madagascar and trying to arrange for the Russian-Swedish war to spread so far afield, went direct to the war and enlisted in the Swedish navy, and then in 1724, after the war was over, having been arrested by the Swedes for disloyal activities, escaped and joined the Russians.

CHAPTER II

INTO THE BLACK SEA
1695–1738

T HE victory of Gangut and the consolidation of Russian sea-power in the Baltic which followed has been chosen as the most appropriate place at which to begin the story of Russia as a sea power, but in fact the Russian navy had made its début as something of importance in world history some twenty years earlier, at the other end of the Empire on the waters of the Rivers Don and Dnieper and of the Sea of Azov and the Putrid Sea.

Before the Great Northern War had begun Peter had built a great river flotilla at Voronezh on the Don, and with this he proposed to descend the river and attack the Turkish position at the mouth. This was the fortress of Azov, between Taganrog and Rostov. His first attack, in 1695, had been unsuccessful because he had not been able to cut the Turkish supply lines which led to Azov through the sea of the same name and through the Black Sea. In the next year he attacked again, his flotillas being under the command of a Swiss admiral named Lefort. They worked their way down the various branches of the mouth of the Don, acting in co-operation with the Cossacks, who, as usual, were engaged in hostilities against the Turks which were half in the nature of a war of independence and half a series of border forays.

In this way Azov was taken and, at the same time, Russian flotillas attacked Turkish shipping off Otchakov and Akerman at the mouth of the Dnieper. These flotillas had not come down the Don, but had been built at Briansk on the River Desna, and all 118 of them had been brought through the inland waterways a distance of about 500 miles to the Black Sea.

Shortly after this a Russo-Turkish truce was agreed upon and during subsequent negotiations a Russian frigate was sent to Constantinople, where her crew caused some confusion by getting drunk and opening fire on the town; Russian historians claim that this had some influence on the Turkish decision to agree to an extended truce which was concluded in 1700 for a period of thirty years, in theory, but which in fact lasted for eleven years only.

In 1711 Charles XII, who had been interned by the Turks after his defeat at Poltava as already related, succeeded in persuading his gaolers—and allies—to attack the Russians, which they did with such success that within a few weeks Peter's army was on the verge of destruction at their hands.

Peter, with his eye on the struggle with Sweden in the Baltic, agreed to the Peace of Pruth, under the terms of which he surrendered Azov, dismantled the fortress of Taganrog and abolished his Black Sea fleet, the units of which were either surrendered to the Turks, scrapped, or transferred by inland waterways to the Baltic. Russia in future was to maintain no warships in the Black Sea—not the last time that she gave this undertaking. An indication of the size of the Russian Black Sea fleet which was now doomed and of the energy with which it had been built is given by the fact that it numbered no less than fifty-eight ships of the line, as compared with the total strength of ninety-eight ships of the line of the British navy at about that time, although in making comparisons it must be remembered that the Russian ships were mostly slightly smaller than the corresponding British or French ships of the epoch.

The use of the great rivers, early canals and portages over land to move ships from the Baltic to the Black Sea, or the Caspian or the White Sea, was a normal thing at the beginning of the eighteenth century. As ships became bigger it was no longer possible to move any but the smallest vessels until quite recently; now, however, 250 years after Peter the Great, Russia's inland waterways have been so developed that medium-sized warships and probably all types of submarines can be moved right across the country.

Of course, when Charles persuaded the Sultan of Turkey to attack the Russians he had high hopes of a joint Turkish-Swedish all-out war against Peter, but as soon as the Turks won their first success and its spoils—Azov and the destruction of the Russian Black Sea fleet—they withdrew from hostilities and left Charles to fight on alone, with the result that has been described in the preceding chapter. This action of Peter's in surrendering his gains in the south for the sake of a chance of a decisive victory in the north may, in some ways, be compared to the fashion in which Lenin in 1918–20 made great territorial concessions, first to the Germans and then to the Allies, in order to save his revolution. Just as a couple of decades later Lenin's successors were to return and take back the lands they had yielded—and more as well—so the successors of Peter the Great were to resume their struggle against Turkey as soon as the more immediate menace of Sweden had been overcome.

In the meantime Voronezh remained the principal Russian naval base looking southward, but it was clear that until the Crimea was in Russian hands they would have no chance of permanently establishing themselves on the Black Sea. Twice already, in 1687 and 1689, they had made unsuccessful attempts to take the peninsula by attack from the land.

It was to be some time after the Peace of Pruth that the Russians reappeared in the Black Sea, for at the end of the Swedish war Peter the Great turned his attention, not to the Turks and the Black Sea, but to the Persians and the Caspian.

In 1721 Persia was being invaded by the Afghans and appealed to both Russia and Turkey for help. An important Russian fleet descended the Volga and occupied Baku and Derbent; at the same time a Russo-Turkish agreement was signed for the division of any spoils that might be obtained either at the expense of the Afghan aggressors or at the expense of the Persian victims of aggression. The Russians claimed territories which they had already occupied, and these with little difficulty they retained; the Turks, on the other hand, demanded lands still in Persian possession, which, in fact, they never got.

The jealousy which this caused was another reason for the outbreak of the Second Russo-Turkish War in 1736. The Turks believed that sooner rather than later they would once again have to defend themselves against a Russian attack, and an arms race developed which was only temporarily halted by the death of Peter the Great in 1725.

Eleven years later, when Anne, niece of Peter, was Tsarina, Russo-Turkish hostilities began again and, in alliance with the Austrians, the Russians started off for Constantinople. There was still no Russian Black Sea fleet, so that one had to be built on the Don. The first Russian objective was again Azov, and with armies commanded by an Irishman and a German and a fleet commanded by a Norwegian, they attacked. The Irishman, Lacy, took Azov, while the German, Münnich, attacked the Crimea with but little result. Bredal, the Norwegian admiral, helped in the successful siege of Azov, but after that was over the Russians found their hands full trying to rescue Münnich from the consequences of his failure to take the Crimea, and it was not until the next year that the advance on Constantinople could be resumed.

By this time the second Russian Black Sea fleet was a really powerful force, at least in coastal waters, for 500 boats had been built on the Don, while at Briansk 400 bigger vessels had been constructed. The smaller craft carried from two to six guns—two- or three-pounders—while the backbone of the fleet was a force of prams, shallow-draft sailing ships, each carrying as many as forty-four guns.

The task of this fleet was to aid the army in its advance along the north coast of the Sea of Azov, both by helping actually to move it and its supplies and by giving inshore support. The army started to move on May 14th and the fleet, forming a bridge of boats, carried it into the Crimea. It was not until July 8th that a Turkish squadron appeared and tried to stop it. This Turkish force comprised fifteen galleys and seventy smaller craft, backed by three bigger sailing vessels which were the capital ships of the campaign, being armed respectively with sixty-four, sixty and thirty guns. This meant that the first two were about equivalent to the smaller British and French two-decker ships of the time, while the third was the size of a frigate.

This Turkish squadron attacked the Russian army from the sea while the Russian flotillas were absent. On the next day a gale blew up and within forty-eight hours 187 out of 217 of the Russian vessels were sunk or driven ashore. Faced with this disaster, Bredal took advantage of the extraordinary geography of the east coast of the Crimea and retired into the Sivash—or Putrid Sea. This is an extremely shallow body of water, almost a lake, separated from the Sea of Azov proper by a strip of land a few hundred yards wide and about sixty miles long called the Tongue of Arabat, which runs parallel to the isthmus, linking it to within a short distance of the mainland, where there is a passage between the Sivash and the Sea of Azov at Genitchesk.

It was here that Lacy had used a bridge of boats to cross from the mainland to the peninsula, operated there for a time without any appreciable influence on the Turks and then withdrew once more to the mainland. So shallow is the sea here that a strong west wind drives back the water and leaves dry land. During his operations Lacy was able to march his soldiers across the sea-bed near Genitchesk, reaching safety just as the wind dropped and the seas flowed back in the manner of the waters swallowing the Egyptians in the Red Sea.

In addition to the Russian naval force in the Sea of Azov and the Sivash, 600 light craft had been assembled on the Dnieper, near Otchakov and Kinburn. These were two Turkish positions at the mouth of the river, which prevented the Russians from getting out into the open sea. In addition to the 600 Russian vessels at the mouth of the river there were 200 more 250 miles upstream and scattered up and down the river there were another 750. Most of these craft were peacetime trading vessels, essential to the life of the country, which at this time possessed very few roads.

But there was nothing that the Dnieper force could do, bottled up as it was by Kinburn and Otchakov. It was Bredal's force in the Sea of Azov that kept the naval war going and it continued to act in support of Lacy's army which was striving to break into the Crimea. To stop them, the Turks had sent ships of the line into the Sea of Azov, and on one occasion in June 1738 came near to winning a decisive victory off Berutch Spit. Two of the big Turkish ships trapped a Russian flotilla off Genitchesk and would have destroyed it had Bredal not run his vessels ashore on the spit, dragged all 144 of them overland and launched them on the other side, so that they were separated from the enemy by the tongue of land. Before the campaign ended Lacy took Perekop and destroyed its fortifications; then he retired to winter quarters.

However, the issue of the war and the fate of the second Russian Black Sea fleet was to be decided a long way away. Although Münnich's army entered what is now Rumania and took Jassy, Russia's Austrian allies were completely defeated by the Turks and made a separate peace. Rather than face the Turks alone, the Russians also made peace, at Constantinople in 1739, returning all their conquests except the town of Azov, which was demilitarised. Once again they agreed not to maintain a fleet in the Black Sea, so that the second Russian Black Sea fleet, with its 1,000 units, great and small, went the way of the first.

CHAPTER III

THE BATTLE FOR THE BALTIC

1725–1761

T HE Russian fleet was the largest in the Baltic at the death of Peter the Great, but it was already beginning a period of run-down. The Russian people were war-weary, the ships, for the most part hurriedly built out of fir, were worn out, and above all the new Tsarina, Catherine I, did not have the same interest in the navy as had her husband and predecessor. A little later Peter II, son of Peter the Great and of Catherine, was to settle the destiny of the Russian fleet for years to come by ordering it to remain in harbour unless he specifically ordered it to sea. Its efficiency and seaworthiness became very low, the officers who cared about the service became discouraged and the rest just bored.

This phenomenon of the waxing and waning of the Russian navy, depending upon the interest in it felt by the rulers of Russia at the time, has repeated itself in Russian history down to the present day.

Although, after the death of Peter the Great, naval affairs were at a very low ebb in the wars that followed during the first half of the eighteenth century, the Russian Baltic fleet was able to play an important part as an auxiliary of the army. Communications by land, apart from the rivers, were almost non-existent for troops or stores, so by far the easiest and often the only way of supplying the Russian armies was by sea.

In the War of the Polish Succession (1733–4), a Russian army was sent to co-operate with the Poles and the Austrians in the siege of Danzig, which was being defended by the French candidate to the Polish throne, Stanislaus Leszczinski. During the siege the Russian fleet held the ring and prevented a French squadron from coming to the rescue of their ally. Stanislaus Leszczinski in consequence abandoned his claim to Poland and retired to western Europe, where he received the Duchy of Lorraine as a consolation prize.

The successful contender for the Polish throne, Augustus III, having won thanks to Russian support, became a Russian satellite.

Five years later the war began between Britain and Spain over Jenkins's Ear which was to escalate into the War of the Austrian Succession. The Russians became allies of the Austrians, who were fighting the French. The latter found it easy to enlist the support of the Swedes, so that another Russo-Swedish conflict took place.

The main theatre of this war was the southern coast of Finland, along which the Swedes tried to advance eastward against St. Petersburg with the support of their fleet, while the Russian army and navy tried to stop them. In 1741 the Russians were successful in this, in part, at least, because an epidemic in the Swedish fleet put many ships out of action and handicapped the rest.

The Swedish army, notwithstanding, continued its advance on the Russian capital but was defeated at Vildmanstrand about 100 miles from its goal.

Mishukov, the Russian admiral commanding in chief, brought his fleet of thirteen ships of the line out of Kronstadt to threaten the Swedish fleet, which with fifteen ships of the line was at Aspö; they withdrew, however, without fighting to Hangö. This exposed the Swedish inshore flotilla, which also withdrew, and this, in turn, caused the Swedish army to fall back on Helsingfors. Here it was blockaded from the sea by the Russian fleet and invested from the land by the Russian army under Lacy, the Irish general, who had already done well in the war against the Turks.

The Swedish and Russian battle fleets confronted each other at the entrance to the Gulf of Finland, but neither side moved. The Russians felt that they did not need to attack, as they were already in a position to cut off the supplies for the Swedish garrison in Helsingfors, and the Swedes, probably because of sickness, did nothing either. Accordingly, Helsingfors capitulated on August 31st, 1742.

In the meantime the Russians had been trying to solve the problem of how to combine the fleets which they maintained in the Baltic and in the White Sea. It was decided that the latter fleet should come down to the Baltic, but, owing to bad weather and probably also to unpractised seamanship, only two vessels got through.

So it was that when the Russians and the Swedes faced each other in the spring of 1743 the former had only a tiny superiority over their enemy—seventeen to sixteen in ships of the line. Golovin, who had succeeded Mishukov, was still under the thrall of the order of Peter the Great that a Russian fleet should not attack the enemy unless in possession of at least one-third superiority. Accordingly he did not challenge the Swedish admiral Utfall, but instead made off towards Reval. The Swedish battle fleet followed him and left the coast, literally, clear for the Russian small craft, which came out of the Gulf of Finland and seized Lemland in the Aland Islands, thus directly threatening Stockholm. As a result a compromise peace was made in the same year between the Russians and the Swedes by which the Swedes received back most of Finland, the Russo-Finnish frontier being fixed along the River Kymmere, about 150 miles west of St. Petersburg and about fifty miles west of the present Russo-Finnish frontier.

Although the war between Russia and Sweden was over, Russia was still, nominally at least, fighting the War of the Austrian Succession and in receipt for that purpose of a British subsidy. A Russian force of 37,000 men and a flotilla of forty vessels was prepared to intervene against Prussia, but it was never used. The Russians, despite their successes, gave easy terms to the Swedes, because the Russian Empress Elizabeth was anxious lest the Swedes be too badly defeated. If this happened they might fall victim to the Danes, who would thus unite all the Scandinavian countries under their rule and completely control the passage in and out of the Baltic.

The process of increasing Danish power had already begun. Denmark, under Christian VI, seeing the Swedes weakened by the Russian victories, had tried to browbeat the Swedish king, Frederick, into recognising the Crown Prince of Denmark as heir to the Swedish throne as well. To bring pressure to bear upon Frederick a pro-Danish rising was started in the Swedish province of Dalecarlia and preparations made to invade Sweden from Norway while the Danish fleet mobilised.

Faced with the threat of a united Scandinavian kingdom of Denmark, Sweden, Norway and Finland under a king in Copenhagen, the Empress Elizabeth sent Russian troops to help the Swedes against the Danes, while her candidate, Adolf Frederick of Holstein-Gottorp, was accepted as heir to the Swedish throne.

This Russo-Swedish alliance endured into the Seven Years' War, when Russia and Sweden fought together on the side of the Austrians and French against the British and the Prussians under Frederick the Great.

At the outbreak of this war the Russian fleet was smaller than it had been since the beginning of the century, having only eighteen ships of the line in the Baltic, with two more based in the White Sea. At this time Sweden had twenty-six ships of the line and the Danes twenty-seven. Twenty-one Russian ships of the line had been condemned between 1750 and 1756, mostly because the fir used to build them did not have the enduring qualities of oak.

The Danes, overawed by the Russians and Swedes, were forced to join their alliance. The British navy was fully occupied in this war with the French fleet, then probably at the highest peak of efficiency it ever reached in the days of sail. Accordingly the Russo-Scandinavian fleets had complete command of the Baltic and proceeded to put it to good use, so good that in 1914–15 more than 150 years afterwards, the British First Sea Lord, Lord Fisher, was striving with might and main to bring about a repetition of the state of affairs which existed in 1760, when a Russian army was landed on the Prussian coast within striking distance of Berlin.

The stages by which this had come about were, first, the Russian attack by land and sea upon Memel, which was successful on July 2nd, 1757; after this the Russians moved on to attack Danzig. The Russian galley flotilla operated in the very shallow and nearly land-locked waters of the Kurische Haff against the coast of East Prussia and also in the Grosse Haff, where they were able to blockade Stettin. While this was going on the Russian battle fleet patrolled off Bruster Ort to the north-east of the Gulf of Danzig, to deal with any British fleet which might come to the rescue of the Prussians.

Plans were made for a joint Russo-Swedish landing on the Pomeranian coast near Kolberg to threaten Berlin from the north with an army of 17,000 men. However, there was dissension between the Baltic allies and chances were missed. This dissension was partly due to the Danish suspicion of the Swedes, and as a result the Danes, instead of waging war wholeheartedly against the British, began to build up their strength in Norway in case the Swedes attacked them there. However, despite mutual suspicion, all three Baltic fleets gathered in Kioge Bay near Copenhagen to withstand a British attack which never came. While nearly all the Prussian Baltic coast was controlled by the Swedish and Russian flotillas, the combined Austrian and Russian armies invaded Prussia from the east, taking Königsberg and defeating Frederick the Great at Kunersdorf, near Frankfurt on the Oder.

All sorts of inter-allied delays occurred, so that it was not until the following year, 1760, that the events took place which so very nearly destroyed Frederick the Great. The Russians and the Swedes bombarded and took Kolberg and, although they almost immediately re-embarked leaving a couple of hundred prisoners in Prussian hands, the Russo-Austrian armies a fortnight later took Berlin. Frederick, however, counter-attacked and defeated the enemy at Torgau on the Elbe (the scene of the Russo-American link-up in the final stages of the European campaign in 1945). Then he re-entered his capital, which had been in the hands of the enemy only four days.

At the end of 1761 Kolberg was again taken by the Russians, but less than a month later the Empress Elizabeth died and her successor, Peter III, at once made peace with Frederick the Great and withdrew his forces into Russia. This was about the sum total of the action taken by Peter III during his reign; he was shortly afterwards murdered under the auspices of his wife, who became the Empress Catherine the Great. The new Tsarina decided upon a policy of neutrality in the north and concentrated her power against the Turks in the Black Sea and in the Mediterranean.

CHAPTER IV

THE FIRST RUSSIAN ARMADA

1769–1774

THE immediate cause of the outbreak of yet another Russo-Turkish war was the uprising of the Poles against the Russian puppet-king, Stanislaus Poniatowski; the Turks were anxious to take advantage of the consequent embarrassment of the Russians and declared war upon the latter, after accusing Russian troops acting in support of Stanislaus of violating Turkish neutrality. At the same time these troubled waters seemed excellent for fishing by the French, who produced their former candidate for the Polish crown, Stanislaus Leszczinski, Duke of Lorraine, as a rival to Stanislaus Poniatowski. Clearly success in the struggle for the control of Poland would be of great advantage to the French; accordingly, the British Government decided to give practically all aid short of war to the Russians.

The results of this decision were to be seen a little later. First, British dockyards in the United Kingdom and in the Mediterranean were open to the Russians. This was greatly to the perturbation of the Mediterranean powers, none of whom wanted to see an operational Russian fleet in their waters, where it was likely to upset a very delicate balance of power. The second product of Anglo-Russian understanding was the fact that a number of British officers were allowed to serve with the Russian fleet.[1]

It was not the first time that this had happened, but there was very nearly all the difference in the world between the English and Scots officers who served under Peter the Great and the British officers who were to serve Catherine II so well. Peter the Great's foreign volunteers—at least the contingent from Great Britain—had been largely Queen Anne's hard bargains, sailors of fortune and Jacobite refugees. On the other hand, the sailors who took part in the expedition to the Mediterranean fifty years later were for the most part serving officers of the Royal Navy and their role was akin to that of a British naval mission on loan to the Russians. They were to do extremely well, but in assessing the part that they played it must be

---

[1] Fred T. Jane wrote in *The Imperial Russian Navy*, W. Thacker & Co., 1904 (p. 78)—'At one time [under Catherine] more than half the entire list of officers were of Anglo-Saxon and Celtic nationality—Scotchmen [*sic*] in particular, showed a partiality for the service.'

remembered that they had—or at least those who afterwards wrote of their doings had—a blistering contempt of the Russians who were their allies. In their writings the British displayed something of an arrogance of which it is still disturbing to read two hundred years later.

The first Russian fleet to sail for the Mediterranean was com- manded by Admiral Spiridov and formed of seven ships of the line, one frigate and five smaller vessels, later reinforced by two more ships of the line from the White Sea fleet at Archangel. In addition, eight ships of the line and six frigates were left behind in the Baltic to watch the Swedes, but later it was decided to form from this Baltic fleet a second fleet for the Mediterranean under Rear-Admiral John Elphinston, a captain of the Royal Navy, who served as a Russian flag officer.

Elphinston, born in 1722, had been commissioned as a lieutenant at the age of twenty-three after more than six years, partly in 'merchants' service', in the Mediterranean. He seems to have specialised in combined operations, serving under Howe in the raids on St. Malo, Cherbourg and St. Cast in the early years of the Seven Years' War. During the latter raid he was taken prisoner while helping to re-embark the troops, but was exchanged in time to be promoted captain and sent on the Quebec expedition of Wolfe and Saunders in command of H.M.S. *Eurus*. Later, captain of the frigate *Richmond*, he drove ashore the French frigate *Félicité* and then went to the West Indies with Rodney under Pocock, where he distinguished himself by leading the fleet through the very imperfectly charted Old Bahamas Passage; Rodney reported:

> Captain Elphinston had been very diligent and careful in his remarks going through and returning back having taken sketches of the land and of the cayos on both sides. He kept ahead of the fleet and led us through very well.

Elphinston was at the siege of Havana and afterwards commanded one of the prizes taken there—the *Infante* of seventy guns—until the end of the war. On his return to the British service at the conclusion of his campaign in the Mediterranean with the Russians, he com- manded various British ships of the line during the American War of Independence, and as captain of *Magnificent* (74) he was present at three actions between Rodney and Guichen. He died in 1785, his eldest son following him into the Russian navy and becoming a captain.

The Russian fleets had a rough passage from the Baltic to the Mediterranean, and Elphinston, whose ships put in to Copenhagen, had some difficulty in persuading his officers to tear themselves away from the joys of the Danish capital.

> The great plenty both of the necessaries and the elegancies of life found here, made it very agreeable to the Russian officers, with which some of them were so captivated, that they seemed to have forgot the service they owed to their country.

wrote a British officer serving under Elphinston.

> They even grew remiss in their duty, and expressed a dislike to the expedition; having, as they said, been forced into it against their inclinations.
> This conduct of some of the officers gave the admiral [Elphinston] great concern, lest it should detain him, which would actually have been the case, had not His Excellency M. Philosoph, the Russian Minister at Copenhagen, exerted his influence and authority to assist him in this critical situation.
> By his assistance, the admiral was enabled to leave Copenhagen just in time; for in a day or two after the harbour was choaked up (by ice) and rendered unnavigable for the winter.[1]

Not all the ships ordered to the Mediterranean could be got ready in time; one was wrecked on the Skaw and one on the coast of Finland and only one made the whole voyage to Port Mahon, in Minorca (then a British possession) without incident; others were driven into the Humber, Spithead and Gibraltar. Disease broke out on the passage; over 300 men died on the way to England and when the fleet arrived there 600 sick needed care.

Catherine was a realist about the state of her navy, but she also knew what could be done. 'Our fleet is rusty, but this expedition will get rid of the rust,' she said, and to Spiridov she wrote:

> If you run out of stores, your expedition will become our shame and will dishonour both of us. I beg you, in the name of God Himself gather all your moral strength and do not *shame us* before all the world.

The two fleets were so thoroughly disorganised that at the beginning of 1770 four ships of the line were at Port Mahon, one at Lisbon and five at Portsmouth. The British dockyards refitted and repaired the Russian ships. Some of these ships were literally prevented from falling to pieces only by wrapping cables round their hulls. It is difficult to see how the Russian enterprise could have been successful without this British help.

---

[1] *An Authentic Narrative of Russian Expedition against the Turks*, anon., 1772, cited as *Narrative*.

Spiridov's first duty on reaching the Mediterranean was to pick up the Russian commander-in-chief, Count Orlov, who had travelled overland to Leghorn. Orlov was not a naval officer but a courtier and a favourite of the Empress. In theory there was everything to be said against putting him in command above two such experienced naval officers as Elphinston and Spiridov, but those two officers could not get on with each other, and it is probable that Orlov was set over them in just the same way as Lord Howard of Effingham was set over the brilliant but quarrelsome professional sailors at the time of the Spanish Armada.

When the Russians opened their campaign in the Mediterranean the Turks held the whole of the Middle East as well as the coasts and islands of Greece, although the Greeks were in a state of endemic rising against their rulers, carrying on a struggle which was not to end until our own day. To support the Greeks and embarrass the Turks, Spiridov began a series of raids, the first of which resulted in the capture of Navarino. However, Greek support for the Russian landing parties was wavering, for experience had taught them what would be their fate at the hands of the Turks if the latter were ever able to return, so that few apart from the most devoted of partisans were willing to commit themselves unless their liberators arrived in overwhelming force. Elphinston, following Spiridov into the Mediterranean, reached Greek waters on May 20th, 1770. Landfall was made off Cape Matapan.

'They discovered, on the top of a hill, a flag and a fire, being the signals agreed on to be made by the Greeks.' An old man and a Greek priest informed them of the proper anchoring-places and gave them good intelligence concerning the situation of the place and the disposition of the inhabitants. The landings began.

> The admiral now hoisted his flag on board the *Nadezhda* (32) frigate, and sailed boldly in. He was followed by the rest of the squadron, and before dark all the ships were moored, and the troops landed. Whilst this was doing, the Greeks, commonly called the Maniots, who live on the shores by fishing, etc., flocked round the ships in their boats, and gave us the most pleasing proofs of their sincere joy at our arrival, by bringing to us all sorts of fresh provisions in the greatest plenty.
> . . . the troops were in high spirits, and desirous of engaging the enemy. Admiral Elphinston was therefore of the opinion that no time should be lost, but that all the land forces should march directly to Mistra the capital of the Morea, which was in possession of the Greeks.

Elphinston was informed that, although the garrison of Mistra was afraid of being driven out by the Turks, they expected on the other

45

hand to be joined by large bodies of Greeks, who only waited for the appearance of the Russians to encourage them to rise in arms.

On the next day came news of the Turkish fleet; with eight ships of the line it had gone to Nauplia to await six more ships of the line and transports bringing troops from Constantinople, which were to be landed at Nauplia and would then move overland to the rescue of Navarino.

Leader of the Turks was Hassan Pasha, born in Persia, purchased in the slave markets of Algiers and successively boatman, soldier, pirate and admiral in the Algerine fleet. He left Algiers pursued by the rage of the Bey and took high office under the Sultan, in command of whose fleet he now was.

Elphinston went off to look for, and engage, the Turkish fleet as soon as wind would permit; for not awaiting the arrival of Orlov and Spiridov and their fleet he has been criticised by Russian writers. On the face of it to attack fourteen Turkish ships of the line with three Russian ships was wrong when, by waiting to concentrate, he could have had the six ships of Spiridov as well. However, he did not wait and on Sunday, May 27th, he found the enemy at the entrance to the Gulf of Nauplia.

> Immediately the admiral threw out the signal for a general chase, Cape St. Angelo bearing north by west and the island of Specia (Spetsai) east north east.
> We bore down upon them with all the sail we could croud [*sic*] with colours flying, whilst the drums and trumpets animated us to battle.

wrote the author of *An Authentic Narrative*. Three Russian ships, the *Ne Tron Menya* and *Saratov* (both of 66 guns) and the frigate *Nadezhda*, led the chase of the Turks, Elphinston afterwards claiming that they were in this position because he had had to open fire on them to chase them towards the enemy; in any event, he followed them in his flagship *Sviatoslav* (80). It would be ungenerous to suppose that the Russians were more afraid of their own admiral than of the enemy; they certainly attacked the latter in fine style. The *Ne Tron Menya* engaged and drove out of the line a ship of greater force, while the *Saratov* after four broadsides against two Turkish ships of the line put them out of action as well and the little *Nadezhda* dealt with the Turkish small craft.

However, the wind failed, the first three Russian ships were left temporarily unsupported and the Turks, still much the stronger force, fought back and 'we were attacked on all sides, and must have been shattered to pieces in a short time or taken, if they had pushed a few

46

ships in the interval between (our) van and rear; but fortunately some shells thrown by the admiral, glowing with destruction, began to fall among the enemy ships, which threw them into confusion'.

This was one of the very first occasions in history in which explosive missiles were ever used in a fleet action and the sight of them caused the Turks to make sail for what they hoped would be the shelter of Nauplia.

Whether or not it was really true that Elphinston had to fire on his three leading captains in order to get them to pursue the enemy, the behaviour of the Russian crews in action seems to have left nothing to be desired, according to the *Narrative*.

> The intrepidity and bravery of the Russian seamen and marines in this engagement deserve the greatest applause; fearless of danger they fought at their guns like lions, and gave hearty cheers, when they were ordered to pour a broadside into the enemy. In this engagement the Russians had only 15 men killed, and 30 wounded on board our ship.

Elphinston continued his chase in the dark, opening fire with his shells whenever a target seemed to offer; both Russians and Turks set their light-oared craft to towing the big ships and at daylight on the next day the Russians came up with the enemy off Nauplia.

The Turks had taken shelter under the guns of the forts guarding the harbour, but as soon as he could Elphinston followed them in with the *Sviatoslav, Ne Tron Menya, Saratov* and the two frigates. After shelling the forts Elphinston attacked the enemy fleet, then moored in a crescent-shaped formation. Within a short time it became an action in which both sides were at anchor, firing upon each other as hard as they could. The fact that the Russians, though numerically much the weaker, were able to stand this for some three hours before withdrawing from the harbour shows, in part at least, the extent to which the Turks were at a disadvantage through the Russian use of shells and also the higher degree of Russian training. The Russian casualties were not high—seven killed and ten wounded in the two days' fighting.

Towards nightfall on this day (May 28th) Elphinston decided to withdraw, as he was afraid of the wind dropping. If that happened his sailing ships would be at the mercy of the Turkish galleys, highly mobile light rowing craft. At the same time he also sent overland an officer with a message to Orlov and Spiridov at Navarino asking for reinforcements.

Meanwhile, the Turks, having seen the smallness of the Russian force, decided to sortie and attack it. Elphinston placed his squadron across the narrow exit from the Gulf of Nauplia and was awaiting the enemy when his second-in-command, Commodore Barsh, sent word that if the fleet did not at once fall back upon the main body of the fleet with Orlov and Spiridov he would do so in any case. Apparently in taking this line he was justified, since the Russian fighting instructions laid down that a junior commanding officer was not obliged to stay with his admiral if the latter insisted in attacking against odds. Elphinston was obliged to give up his attack, although he retaliated, up to a point, by removing Barsh from his command.

It was now the turn of the Turks to pursue, and they very nearly caught up with the retreating Russians, using galleys to tow their big ships up to the becalmed enemy. Only at the last moment did a wind spring up and enable the Russians to escape.

Spiridov was met on June 3rd with four ships of the line who had been to re-embark Elphinston's landing party, in reply to a SOS from the landing party at Levetzova, which had 'sent a trusty Greek to Navarino, with an account of their situation, which indeed was but indifferent'.

This was partly because 'the Greeks were backward in assisting the Russians from the apprehension of the severities they might expect from the Turks in case they were unsuccessful . . .' When the Russians left they were 'loaded with the execrations of the few Greeks who had joined them, and now fled to the shelter of the mountains from their cruel masters'.

The inability of the Russians to land sufficient troops to support a popular rising in Greece and the islands was to bedevil the expedition and finally to render all the efforts of Orlov and the Russian squadrons useless, but that was not clearly seen until later in the campaign. In the meanwhile there was still an excellent chance of dealing a direct and deadly blow against Constantinople itself.

First the Turkish fleet had to be put out of action; there was delay on account of the difficulty of deciding which of the admirals, the Russian or the Scotsman, was in command of the Russian fleet. Elphinston claimed that although Spiridov was the senior the Russian had agreed to take orders from him; Spiridov did not, in fact, do so and a great deal of time was lost.

However, Elphinston, who still had his three ships of the line, came up with the Turks between the island of Hydra and the Greek mainland. The Russian shells once again had effect and the Turks left rapidly, the flagship under tow by the galleys, while three small sailing vessels, thought to be carrying tribute from the islands, made off at once.

'A pleasant gale' filled the sails of Elphinston's ships and they made for Porto Rafti, where troops were landed, water procured, the ships careened and their rigging prepared. A big action seemed imminent, as a French merchantman brought the news that there were 8,000 Turkish troops at Salonika ready to sail for the Morea, where they would have had little difficulty in dealing with the penny packets of Orlov's landing parties.

Turkish troops were already threatening the Russian bases, although on one occasion on the island of Euboea a landing party of 'four English gentlemen volunteers' with thirty Russian soldiers drove off the local Turkish troops without a fight; nevertheless, the position ashore was poor from the Russian point of view and the fleet started back westward round Matapan to protect Navarino. The Russian land front collapsed, Modon fell and Orlov accordingly decided upon the evacuation of Navarino.

The fleet went back into the Gulf of Aegina and made its base at Paros; Elphinston's chronicler, recalling that Paros had been the home of Phidias and Praxiteles says:

> The town retains nothing of its former grandeur and yet, like beauty in distress, it excites our particular regard; we cannot see without regret the many noble pieces of sculpture, consisting of basso-relieves, altars, etc., disgraced by serving as common fences to their fields or to patch up their poor inconvenient habitations.

In addition to these relics of a very distant past there was plenty of good water and excellent wine, as well as pigeons and partridges.

From this pleasant spot they were drawn, on July 1st, by the news that the Turkish fleet was lying between the island of Chios and the Anatolian mainland. Orlov led his fleet against them; nine ships of the line, three frigates and the bomb vessel. Against this force the Turks had some twenty ships of the line and frigates, but the Turkish fleet was so unskilfully drawn up that several ships masked each other's fire. In this way the Turks lost all advantage of their superiority in numbers, only five of their ships of the line being able to bring their guns to bear on the enemy at a time.

On Saturday, July 5th, 1770, at three in the morning, Elphinston's flagship tacked and led the whole fleet before the wind into the passage between the east side of Chios and the Anatolian shore.

> At 11 o'clock each commander was on board his own ship. The signal was made for prayers throughout the fleet to supplicate the Almighty to crown them with victory.
> For some time there was an awful and profound silence in both fleets.

The commanders on each side seemed penetrated with proper ideas of the great importance of the day, what they were to fight for, and how much the success of it depended on their conduct and courage.

The proper disposition for the engagement was formed and at noon Count Orlov threw out the red flag as a signal to attack. The whole fleet, being ranged in battle, moved towards the enemy, like a gathering cloud. Every brave man now wishing to survive with glory or die with honour.

Spiridov led the van in the *Evstafi* (66) and bore on the leading Turkish ship, the *Real Mustapha* of eighty-four guns, the flagship of Hassan Pasha.

The *Evstafi* came under fire from five of the Turkish ships of the line and lost at least 100 men killed outright. Spiridov held his fire until he was within musket shot of the *Real Mustapha*. Then a full broadside struck the Turks and was followed, as quickly as it was possible to reload, by another.

The *Real Mustapha* gave as good as she got; Spiridov's rigging was shot away and his ship, out of control, drifted down aboard the Turk. As soon as they were alongside boarders from the *Evstafi* swarmed over the Turkish flagship and cleared her upper deck. One of the Russian boarding party seized the big red and white Turkish flag and began to tear it down; a Turk cut off his hand with a scimitar and was himself killed; the Russian caught the flag in his other hand; that hand was also cut off, the Russian caught the flag in his teeth and finally brought it to the deck, falling dead with the enemy's flag across his body.

Fighting continued in the darkened 'tween decks; then, after some fifteen minutes, a column of flame and smoke burst from the starboard quarter gallery of the *Real Mustapha*. The whole ship seemed to be on fire at once, and the flames spread to the tumbled rigging and spars of the *Evstafi*. As both the ships blazed their crews ceased firing and tried to save their lives as best they could, but the fate of the *Evstafi* was sealed when the Turk's great mainsail, a huge flaming rag, fell upon the Russian's upper deck. The Russian at once blew up and for fear of being involved in the catastrophe the Turks cut their anchor cables and drifted into Tchesma Bay, which was to be the scene of their ruin.

Altogether, when the Turkish battle fleet had entered the bay, there were present some 200 ships great and small, and the harbour was so very crowded that some of the small vessels were hauled out of the water on to the shore to make room for the bigger craft.

Elphinston as usual was for attack; he wished to send two fireships in at once to complete the enemy's undoing, but was stopped by a wrangle over protocol. The commander of the Russian fleet train— the auxiliary vessels, supply ships and the rest—was General Hannibal, a Negro and son of the famous slave of the same name who had been given to Peter the Great by Louis XIV. Hannibal now maintained that it was his right to give orders to the fireships. Time was wasted in argument, an argument which would have cost the Russians a great deal if the Turks had used the time properly and put their defences in order. As it was, however, when the Russian fireships finally attacked on the night of July 7th, after a delay of twenty-four hours, the Turks had taken no effective precautions at all.

The fireships' attack was covered by the three ships of the line *Rostislav*, *Ne Tron Menya* and *Europa*, under the command of Commodore Samuel Greig, a Scotsman from the Royal Navy 'who, proud of this opportunity to distinguish himself', says the *Narrative*, 'led them into the harbour with great spirit through a smart fire from the enemy ships and batteries. The Russians soon brought their broadsides to bear on the largest of the enemy ships and their balls thundered among them, whilst their shells flew about like burning meteors, threatening destruction wherever they should fall.'

As the Turkish fire was concentrated upon the Russian big ships, the fireships slipped into the harbour at one o'clock in the morning, hardly perceived. There were four Greek coasting vessels converted for the purpose and full of explosives and inflammable material. The names of the commanding officers, in the order in which they came into the harbour were Dugdale, Mackenzie, Illyin and Gagern. Four other fireships had been also prepared, but, according to the *Narrative*, their Russian captains were too drunk to take them in; in any case, they were to prove unneeded.

Dugdale's ship, leading, was set on fire and then deserted by her crew. Dugdale himself, alone aboard the blazing ship, steered her amongst the enemy and only jumped overboard at the last moment, being picked up by a small Greek vessel. The fireship ran aground without doing any damage and burned out; in the meantime, however, the shells of Greig's big ships had already set fire to the bunt of the foretopgallantsail of the weathermost enemy vessel and, the Turkish sails being made of cotton, the fire spread rapidly, soon extending to other ships, so that when Mackenzie's ship came in her target was already on fire. It was left to Illyin to complete the enemy's destruction, which he did by setting fire to yet another ship so that Gagern, the fourth captain, seeing the bay full of blazing enemy from which it was clear that none could escape, decided that it was not worth his while going in.

The *Narrative* says:

> A fleet consisting of 200 sail almost in one general blaze, presented a picture of distress and horror dreadfully sublime.
>
> This description will convey but a faint idea of the catastrophe of the Turkish fleet. While the flames with the utmost rapidity were spreading destruction on all sides, and ship blowing up after ship, with every soul on board that feared to trust the waves to swim to shore, the Russians kept pouring upon them such showers of cannon balls, shells and small shot, that not one of the many thousands of their weeping friends on land, who saw their distress, dared venture to their relief.
>
> Nothing now remained but united shrieks and unavailing cries, which, joined to the martial music and the loud triumphant shouts of the victors, served to swell alternately the various notes of joy and sorrow, that composed the solemn dirge of their departing glory.

When it was all over the Turkish fleet had been destroyed. Nearly two hundred years before much the same kind of attack had been made by the English fireships against the Spanish armada, but Gravelines, where the Spaniards had lain, was an open roadstead; they could slip their anchors, set their sails and, temporarily at least, escape. At Tchesma, however, the Turks were caught in a harbour from which, for them, there was no escape.

On the day after the battle, as the Russian small boats were prospecting through the wreckage which covered the bay, they came upon two Englishmen, escaped slaves. One was Robert Jacobs, who had been in the hands of the Turks for eleven years, and with them was a Maltese who, although in chains, had crawled out through a hole in the side of his sinking ship and managed to keep afloat on a piece of wreckage until his rescuers arrived.

The Russians held a thanksgiving ceremony in the bay, with Greek clergy coming from the mainland and neighbouring islands in small boats, and after a general turmoil of mutual congratulations, victory banquets, salutes, toasts and celebrations Elphinston urged that, with the Turkish Mediterranean fleet destroyed, there was no obstacle to an attack upon the entrance to the Dardanelles. At the best the Straits could be forced and Constantinople would be within the Russian grasp; if the Straits could not be forced they could, at least, be blockaded and Constantinople cut off from the supplies which usually reached it from the Mediterranean and upon which it was said to depend.

Accordingly the Russian fleet went up to the north and made its base at Lemnos, just as the Franco-British force was to do in 1915, and began to skirmish with the forts at the entrance to the Dardanelles. The crews enjoyed life ashore on Lemnos, living on wild hogs, which they found pleasant despite a somewhat fishy taste, and honey.

Elphinston continued to urge an all-out attack on the Turkish defences ashore, where affairs were in the state of corrupt confusion usual under the Sultanate. However, as had happened before and was to happen again, the courage of the ordinary Turkish fighting man and the stiffening given him by foreign experts was to turn form upside down. Since the Russians were carrying on their campaign against the Turks with the support of British naval officers and British dockyards it was only natural, given international politics in those days, that the Sultan should seek and obtain assistance from the French.

At this critical moment there arrived in the Turkish capital a French engineer named De Tott, who is commemorated to this day on the map of the Gallipoli peninsula and in the history of the Gallipoli campaign of 1915. Now, in 1770, he began to organise the ramshackle defences of the Dardanelles. Time was short, and an immediate attack on the Straits would probably have succeeded. De Tott set to work as fast as he could. More important than the slave labour which was put to work on defences which have lasted until today, was a large quantity of white paint which De Tott used to repaint the old fortifications as smartly as he could, so that when Orlov arrived with the Russian fleet he judged that the new fortifications had already been completed and made no serious attempt to attack the Straits.

All of the island of Lemnos was not, however, in Russian hands; the Turks were still holding out in the principal fortifications round Pelari. The blockade of the Dardanelles began on August 12th, when the Turks were seen to have gathered an army of some 8,000 to 10,000 men on the shores of the peninsula. At the same time a blockade was also begun, as far as was possible, of the Turkish ports on the Aegean from which a seaborne raid could be made on Lemnos and rescue carried out of the Turkish garrison that was holding out there. However, there were not sufficient Russian forces to do this properly and, in particular, the port of Enos was insufficiently guarded.

During these operations the *Sviatoslav*, still Elphinston's flagship, ran aground and the *Narrative* describes what happened:

Every method possible was tried to get her off during the day, but all proved ineffectual; the night was very dark, the wind whistled loudly through the rigging, and the boisterous waves, which flashed like fire against the sides of the ship, shook every joint in her and made her groan with the weight of distress. The next morning it blew yet more violently, so that some of the boats which were employed in carrying out anchors, hawsers, etc., were often dashed against each other and their crews immerged in the waves, yet with uncommon dexterity and resolution, they often recovered themselves, determined to do their duty to the last.

All this time the ship laboured very hard, and beat so violently against the ground that it was very difficult to stand on deck.

At three o'clock she had four feet water in her hold, the pumps were set to work, but in vain!—it still increased and at four it was risen to ten feet. The admiral seeing that the ship must inevitably be lost, ordered the provisions to be brought upon deck (which in five minutes more would have been all spoiled); he also ordered the ship to be laced from side to side with strong hawsers to prevent her, if possible, from bulging or going to pieces, which if she had done, it is very probable that the whole ship's company, consisting of about 600 men, including officers, would have perished.

At six the admiral, with a heart full of manly concern, ordered all the masts to be cut away, and thrown overboard, when one of them not being cleared in time, catched fire by the extreme friction occasioned by the violent agitation of the ship, and the whole in another minute would have been in flames, and every soul lost, if a Russian seaman had not instantaneously extinguished it by throwing a tub of Quass [a liquor made with flour and water] which they drink in common. In the afternoon they got a warp from the *Sviatoslav* to the *St. Pavel* and so brought the boats from one to the other, each being filled with one officer and 20 men, beside a chest of money, and great quantities of cloathing, etc. which were put on board the *St. Pavel* . . . the remainder of the men were sent on board the *Ne Tron Menya* the admiral, with his secretary, followed, and soon after hoisted his flag on board that ship.

The cause of this disaster had been a quarrel between the officer of the watch and the master; the former had refused to take advice proffered by the latter—who thereupon disinterested himself in the proceedings and went to his cabin.

The siege or rather blockade—for there were not Russians enough to make it a proper siege—of Pelari continued until the Turkish garrison asked for a truce and negotiations for a surrender began. Agreement was reached but, on the very night the Turks were due to give themselves up Hassan Pasha appeared from the mainland with a scratch collection of coastal vessels with sufficient troops on board to cause Orlov to raise the blockade and withdraw the fleet base to Paros, despite the fact that his was the stronger force upon the island.

54

Shortly after this Elphinston and the majority of the remaining British officers in the fleet returned to Russia and most of them surrendered their commissions; a British warship, the frigate *Winchelsea*, had been sent to seek out the Russian fleet and order the British auxiliary vessels serving with it to return to the United Kingdom. This, and the withdrawal of the British officers, may be set alongside the contention of Russian historians that Catherine the Great and Orlov deliberately refrained from exploiting their successes in the Aegean for fear of British jealousy.

Meanwhile operations in the Aegean went on, mostly raids on Turkish ports and attacks on roads and bridges within reach of the sea.

A more serious campaign began in early 1772, when a small Russian naval force was sent to Damietta at the mouth of the Nile to aid the Governor of Egypt, Ali Pasha, in his revolt against the Sultan, who, however, organised a counter-rebellion of his own. As the result Ali Pasha withdrew to Haifa, which temporarily became a Russian base for operations against Beirut. The first attempt to take Beirut failed, but it was renewed again in the following year, 1773, and after a siege lasting from July 6th to October 10th the place was taken. This was a success of which no use was made, and indeed after Tchesma and the failure to attack the Dardanelles, the whole Russian campaign in the Mediterranean was an anti-climax.

When the war had started in the Black Sea in 1769 the Russians were without a fleet, in accordance with the disarmament clauses of the Treaty of Constantinople of 1739. For the third time it was necessary for them to begin from scratch the building of a Black Sea fleet, although there were still a few ships on the stocks which had been laid down some thirty years previously and never launched. About a dozen miscellaneous small craft, in addition, were laid down and, by the time that they were completed, bases from which they could operate in the Black Sea had been captured for them by the Russian army. These bases were the ports of Azov and Taganrog.

The army having helped the navy by taking bases that were needed, it was now the turn of the navy to help the army.

In May 1771 Vice-Admiral Alexis Seniavin hoisted his flag in the sixteen-gun ship *Chotin*—a ridiculously small vessel by normal standards for a vice-admiral's flagship—and led his tiny fleet to sea to co-operate with the army in an attack on the Crimea. The attack was successful, for the bigger Turkish ships that could have challenged it had been destroyed at Tchesma; it was not until the last months of the war that the Turks again had any big ships in the Black Sea. These were never fully committed, so that it was comparatively easy for Seniavin's force to carry out its task of detaching the Crimea from Turkish control.

This particular war in the Mediterranean and the Black Sea was brought to an end by the Treaty of Kuchuk Kanardji in July 1774. The Russians gained the ports of Azov, Taganrog, Kertch and Kinburn and the Crimea became 'independent'—an 'independence' which lasted only until 1783. Russian agents followed quickly in the wake of the Russian army, and began to organise 'spontaneous' demonstrations for the annexation of the Crimea by Russia. The Turks were not strong enough at the time to protest and the matter was soon arranged. The foundation of Sevastopol, from that day to this the most important Russian base on the Black Sea, followed at once.

CHAPTER V

WARS ON TWO FRONTS
The Black Sea and the Baltic
1787–1791

T HE Russians had defeated both the Turks and the Swedes in their most recent wars, but they had not been able to crush them. Both Sweden and Turkey still had the desire and the power to seek revenge and the reconquest of the provinces which they had lost, and both felt sure that the Russians would soon begin again the process of inching their way westward and southward at their expense. Under these circumstances it was natural that war between Russia and Turkey should break out again in 1787, almost of its own accord. The Russians planned to repeat the successes which they had gained in the Levant during the previous war by sailing the major portion of the Baltic fleet into eastern waters as Orlov, Spiridov and Elphinston had done in 1769–70.

But the sight of the Russians again involved with the Turks was too much for the Swedes; their lost provinces seemed to beckon, and tension between Russia and Sweden grew so rapidly that the Russians dared not let their Levant-bound fleet pass Copenhagen. This meant that the Russian naval effort in the war against Turkey could be assumed only by the Black Sea fleet, which was outnumbered by the Turks roughly in the proportion of three to two.

Apart from the fact that the Swedish threat pinned down the Baltic fleet and prevented it from sailing to the assault of the Turks, there was no strategic connection between the campaigns which Russia was now to wage on two fronts, and it is therefore possible to deal with the two wars, Russo-Turkish and Russo-Swedish, separately.

The first campaigning season—1787—in the Black Sea was devoted to an amphibious struggle for the twin towns of Otchakov, which was Turkish, and Kinburn, which was Russian. These towns faced each other across the narrow passage which gives admission from the Black Sea to a long shallow bay, the Liman of the Dnieper. Into the Liman flows not only the Dnieper but also the Bug. These two rivers were almost the only means of communication in a southerly direction from the Ukraine and Poland. They were of such importance that William Pitt the Younger was soon to be willing to risk a war with

Russia in order to prevent her from holding Otchakov. In the meantime, however, Russia had first to gain possession of the place, the importance of which was increased by the fact that part of the Russian fleet was trapped inside the Liman, in its base at Kherson, before hostilities began.

The Turks were first off the mark; they declared war on August 16th and on the 27th of that month launched their first attack on Kinburn; having command of the sea, the Turks, crossing the Liman, landed on the narrow strip of sand-dunes which linked Kinburn with the mainland. Suvarov, the local Russian commander, soon to become and remain through all the vicissitudes of the next 175 years of Russian history a national hero, was able to repulse the enemy with the assistance of the Russian light coastal forces.

At first his support from the sea appears to have been limited to Lieutenant Lombard and the galley *Lesna* which he commanded; with this ship, whose principal armament was a single thirty-six-pounder carronade, he attacked single-handed the naval force covering the Turkish assault, which comprised two ships of the line, one frigate and thirty smaller vessels, most of them oared craft. This whole force he drove off and, passing to the offensive, attacked the Turkish position at Otchakov.

Two days later the *Lesna* was again in action by herself, this time against twenty enemy craft, and had her big gun disabled; Lombard turned over to another galley and was shortly in action once more, but his luck was out. His ship, with others, attacking the Turkish fleet off Otchakov, was cut off from the Russian main body and driven ashore behind the Turkish lines, where Lombard was made prisoner after having been badly wounded. It was ironical for the Russians that this loss occurred just as fresh ships were arriving to their aid and they were no longer greatly outnumbered by the Turks. At last the squadron (two ships of the line, three frigates and some smaller craft) had been able to leave the port in which it had been bottled up since the beginning of the war. News of its coming reached the Turks, who hastily mounted the biggest attack they had yet put in against Kinburn. This failed thanks to Suvarov—with a loss to the Turks of 4,500 out of the 5,000 men they had landed.

Two days later Rear-Admiral Mordvinov with the Kherson squadron arrived on the scene, and after some desultory fighting the Turkish fleet withdrew to Constantinople for the winter; as the campaigning season ended things were still as they had been at the outbreak of the war—the Russians were still in Kinburn and the Turks still in Otchakov. However, one important change was to be made—Mordvinov was apparently thought not up to the demands of his post and he was replaced by his junior, Commodore Ushakov, one of the greatest of all Russian sailors.

Ushakov had been born in 1735 of a family of poor nobles of Mongolian origin, no member of which appears ever to have seen the sea. He was educated by the village priest and then, probably for reasons of social prestige, at the naval school, from which he graduated at the somewhat venerable age of thirty-one; but he made up for lost time. He did well in the Russo-Turkish War of 1769–74 and began to make a name for himself both as a trainer of men and as a student of tactics.

One sortie during this autumn of 1787 had been made by the Russian squadron based on Sevastopol, against Varna; it ran into bad weather and, badly manned, trained and equipped, it lost two of its ten principal ships without sighting the enemy.

In the spring of the next year the struggle for Otchakov began again. The command set-up, under Potemkin, was that Suvarov commanded the land forces, Nassau-Siegen, a Franco-German soldier of fortune, the inshore flotilla, and John Paul Jones, the American, the seagoing fleet. The admission of John Paul Jones to flag rank in the Russian navy called forth a great outcry from the British officers in the same service. James Trevenen, then serving as a captain, describes how he and his fellow Britons protested in vain at the honour done to the former enemy of their country, whom they regarded as a traitor.

The first casualty of the fighting in 1788 was a Russian sloop commanded by Captain Saken, who was cut off by thirteen Turkish vessels of approximately the same size. When he saw that the fight was hopeless Saken sent his men away in the boats and remained behind alone. Four Turkish galleys came alongside to take the Russian ship by boarding. Saken blew up his magazine, destroying himself, his ship and all four of the enemy.

The Russian army once more began their advance along the north shore of the Liman towards Otchakov, covered from the sea by the inshore flotilla and a detachment of the ships of Paul Jones.

The Russian fleet of light coastal and river craft had been built under the auspices of Colonel Samuel Bentham, brother of Jeremy, who later became Inspector-General of the British navy. One of his creations was a vessel called *Vermicular*, over 200 feet long, with a beam of 16 feet and a draft of 4 inches. Propelled by 100 rowers, her hull was jointed in seven places, so that she could go round bends in the rivers.

On the morning of June 18th the Turkish inshore forces counter-attacked without great result and it was not until ten days later that the decisive action began. Another Turkish attack was checked when their flagship and second flagship ran aground; Paul Jones and Nassau attacked in their turn, but Nassau's flotillas, concentrating on the grounded Turkish ships, left the American's big ships uncovered and they suffered some loss, one of them being sunk. A great controversy broke out between Nassau and Paul Jones as a consequence, each accusing the other of having left him unsupported.

Nevertheless, the Russians had done well; as a result of the action the Turkish Kapudan Pasha, the former commander-in-chief at Tchesma, formerly Hassan Pasha and now styled Hassan-el-Ghazi, decided to withdraw his big ships from the Liman. Paul Jones and Suvarov had built a powerful battery on the south or Russian side of the exit from the Liman and, in avoiding this, the Turks steered so far to the northward that nine of them ran aground. First thing next morning they were attacked by Nassau's small craft and all were destroyed, except one, which was towed off and incorporated in the Russian fleet.

Paul Jones and Nassau disputed as to the actual damage they had done to the enemy and as to the share each had had in the work. Dr. Anderson comes to the conclusion that 'it seems fairly clear that, in the two days fighting, the Turks did lose a total of fifteen vessels of which ten were sailing ships of some size . . . The Turkish loss in men must have been enormous; 885 prisoners were taken on the 28th and 788 on the 29th. The Russian flotilla had eighteen killed and sixty-seven wounded in the series of actions, their loss in sailing ships was probably slight.'[1]

Just after this, on July 9th, the Russians began their final attack on Otchakov. Phase One of the assault was the destruction of the Turkish naval forces still in the Liman and this was done by Paul Jones and the light forces together.

Meanwhile the Turkish battle fleet was committed to aid in the defence of Otchakov and set out in search of its Russian opposite number. On July 10th the two fleets were in sight; three days of alternate manoeuvring and calm followed, until battle was joined on July 14th off Feodonisi or Serpent Island, twenty miles east of the mouth of the Danube.

The Russians under Rear-Admiral Voinovitch had four ships of the

[1] R. C. Anderson, *Naval Wars in the Levant*, p. 327, University Press, Liverpool, 1952.

line and eight frigates, which also fought in the line, while the Turks had seventeen ships of the line and eight frigates. 'Omitting the small craft on both sides they [the Turks] must have had a superiority of strength of at least two to one,' remarks Dr. Anderson.

What followed was the first battle ever fought in the open sea by the Russian Black Sea fleet. Neither side was anxious to come too close, naturally enough as far as the Russians were concerned, since they were so heavily outnumbered, and all that happened was an encounter between the leading ships in both fleets in which Ushakov, the commodore second-in-command, distinguished himself by going to the rescue of the two leading Russians which were in danger of being cut off.

Operations against Otchakov went on; in order to distract the attention of the Turkish fleet from them a flotilla of five gunboats under Captain Seniavin was sent to operate against the coastwise shipping on the Anatolian coast of the Black Sea, and during a three-week cruise the flotilla took or destroyed ten ships.

After the Turks had made a successful attempt to run the blockade of Otchakov in October, Potemkin's dissatisfaction with the leadership of the fleet came to a head. Nassau and Paul Jones were replaced by Admiral Mordvinov. Paul Jones, protesting, went to St. Petersburg, but he could obtain no redress, was made to appear guilty of scandalous conduct and left Russia for good. Nassau received command of light coastal forces in the Baltic, where war with Sweden broke out again in 1788. It has already been explained that this prevented the Russians from sending a battle fleet from the Baltic to the Mediterranean to take the Turks in the rear, as had been done in 1769 by Orlov.

Potemkin had not been the only belligerent leader dissatisfied with the conduct of the war in the Black Sea. Sultan Selim III caused his commander, Hassan, to be executed.

The failure of the Russians to send a fleet to the Mediterranean from the Baltic meant that 1789 was a fairly quiet year for the Russian Black Sea fleet. Dr. Anderson points out that Voinovitch had only four ships of the line under his command, while the Turks had seventeen. Under these circumstances there was little that the Russians could do save keep out of the way of the Turkish battle fleet, raid their coastwise shipping and use whatever advantage was to be obtained from the slow advance of the Russian army. This, on September 25th, took Hadji Bey, near the site of the present-day Odessa, and compelled the Turks to pull back their naval forces, both light and heavy, from the Otchakov area. The Russian army continued its advance, taking Akerman and Bender; while a new naval base, which has remained of first-class importance to this day, was established at Nicolaiev at the entrance to the Bug.

In 1790 Voinovitch was succeeded by Ushakov and a fleet strong enough to challenge the Turks for command of the Black Sea was assembled at Sevastopol. The first Turkish operation planned was a landing in the Crimea; Ushakov broke off commerce-raiding on the Turkish coast and went to intercept the enemy. The two fleets met in the Straits of Kertch, the Russians being slightly outnumbered. There was a series of exchanges of broadsides and the Turks were driven off; thanks to their copper bottoms they had the advantage in speed and could make their escape, but there was no more question of a landing in the Crimea.

The Russian army, free from its need to guard the Crimea, was able to continue its advance through what is now Bessarabia towards the mouths of the Danube, with Ushakov and the Turkish admiral each giving support from the sea to their respective armies.

The two fleets thus engaged met off the peninsula of Tendra, to the south-east of Kinburn. The Turks withdrew despite their superiority in numbers, but, trying to get away, were raked by the Russians and two of their ships of the line, crippled, lagged behind and were overtaken by the Russians after a two-day chase. One surrendered at once, but the other made a great fight. This was the flagship of the Turkish vice-admiral, Said Bey, and she was finally sunk after a single-ship action by Ushakov's flagship *Rozhdestvo Christovo*, with a loss of nearly all on board.

An interesting feature of Ushakov's handling of his fleet in this battle which had begun off Tendra and ended off Hadji Bey was his use of a detached squadron of three large frigates, in a position which, according to the Russians, foreshadowed the disposition of the British fleet in two divisions used by Nelson at Trafalgar.

Once again a Russian victory at sea made possible an advance by the Russian army, which, continuing its advance, took Ismail and Braila on the Danube with the help of the Russian river flotillas. As a result of this, by the time that the campaigning season started in 1791, the Turks were ready for an armistice, which was duly signed at Galatz, while at the same time the Turks, scraping the bottom of the barrel as far as their fleets were concerned, assembled at Varna a force brought from places as far away as Albania, Algeria, Tunis and Tripoli. Altogether, from these various sources the Turks collected

eighteen ships of the line and seventeen frigates, which, with auxiliaries, anchored off Cape Kaliakria to the north-east of Varna.
Although he had six ships of the line and twelve frigates, Ushakov
attacked, leading his ships in between the Turkish fleet just getting
under way and the land. A few Russian broadsides served to break up
whatever unity there existed in the motley Turkish force, which fled
in the direction of Constantinople.

This was one of those useless battles like New Orleans, fought after
the nominal conclusion of hostilities because neither side, in the
absence of modern communications, knew that the war was officially
over.

Thus ended—in 1791—the fourth Russo-Turkish war; the armistice became the Treaty of Jassy and in the next year the Russians were
able to move their frontiers westward from the Bug to the Dniester.

A full exploitation of this victory was made impossible by the withdrawal from the struggle of the Austrian forces which were needed to
put down a rising in Belgium, started by an overspill of the ideas of
the French Revolution.

This Russian advance, which coincided with the virtual extinction
of Polish independence, led to a sudden crisis in Anglo-Russian relations, for Pitt believed that the Russian territorial gains would upset
the balance of power in Europe. As Pitt was opposed to the Russians,
it is not surprising to find that Fox supported them, but the crisis
never came to a head and was eventually submerged in the much
bigger and more alarming events of the French Revolutionary wars.

It had been in accordance with the *mores* of those and of later days
that, in 1787, as soon as the Russians were involved with the Turks in
the Black Sea, the Swedes should begin to seek their own advantage
and the disadvantage of the Russians in the Baltic and that the
Russians should make counter-moves. Gustav III of Sweden began
manoeuvres for the capture of Norway while brow-beating the Danes.
At the same time the Russians stoked up the fires of a pro-Russian,
anti-Swedish fifth column in the Swedish possession of Finland. Of
these moves war was a natural consequence. However, the timing,
from the Swedish point of view, was bad, for matters came to a head
before the Russians had sent a fleet to the Mediterranean to fight the
Turks, so that the Swedes were faced by the undivided strength of
the Russian Baltic fleet. It would seem that one of the reasons for the
delay in sending ships out of the Baltic was diplomatic difficulties met
with by the Russians in organising the expedition—difficulties partly
instigated by the United Kingdom.

Despite the rapidly mounting distrust of Russia felt by Britain, however, and the obstacles put in the way of the Russians obtaining supplies on their voyage, officers of British nationality were not recalled from the Russian service.

When yet another Russo-Swedish war opened in July 1788, after Gustav III had presented an ultimatum of the most unacceptable sort, the Swedish plan was, after defeating the Russian Baltic fleet, to land an invasion force some 30,000 strong at Oranienbaum, and advance upon St. Petersburg. Once again the future of Russia depended upon command of the Baltic; what the Russian Government thought of its prospects may be seen from the fact that its first reaction was to suggest moving to Moscow. Catherine the Great promptly put an end to this idea and the Russian fleet, forty-five vessels strong, in poor repair and badly manned, was ordered out from Kronstadt in search of the Swedish fleet. This latter, to a great extent composed of obsolete ships, commanded by Charles, Duke of Södermanland (later King Charles XIII), was also seeking the enemy, since the landing of troops at Oranienbaum could not be made until the Russian fleet was out of action.

For the battle which took place on July 17th, the Swedes had twenty ships of 1,180 guns, while the Russians had seventeen ships of 1,220 guns; although the Russian fleet was by no means fully efficient it had a great advantage in the flagship of Greig, the commander-in-chief, the *Rostislav*, of 100 guns, by far the biggest ship on either side. In the days of wooden ships of the line a vessel of 100 guns was generally considered the equal of two of seventy-four, and it was just as well for the Russians that that was so on this occasion, for their fleet went into action in scattered groups.

The head of their line with Greig and the *Rostislav* attacked the Swedish van, the *Rostislav* tackling the Swedish fleet flagship *Gustaf III* and another ship of the line, but the rear of the Russian fleet held off at a range so long that it was able to do little damage to the Swedish rear. This, therefore, was able to concentrate at its leisure on the one Russian ship which had tried to close it, the *Vladislav* (74), which was obliged to surrender after having been so badly damaged that she was dead in the water and had lost one-third of her crew. This Russian loss was balanced by the fact that the *Rostislav* managed to capture the flagship of the Swedish van, the *Prins Gustaf* (70).

In theory, this battle which took its name from the nearby island of Hogland, ending with the loss of one ship of the line on each side, was a draw, but in fact it may be counted a Russian success, since the Swedish attempt to attack St. Petersburg was given up.

The Swedes excused themselves as best they could by drawing attention to the large number of British captains in the Russian fleet— nine out of the seventeen Russian ships of the line had British commanders—and by accusing the Russians of a breach of international etiquette in using incendiary projectiles. Greig answered by half denying the charge and adding that 'fire balls' might have been issued to some of the ships which were to have been sent to the Mediterranean, since there were no restrictions upon their use against the Turks, who were not a civilised nation.

After Hogland both fleets withdrew to their bases, the Swedes to Sveaborg and the Russians to the island of Seskari, forty miles west of Kronstadt. Refitting and replenishment over, Greig and the Russians were quicker off the mark and followed the Swedes to Sveaborg. A group of three Swedish ships of the line were found outside in a thick fog and one of them taken, though she was too badly damaged to be brought away and had to be burnt. Greig then settled down to a blockade, but very soon afterwards he died. The Swedes were much encouraged by this, while the Russians and the British alike who had served under him were deeply distressed. Trevenen, one of his British captains, wrote to Edward Riou of Copenhagen fame:

> He was obliged to be in his own person Admiral of the fleet, Captain of his ship and Lieutenant of his watch. In short, I am decidedly of the opinion that he fell a victim to the incapacity of everyone about him and to the honesty of his intentions and zeal for the service of the Empress . . . He has gone through the fiery ordeal of temptation and not a spark of dishonour has branded him with a stain. He has been seven times tried in the fire and is proved pure. The touchstone of virtue has been applied to him and his character remains unchanged and unspotted. In short, after having had the disposal of immense sums of money, which in going through the hands of Russians would have melted like the baseless fabric. [*sic*].
>
> His person was rather large and excessively awkward. His legs very large; his belly and breast rather sunken; his shoulders round and his head stooping forward. In his winter dress at Kronstadt nothing could look more like an old Scotch wife well wrapped up in cold weather.[1]

Clearly Greig was a great man whom the Russians were fortunate to have in their service; but they nearly had an even greater. At this time Nelson, tired of four years' unemployment, was, according to his wife, thinking seriously of offering himself to the Russian navy.

The Swedes set about reorganising their fleet, while Greig was succeeded as commander-in-chief by Tchitchagov.

[1] *A Memoir of James Trevenen*, edited by Christopher Lloyd and R. C. Anderson, published by the Navy Records Society, 1959.

Baulked in their attempt to attack St. Petersburg by means of a landing from the sea, the Swedish forces tried an overland attack, advancing eastward along the Finnish coast with the support of their light coastal forces. However, although they were under the same crown the Finnish authorities would not support the Swedes and the Swedish army had to withdraw. At just about this time the Danes attacked South Sweden and the Swedish position became critical. Because of the Danish threat and because of the doubtful attitude of the Finns, the Swedish battle fleet withdrew through the young ice from Sveaborg to Karlskrona in the southern Baltic.

Meanwhile a small Russian squadron, mostly drawn from the White Sea fleet at Archangel, and based on Copenhagen, had been co-operating with the Danes, who were now besieging Gothenburg, until Britain, the Netherlands and Prussia put diplomatic pressure on the Danes and persuaded them to withdraw. British intervention was, as usual, due to the fact that the protection of Sweden and marine supplies from the Baltic was still a vital concern of British foreign policy.

When the Danes withdrew from the Swedish campaign the Russian fleet from Copenhagen went off to blockade Karlskrona, to prevent the Swedish fleet, on its way from Sveaborg, from entering the port. However, the Russian admiral, von Dessen, remiss in his duties, returned too soon to Copenhagen, so that the Swedes' fleet was able to reach safety undisturbed.

The problems involved for the Russians in trying to maintain a fleet at sea are shown by the events of October, when their ships of the line were blockading the enemy in Karlskrona. On September 30th a ship badly damaged by weather was obliged to return to port. On October 2nd a cutter was damaged. In bad weather on October 4th and 5th two other ships were in distress and were being driven down on to the Swedish coast.

The weather improved on the next day, so that the two ships were able to escape destruction, but another ship damaged her rudder and had to be sent home, together with a ship of the line and another cutter. On the following day—October 7th—the gale strengthened just before midnight and two ships were in distress, but the unfavourable wind did not permit of their being sent home. It continued to blow and sails, rigging, masts and yards suffered throughout the fleet as the ships spent two days and nights clawing themselves off rocks of the enemy-held lee shore. On the 11th another ship sprang a leak, and finally the whole fleet went home, raising the blockade.

At this time the Russians also withdrew from their position off

Hangö and returned home. The season's fighting at sea was brought to an end by the freezing of the Baltic; the ice lasted much longer than usual and it was not until May 1789 that Tchitchagov and the Russian fleet once more left port.

The Kattegat was far to the south, but even so the onset of winter needed special precautions if war was to be waged; these were not taken by the Russian squadron there, which suffered all sorts of woes, ships being caught in the ice, losing their anchors and being driven ashore. Finally, after Christmas, von Dessen was recalled and Povalishin from the White Sea given command.

The scene was now set for the spring of 1789, the melting of the ice and the second round of the war, which began with a couple of smart little performances by the brig *Merkurii* commanded by Lieutenant Crown—or Cronin—an Irishman who, on May 10th, captured the Swedish vessel *Snappup* of ten guns. A little later in his ship of twenty-two guns Cronin chased the Swedish frigate *Venus* of forty-four guns up what is now known as the Oslofiord and took her. He approached disguised as a merchant ship and then, when in striking distance, in a flat calm, came up with the enemy by the use of great oars or sweeps. On board the Russian ship during both these actions was Mrs. Cronin, who distinguished herself looking after the wounded during the fighting.

As the ice began to melt this year the situation was of the kind imagined by those tortuous minds who set problems in war games. The Russian fleet was in three groups—eleven ships of the line at Copenhagen, ten at Reval and fourteen at Kronstadt, while the combined Swedish battle fleet of twenty-one ships was at Karlskrona. The ice, of course, melted first in the south, so that the Swedish fleet would be able to leave Karlskrona before the Russians would have a chance of uniting their three fleets. An additional complication, but to the Russian advantage, was the fact that although the Danish fleet had withdrawn from the prosecution of the offensive against Sweden it was still committed to the defence of the Russian fleet if it were attacked in Danish waters.

Despite the opportunity which the Swedes had of getting to sea and trying to attack one of the divisions of the Russian fleet before the others could stir through the ice to come to its aid, nothing was done until July. Then the Swedes challenged the Kronstadt squadron, only to withdraw when the Reval squadron came to the rescue.

The light coastal forces on both sides, however, continued to carry on a war that was almost independent of that conducted by the big ships, since these latter were incapable of manoeuvre in the narrow waters, inshore, on the coast of Finland. The strength of the Russian light forces had been prodigiously expanded during the winter of 1788–9, about 150 ships having been built, mostly of the same types as those in the service of the Swedes. They ranged in size from rowing frigates 130 feet long, carrying between thirty-two and fifty guns, with masts and sails as well as oars, to small gunboats propelled by oars alone and mounting only a single gun.

The Russian coastal forces were under the command of Nassau-Siegen, from the Black Sea, and their first task was the recapture of Rochensalm, which had fallen to the Swedes. However, before this was undertaken, another fleet action was fought. On paper it was indecisive, but in fact it settled the question of Russo-Swedish rivalry down to the present day. Tchitchagov took his fleet of twenty ships of the line down to the southern end of the Baltic and at the same time ordered Koslanianov, from Copenhagen, with eleven ships of the line to join him in order to be ready to meet the Swedish fleet as it emerged from its hibernation at Karlskrona.

However, before the two parts of the Russian fleet joined, the Swedes with twenty-one ships of the line met Tchitchagov and his twenty vessels off the island of Oland on July 26th. The two sides were well matched numerically and, although the engagement lasted for six hours, neither side was able seriously to damage the other. This was in part due to the fact that the commander of the Swedish rear, Admiral Lilljehorn, failed to keep up with the main body commanded by Duke Charles; it is not clear why this happened, but the consequences were disastrous for Sweden. Fred Jane wrote in *The Imperial Russian Navy*, 'Lilljehorn's inaction may be said to have sealed the fate of Sweden; the last chance to break the Russian naval power was thrown away.'

Dr. R. C. Anderson concurs, saying, in *Naval Wars in the Baltic*, that the Swedes 'lost almost the only good chance of success' which had come their way during the war.

The Russians had started to withdraw as soon as they had sighted the Swedes on this occasion, for Tchitchagov wished for the arrival of Koslanianov's Copenhagen squadron, which would have given him an advantage of thirty ships to twenty-one instead of even terms, and after the Swedish pursuit had been shaken off the Russians continued to avoid decisive action. The Swedes, having been back to Karlskrona to land their wounded, went south to try and intercept Koslanianov's nine ships of the line, but missed them. The two parts of the Russian battle fleet were reunited and the focus of operations shifted back to the Gulf of Finland.

Here the war between the opposing flotillas of coastal craft was soon in full swing. The two sides were more or less equal and the situation was complicated by the fact that both forces were divided into two groups, each of which had part of the enemy between them. Thus, from west to east there were first the Swedes based on Stockholm, then, in Finland, there were the Russians at Porkala, the Swedes at Svenskund and the Russians at Frederikshamn. The Russians at Porkala were able to prevent the dispatch of reinforcements from Stockholm for Svenskund; they decided to take advantage of this and concentrate their coastal forces in an attempt to destroy the Swedish force, which they held blockaded in Svenskund. Nassau-Siegen was in command of the Russians and the attack was made on August 24th. The Swedish ships lay in line abreast across the entrance to the harbour—forty-nine vessels in all, carrying 686 guns; the Russians were in two divisions—Nassau-Siegen with sixty-six ships and a detached squadron under Balle with twenty ships, the total Russian force thus being eighty-six ships with 1,283 guns.

Instead of attacking with both Russian divisions simultaneously, Balle was sent in first and lost heavily, for his ships straggled into action so that the Swedes could easily concentrate against them as they came up in ones and twos. Nassau-Siegen took nine hours to get into action and by the time he was there Balle had been beaten off. Nassau-Siegen, once engaged, fought a muddled but tough fight and the Swedes withdrew. As a reward the Empress Catherine sent him two dressing-gowns.

The year 1789 had been indecisive on land as well as on sea. The Swedes had advanced as far as Helsingförs on the way to St. Petersburg, but after the defeat of Svenskund had pulled back to the original position from which their offensive had started at the beginning of the campaigning season.

The year 1790 was to see the climax of nearly a century's naval warfare between Russia and Sweden. Denmark had finally made peace, leaving the Swedes with their hands free to the south and east, and the lukewarm feelings of the Finns towards the war had been replaced in their hearts by a deep desire to expel the Russians from their country.

At the beginning of the year the Swedes had twenty-five ships of the line, while the Russians had thirty—being divided in three groups, eleven at Kronstadt, ten at Reval and nine in reserve. As usual the Swedes had the more favourable ice conditions and got to sea before the Russians; thus they started off a season's campaigning which they hoped would lead them to St. Petersburg. First they attacked the

Russian base at Baltic Port and burned all the stores they found there. They then made their big move with an attack on the Russians at Reval. Duke Charles had twenty-two big ships against the ten under Tchitchagov, but the Swedes, attacking in a gale, did not press home their advantage and withdrew with a loss of one ship.

However, this Swedish reverse on the south side of the Gulf of Finland was matched by an important success on the north side. The King of Sweden in person with his coastal forces had forced the entry into Frederikshamn, sinking twenty-nine Russian small craft for a loss of only one of his own, and had then gone on to land his invasion force, destined for St. Petersburg, at Viborg, only eighty miles from the Russian capital.

The next move was to be the link-up between the king's light forces and his army on the one hand, and Duke Charles' battle fleet on the other. But on the way to the rendezvous Duke Charles was attacked by the Russian Kronstadt force under Admiral Kruse—seventeen Russian ships against twenty-one Swedish; there was an indecisive but fierce fight on June 3rd. Then, on the next day, Tchitchagov's Reval squadron came up and the Swedes withdrew into Viborg before the superior forces of the enemy (thirty to twenty-one).

The link-up between the coastal and seagoing forces planned by the Swedish king had taken place, but it was of no value to him, since the Russians had command of the sea and proceeded to exercise it by keeping the Swedes shut up in Viborg for a month until their provisions ran short and they decided that the only alternative to starvation was to break through the Russian blockading forces. It was an attempt by a beleaguered fleet to break out similar to that of the Spanish at Santiago in 1898 and the Russians at Port Arthur in 1904.

The venture began late on the night of July 2nd; first the Swedes attacked with light craft to drive off the Russians and then sent out fireships to finish the job. However, one of the Swedish fireships was blown back on their own fleet and set fire to a ship of the line and a frigate, both of which blew up. This disorganised the Swedes completely, and their battle fleet fled, two of their ships being captured by Tchitchagov. Following the Swedish big ships, now that the Russian blockade had been broken, came the light forces under the King of Sweden, who escaped to Svenskund with the loss of thirty ships.

During this operation the Swedish ruler spent a proportion of his time in his cabin aboard the royal yacht drafting an announcement in elegant terms of his own surrender, but it never came to that. This Battle of Viborg, however, did mean the end of the Swedish battle force as a force that had any chance of beating the Russians in a fleet action.

Notwithstanding the result of this battle, however, the powerful Swedish inshore fleet remained intact and Nassau-Siegen moved at once to destroy it. He was as sure of his success now as his enemy, the King of Sweden, had been of his own failure a few days earlier. Before going to the attack at the entrance to Svenskund he fitted up a tent on board his own galley-flagship for the accommodation of the sovereign whom he believed would soon be his prisoner. The first of Nassau-Siegen's attacks was an attempt, made with no preparation, to rush the Swedish position; it failed and the Russians drew off to re-form. Another attack, prepared this time, was then made. It also failed, as did all the other Russian attacks made during the long day of high summer on the threshold of the midnight sun. Only when half the Russian force were casualties—killed, wounded or prisoners, did Nassau-Siegen withdraw, and once again Stockholm was saved.

The defeat of the inshore squadron, the claims of the war against Turkey, the Anglo-Russian crisis over Otchakov and the desire of Catherine to have a hand free with which to seize more Polish territory as that unfortunate State moved towards its penultimate partition in the eighteenth century, all argued for yet another compromise Russo-Swedish peace. However, although it was a compromise on paper, in fact the issue of the struggle between the two countries, which had been waged for nearly a century, was decided. Russia was established as a first-class power athwart Europe and Asia, and Sweden fell back to the secondary role which was made inevitable for her by reason of the smallness of her population.

CHAPTER VI

WAR AGAINST—AND FOR—NAPOLEON
Part One: The Baltic

1795–1814

F ROM the storm centre of the French Revolution the waves, which were to engulf all Europe in wars from 1792 to 1815, spread outward. France was at war with Prussia and Austria, Spain and Sardinia in 1792; in the next year she was at war with Britain and Holland as well, and the Russian Baltic fleet was mobilised as a precaution. In 1794 the armed neutrality of Sweden and Denmark was revived—as usual an anti-British measure, since it was the British who were able to maintain the blockade which was so onerous to neutrals and, in the end, catastrophic to her enemies.

Finally, in 1795, Russia was at war with France as well and a fleet of twelve ships of the line and eight frigates were sent by Catherine the Great to serve under British orders in the North Sea; two years of cruising and blockading by the British and Russian fleets in inter-mittent co-operation under Duncan followed. In 1797 came the mutinies of the British fleets, first at Spithead and then at the Nore, and Russian writers, naturally enough, make much of their claim that for a time the Allied blockade of the enemy's North Sea coast was exercised by the Russian fleet alone.

This the enemy never discovered until it was too late, thanks to Duncan, who took his one loyal ship of the line, the *Venerable*, close to the hostile shore and then flung out a series of signals supposedly to the other ships of his squadron just over the horizon, although, in fact, the ships were a long way over the horizon—and in a state of mutiny at that.

In 1796 Catherine the Great died and her insane son, Paul I, whom she had kept off the throne which was rightfully his for forty years, ruled in crazy tyranny, dining in his crown and suffering subsequent agonies with indigestion, while filling his officers and courtiers with dread that they would be in the next transport for Siberia.

One of the manifestations of Paul's madness was a mania for uniforms which led to his trying to put all his principal subjects, soldiers, sailors, courtiers, landowners and officials, into uniforms of his own design but based on the clothes worn at the Court of Prussia forty or fifty years before. Naval officers received a uniform of green which they were to wear for nearly a century—almost the only naval officers in the world who did not wear blue or white. The first Russian naval uniform had, in fact, been white with green facings, selected by the Empress Elizabeth, as this was the colour scheme of a gown which she was wearing when called upon to decide how her naval officers were to be dressed.

The new Tsar's idea of the sanctity of his uniform was such as to cause him, when he berated an officer for some fault, to order him to take off his uniform at once. The luckless officer was then sent home in his underclothes, even in a Russian winter.

But Paul, though cruelly mad, had a very clear idea of the importance of his navy, the uses to which it could be put and the necessity for strengthening it. A fleet under Makarov was sent from the Baltic into the North Sea, and at about the same time—in a manner to be described in the next chapter—another fleet was sent from the Black Sea through the Dardanelles. Fear of the French Revolution and of Napoleon Bonaparte was such that, for once, Russo-Turkish antagonism abated sufficiently for the Turks to give their consent to the passage of the Straits by the Russians. At the same time a Russian army under Suvarov was operating in Switzerland until its defeat by Masséna outside Zürich.

Meanwhile, in the North Sea, the British and Russian forces were planning a combined operation against the enemy-held coast in North Holland—one of a series of attempts to open a second front against the French. A British squadron under Vice-Admiral Mitchell, with the Russian ships of the line *Retvisan* (74) and *Mistislav* (66), captured thirteen Dutch warships laid up at Den Helder, and followed the rest of the Dutch fleet to the Vlieter. The pursuit through shallow and badly marked waters was difficult and dangerous, the *Retvisan* and two of the British ships running aground. The Dutch, unwilling to fight against their lawful ruler, the Stadhouder William V, and for Bonaparte, surrendered without firing a shot. Twelve more ships, including eight of the line, fell into British hands.

The landings of the Anglo-Russian forces were successfully made, but the same sort of paralysis as that which crippled the landings at Suvla in 1915 and at Anzio in 1944 descended upon the Allied commander-in-chief, the Duke of York, famed in nursery rhyme if not in history. It was therefore comparatively easy for the French to concentrate sufficient forces to drive out the invaders—the Russian component being withdrawn to garrison duties in the Channel

Islands, after a riotous passage through Yarmouth, where they surprised the East Anglians by drinking the oil out of the street lamps.

In Jersey and Guernsey the Russians passed the winter; local observers agreed that they behaved reasonably well—there was only one death sentence—but they had what seemed to the islanders a remarkable tendency to take off all their clothes, and bathe in the local streams. Units fell into two sharply distinguished categories— those whose officers looked after their men, and those whose officers spent their time and the British tax-payers' money on feasting without thought for their soldiers for whom the money was intended.

When the Russians finally sailed away the event was marked by the granting of a free pardon to the man under sentence of death.

Altogether these operations were not a happy exercise for the Russians in Anglo-Russian co-operation. In the first place the political liaison officer sent by the Russian Embassy in London to help the squadron at Yarmouth went around to the tradespeople of the town warning them not to give credit to his fellow countrymen from the navy. This was perhaps good advice, for the Russian scales of pay were such that the pay of a Russian post captain was equivalent to that of a British able seaman, at a time when the British navy was on the point of mutiny because the rates of pay of the lower deck had not been raised for over a hundred years.

In addition, the *Retvisan* and *Mistislav* were terribly slow carrying out sail drills and exercises, trailing miserably behind the British ships. All in all the Russians were very unhappy—except for Tchitchagov, son of the admiral, who spent his spare time courting, successfully, the daughter of an Admiralty official at Chatham.

A little later a combination of the French victory over the Russians at Zürich, its skilful exploitation by Bonaparte from the point of view of psychological warfare—or rather peacefare—and the crazy delusions of Paul I caused the Russians to withdraw from the war and to adopt a position of malevolent neutrality to Britain.

The causes of this were two: first, Bonaparte treated the Russian prisoners taken in Switzerland very well and sent them home with new uniforms; second, Paul had conceived the idea of getting himself made Grand Master of the Knights of Malta—the Knights having been driven out of their island by the French, who were in turn besieged in the island by the British. Paul took his position of Grand Master with such boundless zeal as to order his warships to fly the flag of the Knights rather than the Russian Cross of St. Andrew, which for a century had been the Russian naval ensign, a measure which was, of course, most unpopular with his own officers. At the same time, the

British made it clear that they had no intention of letting Malta go to the Russians, once they had captured it—which they did in 1800.

Before the siege was over the Russian fleet under Ushakov had withdrawn, its commander being followed by the execrations of Nelson which have come down the ages to us. The British admiral said, amongst other things, of Ushakov that he was 'a blackguard' and 'polished outside, but the bear is close to the skin . . . He is jealous of our influence.' The Russian ships could not be expected to keep the seas during the winter, said Ushakov, and, commented Nelson, they had shown no sign of wishing to do so in the summer either.

This exemplifies one of Nelson's few really unpleasant characteristics, a scathing contempt for nearly all foreigners, and below all the rest he seems to have put foreign naval officers, enemy or allied. However, a few of his own brother officers in the Royal Navy, of course, occupied an equally low place in his esteem.

Nelson, having been involved in the Mediterranean with Ushakov and the Russian ambition to possess Malta, soon found himself at the entrance to the Baltic faced with the situation which had arisen from the British action in thwarting that ambition. Once Russia had withdrawn from the war and become a neutral, the rights of neutrals in the face of the British blockade became a vital question to the Tsar. With the co-operation of the Danes and the Swedes, whose commerce was, as usual in wartime, suffering greatly, he once again set up an Armed Neutrality; it is a matter of note that all three sovereigns of this alliance were mad—Paul, Christian VII of Denmark and Gustav IV Adolf of Sweden. To suppress this the Battle of Copenhagen was fought, so quickly that the Swedes and the Russians did not have time to come to the aid of their Danish partners, and the Swedes made peace, once a face-saving formula could be reached. Nelson was left facing the Russians—Hyde Parker, his commander-in-chief at Copenhagen, having been recalled to the United Kingdom.

A few days before the victory of Copenhagen the Tsar had been murdered by his own exasperated officers. His son succeeded him as Alexander I; he was very nearly as strange a character as his father, but without the same bent for war, torture, murder and imprisonment.

Nelson learned of the accession of Alexander I from the Russian Minister in Copenhagen, who added that the new Tsar had ordered his fleet to abstain from hostilities. Nelson believed that the danger of war between Britain and Russia was over, but in fact the relations between the two countries remained difficult for several weeks.

As usual the Russian Baltic fleet was in two groups, separated by the 180 miles from Reval to Kronstadt and by the ice in the Gulf of Finland. Nelson moved to be ready to cut off the Reval squadron, at the same time warning the Swedes that if they interfered he would attack them, but when Nelson arrived at Reval, in theory on a courtesy visit, he found that the Russian squadron had left for Kronstadt ten days before.

As soon as the news of Nelson's arrival came to St. Petersburg, Count Pahlen, the new Tsar's principal adviser and leader of the plot that had killed his father, sent the British admiral a message that the only way in which the British could show their wish for peace, which Nelson stressed on arrival, was by leaving at once, and this the British fleet did. Following this there was an Anglo-Russian exchange of courtesies and of good wishes while Nelson, succeeded by Sir Charles Pole as commander-in-chief, went home.

Half-time in the struggle between Britain and France came in 1802 with the Treaty of Amiens. The pause for the main contestants lasted just over a year, and when the war was recommenced it once more spread over most of Europe; by April 1805 there was again a war going on in the Baltic, with the Russians and the Swedes in alliance with Britain against Napoleon.

Russian troops landed on Rügen, prepared to advance from Stralsund against the French to drive them out of Hanover and rescue that kingdom for George III. But the French victories at Ulm and at Jena broke up the anti-French combination, and a British fleet again entered the Baltic to support its allies and overcome its enemies. In 1807 the Danish fleet was once more 'Copenhagened'; most of it fell into British hands after an ultimatum, without a declaration of war, and the bombardment of the Danish capital. At the same time the British took the islands of Heligoland and of Anholt to help secure the entrance to the Baltic.

Russia declared war on Britain in November 1807, the Russians and the French being allies after the Treaty of Tilsit, and the Russians once more prepared to attack Sweden through Finland. A British fleet and expeditionary force was sent into the Baltic in the spring of the next year. The fleet was under Sir James Saumarez, with his flag in Nelson's *Victory*; the expeditionary force was landed at Gothenburg under Sir John Moore, who within a year was to be buried 'darkly at dead of night' at Corunna and to live until the present day and beyond in a poem.

The function of the British was to prevent the union of the Danish and Norwegian troops across the Skagerrak and to prevent the Danes from invading Sweden. In the meantime the Russians won their final great success of the war against Sweden with the capture of Sveaborg, with which went, as Sir John Moore noted at the time, Sweden's last hope of retaking Finland.

Meanwhile the crazy King of Sweden was planning all sorts of large-scale schemes for attacks, and the British fleet was doing what it could to hold the Russian navy in check and handicap French military moves on the south shore of the Baltic by raids, landings and threats of raids and landings. In these operations under Captain T. B. Martin, R.N., who played something of the role given Hornblower by C. S. Forester in *The Commodore*, skilful use was made of what much later became known as 'psychological warfare' against the French, the Russians and their rather unwilling allies. First and foremost came the need to tell the enemy what was going on, as opposed to what Napoleon said was going on. Cracks were beginning to appear in the Napoleonic empire, especially in Spain, and Martin spread the glad tidings, particularly amongst the theoretically enemy Spanish troops brought by Napoleon to the Baltic to fight his battles.

In the meantime, a combined Russian and French force, 1,600 strong, had landed on May 21st on Gotland and taken Visby, the principal port of the island. There seems to have been no command of the sea—the Russians and French had been able to land without the Swedes stopping them, and now the Swedes sent a force to the island which got ashore without the Russians being able to interfere. The result of this move and counter-move was a truce, under the terms of which the Franco-Russian force evacuated Gotland and, at the same time, the Russians also withdrew from the Aland Islands, which they had captured during the previous winter by marching across the ice.

A Russian move against Stockholm was checked by the Swedish and British fleets, although the Swedes had been weakened by the loss of their light coastal forces during recent operations in the Gulf of Finland.

In August 1808 the combined British and Swedish fleets met the Russians—the combined fleets had twelve ships of the line and the Russians nine—and the Russians withdrew, pursued by the Allies, whose two fastest ships, the British *Centaur* and *Implacable*, caught the rearmost Russian, *Vsevelod*, chased her aground and destroyed her. After that the Russians were blockaded in Rögersvik for several weeks, eventually getting free and returning to Kronstadt at the beginning of the autumn.

77

Attempts to use the British expeditionary force brought to Sweden by Sir John Moore had failed—no agreement with the mad King of Sweden was possible and the army was taken away—after Sir John Moore had been briefly placed under arrest by Gustav for refusing to fall in with his madder plans for an all-out attack against the Russians. Moore went to his death at Corunna and Saumarez, the *Victory* and the rest of the fleet came back to the Baltic in the spring of 1809.

Raids were carried out in Finnish waters by boats of the British and Swedish fleets, but although the Russian big ships were at least equal in strength to the combined British and Swedes, they remained in Kronstadt, while a Russian attempt to invade northern Sweden overland via Umea was defeated by the Swedes.

In this same year, 1809, Gustav IV Adolf was deposed and carried off, vomiting with fear, to an exile in which he lived many impoverished and miserable years. His successor was his uncle, Charles XIII, who as the Duke of Södermanland had commanded the Swedish fleet in the last war with Russia. He was soon forced to side with Napoleon, for in those days Napoleon and his ideas had the same thrill for the bored and frustrated middle classes of Sweden and indeed of Europe that National Socialism and Communism had over a century later.

Peace between Russia and Sweden followed in September 1809. Sweden gave up the Åland Islands, all that remained to her of Finland, and part of her northern territories.

Then in the following January a Swedish-French alliance was formed which meant that Sweden was forced definitely to declare war on Britain. Now, in theory, Britain was at war with both Russia and Sweden, but it was a very limited, if not a phoney, war. Saumarez took great care to avoid action of any sort with the Swedes which would make the conclusion of peace with them more difficult when once they decided to detach themselves from the French. At the same time there seems to have been a general disposition to refrain from an attack upon the Russians, perhaps for the same reason.

Saumarez, in addition to conducting this diplomacy, was British naval commander-in-chief in the Baltic and responsible for keeping the sea open so that the vital shipbuilding supplies reached the United Kingdom. In October 1810 a convoy of 1,000 ships was concentrated for the passage home; it was expected that this immensely valuable target might be intercepted either by the Russians from Archangel or the Franco-Dutch fleet from Antwerp, but nothing happened and the vast convoy reached home safely.

Saumarez spent 1811 as he had spent 1810, watching the Russians and the Swedes from on board *Victory*, but in the next year the situation was turned upside down by the French invasion of Russia. A peace was hastily patched up between Britain, Russia and Sweden, while Saumarez' first concern was to arrange the evacuation of the Russian Baltic fleet, with some eighteen ships of the line, to England, as it was feared that the French would succeed in taking Kronstadt and St. Petersburg. The retreat from Moscow removed that danger, but part of the Russian fleet did come to Britain in the following year and was still serving with the British in the North Sea when Napoleon went into exile in March 1814.

In the meantime British ships had been carrying on coastal operations on the seaward flank of Napoleon's beaten armies, their operations being in part at least responsible for the liberation of Danzig and Stettin.

At the beginning of 1814 Denmark surrendered to the anti-Napoleonic coalition, Norway was separated from her and joined to Sweden under conditions approaching 'Dominion status'. Although the Danish battle fleet had twice been destroyed during the war, Danish small craft had fought persistently and well to handicap the passage of the British and Allied convoys through the Skagerrak and the Kattegat.

Thus ended the Napoleonic wars in the Baltic. Theoretically the Russian navy had come out of it reasonably well, with an almost unchallenged position on paper, but the officers and crews felt neglected and the ships certainly were, for the Tsar Alexander I had none of his otherwise mad father's understanding of, and enthusiasm for, the navy. In 1818 the degree of neglect from which the Baltic fleet was suffering could be clearly seen. In that year Ferdinand VII of Spain called upon his fellow monarchs of the Holy Alliance to help him reassert his rule over the provinces of Spanish America then in revolt. The Tsar Alexander sent a fleet of five ships of the line and three frigates, but they never got beyond Cadiz, for, of the eight ships, only two of the frigates were seaworthy and the expedition was given up, most of the ships being sold to Spain.

Apart from their generally run-down state, the principal trouble with the Russian ships seems to have been the inferior quality of timber—much of it larch, which was two years on its way from the forests where it grew to the shipbuilding yards; in addition, during the winter when the ships were laid up in the ice, the timber once again suffered from cold and it was some time before it was discovered that, contrary to previous belief, these very rugged conditions were not good for it. The foregoing remarks apply largely to ships of the

Baltic fleet; the ships of the White Sea fleet, based on Archangel, were generally much more robust.

But, while the sailing warships of the eighteenth and nineteenth centuries were ending their lives in depressing circumstances, the very first beginnings of a new fleet date back to those same years. In 1817 the first Russian steam warship, *Skoryi*, was laid down.

CHAPTER VII

WAR AGAINST—AND FOR—NAPOLEON
Part Two: The Mediterranean
1798–1808

RUSSIA's war with France spread to the Mediterranean in 1798. As a result of Bonaparte's expedition to Egypt, Russia and Turkey, who had been enemies almost constantly for over a hundred years, became allies. On October 1st, 1798, a joint Russo-Turkish fleet sailed from the Dardanelles to make war on France in the Mediterranean. The Russian fleet, coming from the Black Sea, consisted of six ships of the line and eight frigates; the Turkish fleet was of about the same size. The Russian commander-in-chief was Vice-Admiral Ushakov, the officer who had made a considerable reputation for his handling of his ships in the successful campaign against the Turkish fleet in the Black Sea during the Russo-Turkish war which had lasted from 1787 to 1791.

In the joint war against France the first objective of the Allied fleet was the Ionian Islands, which, formerly Venetian, had come into the hands of the French when the republic of Venice had ceased to exist.

Cerigo, Santa Maura, Zante and Cephalonia fell swiftly, and by November 20th the Russians and Turks, together with 4,000 Albanian irregulars, were able to begin a blockade and siege of Corfu, the only remaining French base. This lasted for four months; in March 1799 the French surrendered, and among the ships which fell into the hands of the Russians and Turks was the former British ship of the line *Leander*, which had been captured while bringing home dispatches from the Battle of the Nile. She was now returned to the British navy.

Having cleared up the situation in the Ionian Islands, the Turks and the Russians then began operations in the Adriatic, against the southern part of the French-dominated Italian peninsula, which was also threatened, from the north, by the Russian army under Suvarov.

Ushakov started his campaign by sending a frigate squadron to the coast of Apulia, where they were able during May to 'liberate' Bari and Brindisi, 'liberation' in this case meaning a return of the Bourbon rulers of the kingdom of Naples.

On May 17th another Russo-Turkish force under Rear-Admiral Putoshkin attacked Ancona without success, and then began a blockade, in which they were eventually joined by a small Austrian flotilla which had been working its way down the coast from the north.

While this had been going on the French hold on the west coast of Italy had similarly been loosened by British naval forces, but although Ischia and Procida off Naples fell to the British in April, the final blow to the enemy in this area was struck by the Russians, who landed, on the east coast at Foggia, a small force under Lieutenant Belli, who is said to have been originally an Irishman named Baillie. This force, 500 strong, crossed Italy, joined up with the Italian partisans under Cardinal Ruffo—no priest but a man upon whom the rank of Cardinal had been conferred for political services—and together the Russians and Italians dashed on into Naples, with British marines and Portuguese artillerymen, and captured the city.

Other operations on the coast of Italy were suspended at this time on account of the arrival of a large French fleet in the Mediterranean, commanded by Vice-Admiral Bruix, which had broken out of Brest on April 25th and come round to Toulon. After a brief intervention on the Ligurian coast in support of the French army, he left the Mediterranean and went back to Brest, after having missed a number of very good chances to do harm to the Allied cause. In fact, it would seem that Bruix had the best opportunity at his disposal that any French admiral had had since the American War of Independence.

When the alarm occasioned by Bruix's sortie had died down, the Russians and the Turks resumed the blockade of Ancona, in which they were presently joined by the Austrians, but the main body of the Russo-Turkish fleet was moved to Messina and then to Palermo, after which it split up in September, the Turks returning to Constantinople in some disarray.

With southern Italy liberated and the British flag flying over the Capitol in Rome, where it had been hoisted by Captain Louis, R.N., an illegitimate great-grandson of Louis XIV, the principal naval operation in progress in the Mediterranean was the siege of Malta, conducted under Nelson by the British and Portuguese fleets and then by the British alone.

At this stage Nelson expressed his lively scorn for the Russians on the ground that they did nothing but blockade Ancona, but it is not possible to say where the truth lay. Certainly this period of Nelson's life, when he was based on Naples, was his worst hour, and his strictures on the Russians appear unreasonable. While he claimed that he was most anxious that the Russians should join him in the blockade of Malta, Russian historians state that in fact everything was done by the British to dissuade Ushakov from taking part, a view which is supported by Sir John Fortescue, the historian of the British army.

Certainly, however, the participation of Russian force in the reduction of the island would have clearly reinforced Russian claims to the place at the subsequent peace conferences, claims which the British were determined to resist to the point of war, as subsequent events were to show.

The siege of Ancona by the Russians, the Turks, the Austrians and the Italian partisans went on, with constant disputes between the Allies, until November 13th, when the French, making the best use they could of the inter-Allied disagreements, surrendered to the Austrians, but not to the Italians or the Russians. The Russians, not having been consulted in the negotiations, seized the French warships in the harbour as soon as the surrender took effect, and it was with difficulty that they were compelled to give them up.

At the end of 1799 Ushakov set out for Malta to take part, at last, in the siege, but on the way he received a letter from the Tsar ordering him to bring his fleet back to Russia. This measure was followed shortly afterwards by Russia's withdrawal from the war against France and by the creation of the Armed Neutrality of the North.

In addition to setting up this alliance, Paul had planned to widen the field of his anti-British activities by dispatching an army overland through Persia to attack the British possessions in India; he made no plans for supplying the army on the march, and the fact that this force was therefore faced with certain death from starvation long before it reached India was one of the reasons why the Tsar was finally murdered by his own officers.

The Treaty of Amiens, which brought the French Revolutionary Wars to an end, was concluded in 1802. Under the provisions of the treaty Malta was to be restored to the Knights, Egypt returned to Turkey, and the Ionian Islands became nominally independent but in fact remained under Russian control. Within a very short time after the conclusion of the treaty it was clear that Napoleon had no intention of keeping his word, and the British Government decided not to surrender Malta until after the French had withdrawn from Holland and Switzerland.

This refusal to hand over Malta to the Knights was the direct cause of the recommencement of the wars with France in 1803. By 1805 an

Anglo-Russian alliance was concluded under the impulse of Napoleon's decision to turn his forces eastward after the failure of his plan
for the invasion of England.

Russian troops were brought to Italy from Corfu, but they were
withdrawn shortly afterwards to the island, while British troops, also
assembled to protect Naples, went to the safe side of the Straits of
Messina, because, after the Austrian defeat at Austerlitz it was clear
that the Allies did not have sufficient strength to defend the Italian
mainland. It had been to try to drive the British and the Russians out
of Naples that Villeneuve had sailed from Cadiz in October 1805,
into the arms of Nelson at Trafalgar.

Meanwhile, a small Russian force, which had been left behind in
the Mediterranean to look after Russia's interests in the Ionian
Islands, was joined by a bigger squadron under Vice-Admiral
Seniavin from the Baltic, so that by the end of January 1806 the
Russians had at Corfu nine battle ships and six frigates as well as
smaller vessels. However, by the time this fleet was on the scene, the
Austrians had been knocked out of the war and compelled to sign the
Treaty of Pressburg, under the terms of which Austria ceded to
France the whole of the Dalmatian coastline, except for the territory
of the republic of Ragusa (Dubrovnik), which was then enjoying the
last few months of its independent existence. This involved Cattaro
(Kotor) and Montenegro becoming French; the native population,
taking advantage of the dilatoriness of the Austrians in handing over
the territory, staged a series of risings and asked Seniavin for help.
The Russian admiral replied by sending Belli, now a captain, with a
ship of the line, a frigate and a schooner to Cattaro.

On his arrival the Austrians surrendered Cattaro to him, but no
sooner had Seniavin consolidated his position there than he received
orders to withdraw to the Black Sea, because of the conclusion of
peace between France and Austria. These orders he disobeyed, for he
realised that the news of his occupation of Cattaro had not yet reached
St. Petersburg at the time that his orders had been sent. He was
confident that the new Tsar, Alexander I, would change his mind as
soon as he heard what had happened. In this he was right, and he
shortly received counter-orders telling him to hold on.

In the meantime Belli was busy. He sent a ship of the line to
Ragusa to overawe the republic, and then took the island of Curzola
(Korcula), raided Lissa (Vis) and attempted to take Lesina (Hvar),
without success.

Seniavin, anxious to follow up this success, came north with the
main body of his fleet, but, arriving at Curzola itself, found that it had

been recaptured in a commando-type raid by the French from the mainland. It was, however, an easy matter for him to expel the French garrison, release their Russian prisoners and once more hoist the Russian flag.

A crisis now developed in Austro-Russian relations at Trieste, for the Austrians had ordered Russian merchant ships to leave the port within six days on pain of seizure. The Russian merchant captains hung on in port for fear of French vessels outside, and were accordingly declared forfeit; Seniavin now arrived and asked for their release. He was told by the governor of the port not to come within range of the Austrian guns, to which he replied by inviting the governor to open fire, so that he might see what that distance was. He prepared to attack the port, but the hearts of the Austrians were not in carrying out French instructions and they capitulated, allowing Seniavin to carry off the rescued ships.

The affair of Trieste having been dealt with, Seniavin was immediately faced with another crisis—the French had occupied Ragusa and announced their intention of remaining there until the Russians yielded Cattaro and Corfu.

Seniavin attacked Ragusa unsuccessfully, blockaded the town and then was driven off on July 6th by the arrival of French reinforcements. He withdrew to Cattaro, while his light coastal forces interfered as best they could with the French coastwise traffic, which was of great importance to the support of the enemy in view of the poor roads along the Dalmatian coast.

Orders once again arrived for Seniavin to cease hostilities—on this occasion because France and Russia had concluded a treaty of peace on the previous July 20th; under the terms of this treaty Cattaro was to be returned to the Austrians, who agreed to hand it over to the French. Seniavin once again disobeyed orders to withdraw, contenting himself with ordering a suspension of hostilities, and a withdrawal of his forces to Cattaro.

Once again subsequent events bore out his judgement, for the Tsar refused to ratify the treaty, and by September Seniavin had orders to resume fighting, and Ragusa was blockaded, while the French, advancing overland, began an attack on the forts protecting Cattaro.

This produced something of a stalemate on land, but the Russians had command of the sea and Seniavin used it to start another series of attacks on the islands which he had evacuated, Curzola being taken by the Russians for the third time in the campaign and Lesina once again attacked.

However, before Seniavin made much further progress on the

Dalmatian coast he learned that Ali Pasha of Janina, who in theory was the Sultan's overlord of Epirus and who in fact did pretty much as he pleased, was believed to be planning an attack on the Ionian Islands. The Russian admiral withdrew his ships from the middle Adriatic to cover the threatened islands and then received news of the official outbreak of war between his country and Turkey. The pretext was the action of the Turks in dismissing, contrary to Russia's treaty rights, the governors (Hospodars) of Moldavia and Wallachia. These dismissals had been brought about by the activities in Constantinople of the French representative, Sebastiani.

Britain and Russia were still allies and accordingly Collingwood, Nelson's second in command at Trafalgar and now commanding the Mediterranean fleet, was told to send ships to the Dardanelles to hold the Turks in check when Russo-Turkish tension became acute. The squadron, commanded by Rear-Admiral Sir Thomas Louis, reached Constantinople before war broke out, but, because of the French victory at Jena and the Russian action in entering Moldavia, the Turks finally declared war on Russia.

Louis then withdrew into the Mediterranean and made his base at Tenedos, where he was joined by reinforcements under Vice-Admiral Duckworth, who took over command of the British fleet. Seniavin was ordered to join the British, but, before he arrived from the Adriatic, Duckworth had entered the Dardanelles, appeared before Constantinople, negotiated, achieved nothing and had been forced to return to the Mediterranean after a running fight with the Turkish batteries in the Dardanelles.

Seniavin was anxious to make a joint Russo-British attack, but Duckworth believed that success would be impossible and refused to co-operate, saying, smugly, that 'where a British squadron had failed no other was likely to succeed'. The British then left the Aegean, and Seniavin, based on Tenedos, settled down to blockade, with eight ships of the line, a Turkish fleet which numbered twelve similar vessels, while, at the other side of the Bosphorus, was the Russian Black Sea fleet of six more ships of the line.

As Seniavin waited this Black Sea fleet began to move. A plan to attack the Bosphorus and Constantinople from the sea had to be abandoned for lack of troops, but a successful attack was carried out on Anapa, then in Turkish hands, at the extreme east end of the Black Sea.

Seniavin's problem was somehow to lure the Turks out to fight. He sent ships to demonstrate off Salonika and then went himself to simulate an attack on the Gallipoli peninsula from the rear, at more or less the position of the Bulair lines.

This demonstration took place on May 3rd, 1807, and ten days later the Turkish fleet emerged from the Straits. There were eight ships of the line against ten Russians. Said Ali, the Turkish commander, headed for Tenedos, the Russian fleet being away to the north-west off Samothrace. Seniavin felt that he could afford to leave the garrison of Tenedos to stand off the Turkish forces while he manoeuvred to get between Said Ali and the entrance to the Dardanelles, but he was thwarted by unfavourable weather and finally, on May 22nd, had to come straight to Tenedos, where the hostile fleets lay side by side at anchor until the wind changed and the Turks made a dash for the Dardanelles. The Russians followed, but although they caught up with the enemy they did not have time to destroy him before he was once more under the shelter of the forts. However, three Turkish ships had been lost during the chase.

The blockade of the Dardanelles continued. The hardship thus inflicted on the Turks is claimed by Russian writers to have caused the revolt of the janissaries which deposed Sultan Selim on May 31st and replaced him by his nephew Mustapha.

However that may have been, the change in rulers did not affect the Turkish determination to make war, and on June 22nd the Turkish fleet once more left the Straits, with eight ships of the line and five frigates.

After a feint in the neighbourhood of Imbros, the Turks landed troops on Tenedos, but Seniavin was too quick for them and forced them to withdraw their fleet, leaving the troops stranded ashore. Seniavin replenished the garrison of the island and then, taking advantage of a favourable wind, succeeded in obtaining the position he wanted off Mount Athos between the Turkish fleet and the Dardanelles. A battle followed on June 30th.

Each side had ten ships of the line apiece. The Turks were, more or less, in line ahead and Seniavin attacked them from abeam in two columns, as Nelson had attacked the Franco-Spanish fleet at Trafalgar.

The Turks had concentrated their three flagships in the middle of their line, and Seniavin's plan was that as his first six ships came up each pair should engage one of these ships, the last four vessels forming a reserve. The leading ship of Seniavin's own line, the *Rafail* (74), however, was so badly damaged on her run up to the enemy that she was unable to turn to come broadside to broadside with her Turkish adversary and went straight through the enemy line; the next five Russian ships, however, took up their positions correctly, while

Seniavin, who had been fourth in the line in the *Tverdyi* (74), with the smaller *Skoryi* (64), went to the head of the Turkish line and began to engage it, while Greig, his second in command and son of the former commander-in-chief in the Baltic, with two ships followed astern, so that there were nine Russian ships engaging the first six or seven Turks in line.

The leading Turkish ship was quickly knocked out and, lying dead in the water, caused the ships following her astern to bunch up in confusion. The *Rafail*, with the whole enemy fleet between her and her friends, was able to get away. Seniavin's *Tverdyi* attacked two Turkish battleships and a frigate simultaneously, and the other Russian ships, all fighting hard, had the Turks withdrawing within an hour of the beginning of the battle; at first the wind threatened to drive them ashore on Cape Pinnes, the promontory of Mount Athos, but the wind dropped and neither fleet could move in the calm.

When the wind came up again the Turks were able to start for the mouth of the Dardanelles and home, but on the evening of the next day and on the morning of July 2nd the Russians began to pick off the enemy stragglers.

In the end only twelve of the twenty Turkish ships of all sizes which left the Dardanelles were able to return, the rest having been sunk, burnt or driven aground underneath the cliffs of Mount Athos.

Dr. Anderson writes: 'Collingwood, judging by the standard of Trafalgar, referred to the Battle of Athos as "a sort of battle" ', and adds 'there was little reason for the sneer'.

While operations had been going at the western end of the Dardanelles, the Russian Black Sea fleet had been giving what support it could. The usual Russian dream of an attack on Constantinople had had to be abandoned for want of means, but the fleet, under Putoshkin, went off to attack Trebizond instead, only to abandon this idea as well when the strength of the Turkish position was seen. After this it was easy for Seniavin to deal with the Turkish forces ashore on Tenedos.

But, while the Russian navy was doing well, the Russian army was being thoroughly defeated by Napoleon, and at Tilsit in July 1807 the Russians once again made peace; the naval consequence of this was that Seniavin was ordered to cease hostilities and take his fleet back to the Baltic.

To carry out this order proved impossible, for, although Russia and Britain were not at war, the British navy took 'precautionary' action and Seniavin's fleet was first blockaded in the Tagus and then interned in British home waters until Britain and Russia once more became allies when Napoleon marched on Moscow.

Seniavin went home to semi-disgrace and poverty; only when he died in 1831 were the tributes paid to him that he deserved. He asked for the simplest of funerals, and received it, 'but the bearer party of seamen who took his body to the grave was commanded by the Tsar himself', according to the Russian naval historians Monasterev and Tereschenko. This chivalrous action is almost the only one to the credit of that very unchivalrous monarch Nicholas I.

CHAPTER VIII

NAVARINO
1827

Tᴴᴱ departure of Seniavin and his squadron from the Mediterranean in 1807 did not mean the end of Russian influence in
that sea.   During the closing stages of the wars against
Napoleon pro-Russian partisans in what is now Yugoslavia were
active, not only in fighting the French but also in providing problems
to be solved by Allied diplomatists as the war went on.   Along that
shore of the Adriatic the British navy was engaged in mopping up
French strongholds—from Corfu in the south to Trieste and Fiume in
the north.

On the Dalmatian coast, and especially in the operations against
Cattaro and its garrison, it was found by the British squadron
under Captain William Hoste, in the frigate *Bacchante*, that the local
inhabitants were in two groups as far as their attitude to the war was
concerned.   First, those living on the coast and largely of Italian
origin took little interest in the fighting.   Prior to the war they had
been Austrians, then they had become French, and when the war was
over they would, presumably, be either French or Austrian once
more, and they showed no sign of caring which.

Very different was the attitude of the Slavs living inland among the
mountains.   Under their leader, the Prince-Bishop of Montenegro
and under the Russian flag, they came down from their fastnesses and
attacked the French with ferocious courage and enthusiasm.   To
assure himself of their support Hoste flew, along with the British and
Austrian flags, that of Russia.   For this he was rebuked by the Earl of
Aberdeen (the British Ambassador in Vienna), since the liberated
Dalmatian ports were to be returned by international agreement to
the Austrians, and it was feared that the Russians would use Hoste's
acknowledgment of their services to support a claim for the territory.
Answering the Ambassador's complaint, Hoste pointed out that he
had not had much choice in the matter.   First, he said, the pro-
Russian partisans had already been in action before he began
operations and, in addition, they were willing to fight the enemy,
while the ex-Austrian inhabitants, for whom in theory the place was
being liberated, were not.

In the end Dalmatia was returned to Austria and the Montenegrins went back to their mountains, but the Russians retained prestige and support in the area for more than a hundred years, and when they lost it this was due to the ideological dispute between Marshals Stalin and Tito as to the proper lines of development of Communism in the post-war world of the late 1940s.

The Montenegrins looked to the Russians in 1814–15 for help as fellow Slavs, and a little later farther down the same coast the Greeks soon afterwards also looked to the Russians for aid. In this case there were no racial ties—though there was a religious one. In addition the memory of Orlov's operations against the Turks in 1769–74 had remained amongst the Greeks, despite the fact that they had failed to secure the liberation of Greece. After the Napoleonic wars had loosened the hold of almost all the Governments in Europe on their peoples it was natural that the Greeks should take hope and Russian help looked the most easily forthcoming.

However, it was not from Russia that aid came in the first place. Prince Alexander Ypsilanti, a Greek officer in the Russian army, had made an unsuccessful attempt to start a rising in Rumania, but Russia was too monolithic and autocratic to permit what happened in 'free enterprise' France and Britain, where private citizens volunteered to give their money and their services to the cause of Greek independence. While private Britons such as Cochrane and Byron were 'going it alone', the British Government dispatched naval forces to the eastern Mediterranean to put down 'piracy'—committed by the same 'pirates' that the unofficial British and French were helping. Eventually the anti-piracy forces came to the aid of the 'pirates' against whom they were supposed to be acting, by destroying the fleet of the 'pirates' ' legal ruler, the Sultan. But this development took six years, starting in 1821 when the sailors of the Greek islands began a seaborne campaign of guerilla warfare, reminiscent of the struggles of the Dutch 'sea beggars' against Spain.

The islanders were able to do this because, although nominally under Turkish rule, they had had a large measure of independence, and they also had their ships. These were, for the most part, large armed trading brigs, very nearly equal in power to a frigate, carrying from twenty-two to thirty guns. Within a short while they were able to effect the independence of their own island homes and then to bring help to the Greeks on the mainland, so that within a short space of time most of the southern part of modern Greece was free. In 1824, however, the Sultan asked for help from his very independent vassal, Mahomet Ali, the Viceroy of Egypt, promising him as a reward Crete and the Morea. At that time the Egyptian navy and the Egyptian army were both efficient forces and soon had the Greeks on the defensive.

But not before help was reaching Greece from the outside world. Byron was first amongst the famous to come. The defence of Missolonghi, in which he lost his life, was only possible because the Greeks had command of the sea; Missolonghi was a kind of Tobruk operation, with a Greek garrison holding the town and supported by supplies brought from the sea.

Other European volunteers who followed included Thomas Cochrane, Earl of Dundonald, who had distinguished himself as a brilliant frigate captain in the war against the French, been sent to prison for alleged complicity in an attempt to commit frauds on the Stock Exchange, been carried protesting out of the House of Commons, and then gone off to lead in succession the navies of Chile and Brazil in their struggles for independence against Spain and Portugal.

Cochrane had always quarrelled with his seniors, equals and juniors, and it is therefore not surprising that he also fought with his associates in the Greek wars. In the first place he found that the Greek captains of the trading brigs, which were, for the time being, the capital ships of the war, were completely unused to taking orders from anyone, and, of course, they also had the full measure of Greek self-assurance and confidence in their own ability to do anything necessary. In the second place their ships were the only possessions which they had in the world, and they were unwilling to risk them or even withdraw them from profitable trading ventures in order to take part in the war without being sure of having their pay in advance. Nevertheless, despite all the frustration and anguish which they caused Cochrane and other foreign friends of Greece and their unreliability ashore, they did the job; they carried the aspirations of the Greek people from words into deeds, and by the time the Egyptian forces arrived to extinguish those aspirations it was too late. Modern Greece had been born.

In the meanwhile public opinion in favour of the Greek rebels had grown throughout Europe, and Britain, France and Russia, as the principal major powers interested, agreed upon the dangers of a situation in which war was endemic. This was at least in part the case because any weakening of the Turkish position might very well leave Russia in command in the Middle East, with Constantinople and the Dardanelles in her possession. Hence Britain and France were determined to associate themselves with anything the Russians did, and an agreement was made by the three Governments to intervene together, by the Treaty of London of July 1827.

British, French and Russian squadrons were sent to the spot under the terms of this agreement and the situation which they found on arrival was this: to help crush the Greeks a large force of Egyptian warships and transports—about 100 ships in all, carrying 11,000 men —had sailed from Alexandria for Navarino on the west coast of the Peleponnese in order that the troops embarked might deal with the Greek forces ashore. The Allied forces followed them to Navarino, where in the middle of the harbour is the island of Sphaktena, where the Spartans once—on the only occasion in their history—surrendered. The supreme Allied commander-in-chief was the British admiral Sir Edward Codrington, in his flagship *Asia* (84), with two other ships of the line, three frigates and six smaller ships; then came three French ships of the line, two frigates and two smaller ships, and finally the Russians with four line-of-battle ships and four frigates under Admiral Heyden, an officer of German descent who had taken over command of the squadron from Seniavin after that veteran had been given the honour of leading it out of home waters.

In the circular bay of Navarino the mixed Egyptian and Turkish fleet of warships and transports lay at anchor under the command of Tahir Pasha. The supreme overlord of the Turco-Egyptian force; Ibrahim Pasha, son of Mahomet Ali, was ashore. The warships of this force numbered twenty, carrying 1,150 guns, compared with the nineteen Allied ships with 1,190 guns.

At this time Greek ships under Cochrane were planning an attack on Patras, and Ibrahim ordered his ships to sea to stop them. Codrington answered by taking his fleet into Navarino Bay and starting to moor it between the Turks and the Egyptians and the sea, so that they could not leave port unless they were willing to fight their way out. It was obviously an explosive situation and very soon it exploded. Before the Allied vessels were all in position the last battle between sailing ships of the line had begun. The British frigate *Dartmouth*, entering the harbour, saw or thought she saw, one of the Turkish fireships preparing an attack and sent boats to get the Turk to move, on the ground that *Dartmouth* needed more room. The British naval historian Sir William Laird Clowes remarks:[1]

> This, of course, was scarcely a politic measure, seeing that the new comers, and not the vessels already in the bay, were obviously the cause of any crowding that might be objectionable. The despatch of the

[1] *The Royal Navy: A History*, vol. 6, p. 258, Sampson Low, Marston & Co., London, 1897–1903.

boats was, moreover, a measure likely to be misunderstood, and, in fact, the Turks, supposing that force was about to be employed, opened fire and killed Lieutenant George William Home Fitzroy and several men.

For a while only *Dartmouth* and the French flagship *Sirène* answered with what was called defensive fire. Codrington was so little expecting to have to fight that he had furled his sails and had *Asia*'s band up on deck; but soon firing became general. The French and Russians were still entering the harbour, the French taking up station opposite Egyptian vessels known to have French officers in Mahomet Ali's service aboard. This seems to have had the desired effect of causing the Frenchmen in the Egyptian ships to go ashore rather than to fire upon the ships of their own country.

By the time the Russians came into action the bay was covered in smoke and filled with ships, but Heyden's *Azov* (74), followed by *Gangut* (84), *Ezekiel* (74), *Alexander Nevsky* (74) and the four frigates came in and took up their stations—not without difficulty, for one of the frigates fired into H.M.S. *Talbot* in error. Two British midshipmen were ordered by the captain of *Talbot* to go on board the Russian ship to 'remonstrate' and came back to report several of the Russian officers drunk and the captain 'not much better'.

The Russians were relatively weaker than the British or French—by comparison with the strength of that part of the enemy fleet against which they were fighting—and the *Azov* was badly damaged. Heyden was wounded, while his flag captain Lazarev greatly distinguished himself by his skilful handling of the ship. Serving under him were three officers who were all to rise to high rank and fame—Kornilov, Istomin, and Nakhimov.

Once the Allied fleet was inside the bay, there was no manoeuvring. Each ship selected a target and got to work. At the end of the Allied line the Russians came in silently, took up their positions, anchored, furled their sails and then, everything being ready, opened fire. The Turks could clearly be seen, wearing turbans, brown jackets and with bare legs, fighting as hard as they could, pausing only from time to time to push through the gun ports the bodies of those who had been killed. Their ships were crowded—partly with troops of the expeditionary force—and casualties were accordingly high. The *Azov* was for a time engaged with five enemy ships and had the highest casualties of any ship in the combined fleets—ninety-one killed and wounded. Astern of her were the three other Russian ships of the line, engaging five heavy frigates, sinking two and capturing one. The Russian frigates, following the big ships, attacked enemy ships of the same type, and by about six o'clock in the evening the battle was over, the waters of the bay being covered with wreckage, burning ships and small boats from the Allied fleet rescuing Turkish and Egyptian survivors and landing them ashore—no effort was made to keep them as prisoners.

The firing had continued until the Turkish-Egyptian fleet was no longer an organised force—twenty-one vessels—warships and transports—had been sunk and 7,000 men killed or wounded. The Allied casualties were: British, seventy-five killed, 197 wounded; French, forty-three killed and 144 wounded; and Russians fifty-nine killed and 139 wounded. For the Russians the most dangerous moment of the battle had come an hour after the fighting ceased, for at midnight a Turkish fireship had come drifting down, ablaze, upon the *Gangut* and the *Azov*. The *Azov* slipped her anchor and escaped, but the bowsprit of the blazing Turk caught in the rigging of the *Gangut's* mainmast and the weary Russians barely succeeded in freeing their ship from the enemy and getting the fire under control.

No Allied ships were sunk, but all three British ships of the line were so badly damaged that they had to be sent home to England to be repaired, as the task was found to be beyond the dockyards at Malta or Gibraltar. The *Asia* and *Genoa* both lost their mizzenmasts and Bathurst, the captain of *Genoa*, was killed.

The Tsar was pleased with the performance of his fleet at Navarino and ordered that in future one of his ships should always be named *Pamiat Azova* (Remembrance of *Azov*) and carry on her ensign the badge of the Order of St. George. No other ship ever received this honour.

The only person who reacted logically to the Allied victory at Navarino was Heyden, who wished the Allies to attack the Dardanelles *en route* for Constantinople, while the Russian Black Sea fleet attacked the Turkish capital through the Bosphorus. The French and British, however, refused to co-operate. The independence of southern and central Greece had been secured and they were not willing to see Turkey further weakened. Turkey, however, declared war formally on Russia and yet another Russo-Turkish war began.

At a time when there is universal anxiety about the possibility of war starting by accident Navarino has a macabre interest, not least because, having been fought and won, it was a source of great embarrassment to the British Government, who had had no desire to strengthen the Russians by destroying the Turks and who referred afterwards to the battle as an 'untoward event'. Codrington was much annoyed and soon returned to England.

In the spring of 1828 the Russian army once again set out to invade Turkey, both through the Balkans and through the Caucasus. In neither the Black Sea nor the Mediterranean had the Russian navy much to do, as most of the Sultan's fleet had been wiped out at Navarino. Accordingly most of the Russians' work was escorting and supporting amphibious operations in the Aegean and on the European and Asiatic coasts of the Black Sea.

Coastal operations continued through 1828; at the beginning of the next year a new Turkish fleet had been formed and sailed out of the Bosphorus to do battle. Its first success was the capture of the frigate *Rafail*; the Russian ship was alone and the Turks had six ships of the line as well as nine smaller vessels. Nevertheless, the Tsar was much enraged by her surrender—it was, in fact, the only time in history when a Russian warship surrendered to the Turks. He ordered that, if the *Rafail* was retaken she was to be burned as unworthy to fly the Russian flag, and her captain on his return from a Turkish prison was never to marry, so that his family would cease to exist.

In contrast to the premature surrender of the *Rafail* was an action which took place three days later when the same Turkish fleet of fifteen vessels came up with the eighteen-gun brig *Merkurii*. The Russian tried to escape with the aid of her sweeps, but was pursued and finally caught by two of the enemy ships of the line, one of 110 guns and one of seventy-four. *Merkurii*'s captain, Lieutenant-Commander Kazarski, decided to fight it out and placed a loaded pistol on the capstan with the order that the last surviving officer should use it to blow up the ship's magazine.

After an hour's manoeuvring the Turks succeeded in getting on each side of the brig and the fighting went on, the Turks using red-hot shot to start fires, which, however, were soon put out. The Russians replied with their tiny broadside and with small arms fire and succeeded, in four hours' fighting, in shooting enough of the enemies' rigging away to cause them to fall astern when the wind freshened. Thus the *Merkurii* was able to escape, having been hit twenty-two times and having lost only four men killed and three wounded. As a reward all her officers were ordered to add a pistol to their crest. There is no denying the courage of the Russians, but the state of the Turkish gunnery which made possible such an action is worth notice.

The Russian army, in 1829, crossed the Danube with the aid of the Russian Danube flotilla and advanced through Bulgaria into Thrace against Constantinople, while the navy landed a small force at Midia on the Black Sea, only fifty miles from the capital. Adrianople (now Edirne) was taken and a Russo-Turkish treaty was signed there, by which the provinces of Wallachia and Moldavia passed from being semi-independent Turkish provinces to being semi-independent Russian satellites, while the Dardanelles were opened to merchant shipping.

The last Russian naval operation in the series which had started in Navarino in 1827 took place in 1831, when a Russian squadron was used at Poros, on the request of the Greek Government, to put down a rising started by Andreas Miaoulis, one of the original leaders of the Greek patriot movement, who had become dissatisfied with the independent Government which he had done much to create.

In 1833 came an incident which seemed to make nonsense of the Russo-Turkish war that had just ended. Mahomet Ali and Ibrahim, allies and vassals of the Sultan in Greece and at Navarino, rose in revolt and so thoroughly frightened the Turkish sovereign that he sent for the Russians to come to his aid. This they did, at a price. A squadron under Lazarev, Heyden's flag captain at Navarino, and an expeditionary force of 12,000 men arrived in the Bosphorus, and Constantinople was once again saved. The Egyptians, who had defeated the Turks at Konia in Anatolia and then advanced as far as Kutalia, 180 miles from Constantinople, withdrew, but Mahomet Ali had collected for himself the virtual overlordship of all of Syria, including Palestine and the Lebanon, as well as of the province of Adana.

The Russians collected for themselves the Treaty of Unkiar Silessi, under the terms of which the Turks agreed to shut the Straits whenever the Russians asked them to do so, while no foreign warships were to be allowed in the Black Sea. Twenty years after this Turkey and Russia were once again at war.

In the meantime, on the perimeter of their Empire, two quick tricks had been picked up by the Russians; a successful campaign had been fought in the Caucasus and, in 1848, a naval transport, commanded by Captain Alexander Nevelskoi, had arrived at the mouth of the Amur River on the Gulf of Tartary. Hitherto there had been no outlet for eastern Siberia on to the Pacific and all communications with it had been west-ward overland—without roads and with most of the rivers flowing from south to north.

CHAPTER IX

THE CRIMEAN WAR

1853–1856

ACCORDING to legend the cause of the Crimean War was a three-cornered dispute between the French, the Russians and the Turks concerning the possession of keys to the Holy Places, but, of course, even at the time of the Crimean War, people did not really go off to fight on such a frivolous ground as that. What, in fact, happened was that, as usual, the Russians were probing their enemy, on this occasion the Turks, looking for a political soft spot. The French, and later the British, were determined that if such a soft spot were found it should not be exploited.

Whether a definite statement earlier by the Anglo-French allies of their intention to support the Turks would have prevented the Russians from actually attacking is not clear. However, the Russians did attack and one of the most important battles of naval history took place—the last fleet action ever fought between wooden ships, the first fleet action in which high-explosive shells decided the conflict. That the first fleet action in which shells were the decisive weapon should have been the last in which wooden ships fought each other was natural enough, because shells—as opposed to the solid round shot hitherto employed—showed that they could completely destroy wooden vessels.

The first part of the sequel to this was to be observed in the Crimean War itself, for within two years of the destruction of the Turkish fleet at Sinope on the Black Sea by the shell guns of the Russian fleet French ironclad warships were in action and the century of the battleship had begun. From the time that the first of these revolutionary ironclads were ordered to the time that they were in action only fifteen months elapsed. To design, build and put into operation a brand-new heavy weapon of war within that time was extremely creditable to the naval architects and shipbuilders of those days, and appears even more creditable when contrasted with the general inefficiency and inexperience which marked the opening months of the Crimean War.

The circumstances under which the Battle of Sinope was fought on November 30th, 1853, were as confusing as any which have attended our 'cold war' during the last two decades. There had been no formal declaration of war by France and Britain until hostilities were well under way. In the meantime as tension built up during 1853 Russian troops had moved into the provinces of Wallachia and Moldavia, which were nominally under Turkish rule, and taken up position along the Danube. This was much to the satisfaction of the inhabitants of both those provinces, who were as anxious to be liberated from Turkish rule as were most of the peoples of the Sultan's Empire. To protect Constantinople from a further Russian advance an Anglo-French fleet was sent to that place, but on arrival was left without any other instructions.

The Turks issued an ultimatum to the Russians on October 4th and moved a squadron of seven frigates, three corvettes and two steamships to Sinope. The Russians began naval operations off Batum; the Turks moved reinforcements eastward by sea—this they were obliged to do because there were practically no roads along the north coast of Anatolia. The Turkish reinforcements went to the port of Sinope, the only natural harbour on the entire coast. The Russians moved to stop these troop movements; the Anglo-French fleet in the Bosphorus had orders to protect Constantinople and its environs, but no orders to protect the Turkish fleet at Sinope and 'the massacre' at that place followed.

A greatly superior Russian force of six ships of the line, two frigates and three steamers, these latter small vessels used chiefly to tow the bigger sailing ships, attacked the Turks, who had seven frigates, three smaller sailing vessels and two steamers. Not only did the Russians use shells, but in addition their big ships had much longer-range guns. Once the weather became suitable on November 30th—after a three-day wait—the Russians were able to lie off Sinope out of range of the Turks, set fire to them and shoot them to pieces. The casualties on both sides give an idea of the odds in favour of the Russians: Turks 3,000 killed and wounded, Russians 266. Only one Turkish ship escaped, the steamer *Taif*, which had on board Captain Adolphus Slade, R.N., who was on loan to the Turkish navy. This escape of the British officer when the rest of the fleet to which he belonged was destroyed naturally figured largely in Russian propaganda at the time and still does so to this day. One of the Turkish ships destroyed was the *Avni-Illah* ('Gift of God'), formerly the Russian frigate *Rafail* which had been reproached for surrendering too easily during the previous Russo-Turkish conflict.

The victorious admiral at Sinope had had, on that occasion, no need of special talents, but he was, in fact, an outstanding product of the Russian naval service and one of the few Tsarist officers honoured by having a ship named after him in the Soviet navy today. Vice-Admiral Paul Stepanovitch Nakhimov was fifty years old at the time of Sinope. He had been with Lazarev in the *Azov* at Navarino, but much more important was the fact that he had been with Lazarev on his voyage around the world in 1819–23, which had given him deep sea experience of a type which Russian officers, confined mostly to the Baltic and the Black Sea, very rarely had.

Lazarev wrote of him after this cruise, 'Has a pure soul and loves the sea'; and thanks to Lazarev he received command early. When captain of the *Silistria* Nakhimov was in collision with the ship of the line *Adrianopol*, which rammed him from astern. When he saw that collision was inevitable he ordered everyone on the upper deck forward of the mainmast, but remained himself on the quarter deck. The *Adrianopol*'s bowsprit cut across the deck and brought the *Silistria*'s mizzenmast down a few feet from where Nakhimov was standing. Afterwards the *Silistria*'s first lieutenant asked his captain why he had not taken cover.

Nakhimov answered: 'You don't often get a chance like that, when a captain can show his nerve. One of these days I may have to fight this ship with this crew and then I'll get my reward.'

In these days it is recognised that a young leader, given the chance, can get great benefit from an opportunity to display his courage before his men—two or three instances and he is, in that sense, made —and need never worry again about what his men think of his personal courage. He can get on with other problems.

Nakhimov was an engaging character. When rebuking a subordinate for some shortcoming he would say: 'I may do that sort of thing, but I don't want you to.' He had a lofty view of his duty and that of his officers—years and years in advance of other officers of the Imperial Russian Navy and quite valid today.

'We must stop thinking that we are lords and the men serfs. The men are the strength of the ship and will do anything that we want, provided that we are not just using them as steps to promotion in our own careers.'

When congratulated upon his success he said, thinking of his old commander-in-chief: 'Michael Petrovitch Lazarev did this.'

Although Sinope caused a great sensation in western Europe and was much employed in propaganda against the Russians, war between France and Britain on one side and Russia on the other did not begin until March 27th of the following year, after four indecisive months.

The naval side of the Crimean War did not make much more sense than any other aspect of the struggle until the arrival of the ironclads, too late to be of decisive value. The war was between the Whale and the Bear with neither strong enough, out of its element, to do the other much harm. The two Russian battle fleets, one in the Black Sea and the other in the Baltic, shut themselves up in harbour as soon as the Franco-British fleets arrived on the scene. French, British, Turkish and Sardinian troops landed in the Crimea, thanks to the British and French navies, and fought the campaign which gave the war its name. In the Baltic the Franco-British fleet operated without achieving very much, largely because the troops required to exploit the Allied command of the sea were engaged in the Black Sea. On the other hand, the threat of an Allied attack in the Baltic tied down some 170,000 Russian troops who might have been useful in the Crimea. Efforts to harass the Russians were made in the White Sea and the Pacific—the latter attempt ending in an extremely inglorious failure.

After Sinope and the Allied entrance into the war, the first pre-occupation of the Russian navy was to carry out the evacuation of the Russian land forces from places along the Black Sea coast where they might have been cut off, since, as has been said, there were no roads and the Allies had firm command of the sea, for the Russian Black Sea fleet under Nakhimov had shut itself up in Sevastopol.

The first of a number of fairly pointless bombardments of Russian Black Sea ports took place on April 22nd, 1854, with an attack on Odessa by the British and French.

Tribes in rebellion against the Russians in the Caucasus—notably under the leadership of Shamyl—were helped by the British and French as far as possible. However, owing to the fact that the Western Allies had as their associates the Turks, who were nearly as much disliked by the tribes as were the Russians, very little could be done. British naval officers co-operating with these rebels had the oppor-tunity of admiring the charm and courage of one of their chieftainesses, but complained that the rigours of campaigning had ruined her complexion.

The British sloop *Tiger* (16) ran aground off Odessa and had to be abandoned on May 12th, and various bombardments of Sevastopol took place, but the first effective Allied naval intervention in the war occurred off the mouths of the Danube, which were blockaded at a time when the river formed an important means of communication in the rear of the Russian troops who had crossed over it and were pressing southward against the Turks.

This blockade of the Danube relieved the pressure on the Turks, and the Franco-British expeditionary force, which had been sent first to Gallipoli on the Dardanelles and then to Varna on the Black Sea, was available for further service. Up to that time it had never been seriously engaged; now Sevastopol was decided upon as the most important target. Nobody cared for the idea of following up the Russians as they withdrew from the Danube—Charles XII and Napoleon had both tried an invasion of Russia by land. On the other hand, Sevastopol was a first-class base from which Nakhimov's fleet could sortie whenever it might wish, and his screw frigate *Vladimir* had shown what might be done in a cruise during July, when she had sunk or taken several Turkish merchant vessels off the coast of Anatolia.

A landing in the Crimea and an attempt to take Sevastopol was accordingly decided upon and finally begun in September. Like nearly all the operations of this war, the move was carried out with nightmare slowness and inefficiency. This was a war fought by over-age officers who had had no experience of hostilities against a great power for forty years, without trained staffs or organised supplies. Its fighting reached a climax in cruelly bad weather against an enemy extremely tough and brave and just as badly led as their opponents.

An indication of the poor quality of Russian leadership is given by the fact that, despite the possession of a considerable fleet—sixteen ships of the line, four big frigates and a large number of smaller vessels—no attempt was made, even by the able Nakhimov, to interfere with the transport of the Allied expeditionary force from Varna to the Crimea or with its subsequent landing there. Vladimir Alexeievitch Kornilov, flying his flag under Nakhimov, urged that this be done, but the overall Russian commander-in-chief, Prince Mentschikov, a soldier, forbade it.

Instead, as soon as the Allied intention to make an all-out attack on Sevastopol became clear, the Russian ships were scuttled to block the entrance to Sevastopol harbour, and their crews landed to fight ashore. It is true that the sailors of the Black Sea fleet were so important a reinforcement of the garrison of Sevastopol that they may have made a decisive difference in the ability of the fortress to hold out for the period of a year; on the other hand, the British and French fleets, once the enemy ships were at the bottom of Sevastopol harbour, were also able to land sailors, marines and, above all, heavy guns which played an important part in support of the Allied armies.

But the most interesting thing at the present time about the decision of the Russians to scuttle their fleet was the way in which it was represented in one of the classics of the Soviet cinema—the film made on the life of Nakhimov just before World War II. This film was in many ways remarkable—perhaps the best ever made of the fighting between sailing ships—and was part of a big propaganda campaign explaining to the Russian peoples why they had a navy. Nevertheless, in this film Nakhimov is shown as upholding to his disappointed officers the decision to scuttle the fleet. The curious lesson seemed to emerge that the best thing to do with a Russian fleet when it was confronted by an enemy superior in force was to scuttle it.

The siege of Sevastopol went on for a year. It was a partial siege only, because the Russian fortress was never completely cut off from outside sources of reinforcement which reached it overland. By the time that it had ended all three of the senior Russian admirals—Nakhimov, Kornilov and Istomin—had been killed.

In March 1854 a British fleet was assembled for dispatch to the Baltic—a French component of the Allied fleet was not available until later, as nearly all the French heavy ships in seagoing condition had been sent to the Black Sea. The Russian Baltic fleet at that time included some twenty-seven ships of the line, with smaller craft including fifty or sixty gunboats, the lineal descendants of the little ships which had proved so important against the Swedes.

The British fleet, consisting of nine steamships of the line and six sailing ships of the line, was commanded by Sir Charles Napier, a man of sixty-eight years of age on the worst of terms with the Board of Admiralty, whose members he had insulted after a dinner at the Reform Club just prior to sailing. Worse still, though he had had a brilliant career as a young captain in the French wars, he lived now in a morass of indecision, and his natural inclination either not to act or act too late was heightened by the fact that, when the French squadron arrived in the Baltic, it was almost entirely composed of sailing ships which, in unfavourable winds, could only be moved under tow. At the same time the French admiral, Parseval Deschenes, was desperately anxious not to miss any action—partly from professional zeal, partly because he knew that the political effect at home of a British victory over the Russians in which the French had not taken part would be very unfavourable.

'There will not be enough paving stones in Paris to throw at me if there is a battle and I miss it,' he said.

But there never was a battle. It was generally thought at the time that Sir Charles Napier missed an opportunity of cutting off part of the enemy fleet near Helsingfors, but no one ever seems to have cared enough to find out afterwards whether this was really true.

As it was, there was nothing to do during two campaigning seasons in the Baltic but blockade Russian ports and bombard Russian ports —except Kronstadt, which was judged too strong to trifle with. There were no Allied forces available to form landing parties; Bomarsund, in the Åland Islands, was destroyed by shelling, occupied and offered to the Swedes, who quickly declined it, for fear of compromising their neutrality. Sveaborg, outside Helsingfors, was also bombarded, and badly damaged, without any real effect. Small shallow-draft vessels throwing high trajectory bombs or mortars or howitzer shells were not available until the closing stages of the campaign, and no real damage could be done with the more conventional weapons.

During one of these bombardments, at Bomarsund, on June 21st, 1854, the first Victoria Cross was won by Acting Mate Lucas serving in H.M.S. *Hecla*. A live bomb fell on board the ship and, while the primitive fuse was still spitting and burning away, Lucas picked up the bomb and threw it overboard. Lucas lived for sixty years afterwards in the enjoyment of his unique honour, dying, a retired rear-admiral, on August 4th, 1914.

During all the operations in the Baltic the Russian warships remained in harbour. They were safe, but as far as they contributed to the Russian war effort they might just as well have been on the bottom of the sea with the Sevastopol ships. But if weapons conventional at the time in sea warfare were left unused by the Russians, they attempted by unconventional means to redress the balance between their enemies and themselves. Off Kronstadt, mines—then called 'torpedoes'—were used for the first time to keep the Allied fleets at a distance, while the Allies attempted to counter these primitive mines by the earliest known minesweeping devices.

However, another revolutionary and more important weapon was soon to be introduced—the armoured ship of war.

After Sinope the French had been first off the mark with the design and construction of the new ships, thanks to Napoleon III and his willingness to back his very expert and ingenious naval architects, Garnier and Gineysse. His first idea was for shallow-draft wooden-hulled steam vessels—literally 'ironclad', with iron armour on their exposed sides above water—with which to attack the Russian coastal fortifications. The conception of oceangoing vessels with iron hulls instead of wooden ships with armoured covering followed later, though here, too, the French were first.

On October 17th, 1855, the first of the ironclads, *Lave*, *Tonnante* and *Dévastation*, were 'stoked up' and, at a full speed of just over three knots or a moderately brisk walking pace, attacked the fort at Kinburn. The action lasted three hours; during that time each ship fired about 1,000 rounds, putting out of action most of the Russian guns. Allied troops landed on the spit behind the fort, thus cutting it off from the mainland, and the Russian garrison surrendered. The *Lave* was not hit; the *Dévastation* was hit sixty-four times, but suffered no damage to herself, though she lost two men killed and thirteen wounded from shells which entered either her gunports or her main hatch; in the same way *Tonnante* had nine men wounded. She was hit seventy times, but only one caused any damage—to her starboard rudder. For the rest, the shells simply left rust-coloured marks on the armour. In comparison with the French casualties of two killed and twenty-two wounded, the Russians lost forty-five killed and 130 wounded.

This was the last important engagement of the war; the limited success of the Allies in the Crimea had been balanced by the limited success of the Russians against the Turks in the Caucasus, and the Allies had no idea as to how they were to exploit such victories as they had had. So there was peace; but to set against Sevastopol, Kinburn, Sveaborg and Bomarsund there was what would have been termed in a later war 'a bloody nose', suffered by an Anglo-French force in an attack on Petropavlovsk in the Pacific.

At that time Vladivostock did not exist and its site was not yet in Russian hands. Petropavlovsk, on the peninsula of Kamchatka, was accordingly the base of the Russian Pacific squadron—composed of three ships, *Pallada* (60), *Avrora* (44) and *Dvina* (12) under Rear-Admiral Putiatin. A first attack on August 30th, 1854, was broken off almost as soon as it had begun by the suicide of the British commander-in-chief, Rear-Admiral David Price, another of the veteran heroes of earlier wars whose great age contributed to so many failures on land and sea in this war. He was succeeded by Captain Sir Frederick Nicolson, Bart. (father of the distinguished diplomatist, Sir Arthur Nicolson, afterwards Lord Carnock, and grandfather of Sir Harold Nicolson, the historian).

No new attack was possible that year, but in May 1855 the British and French came back again—the British base was at Vancouver and the French at San Francisco—and landed 700 sailors and marines outside Petropavlovsk. The beach selected was commanded by enemy fire, and before the Allied force could be withdrawn it had suffered over 200 casualties. The Allied ships made off, first investigating reports that Sitka, in Alaska, then a Russian possession, was being developed as a base. The reports proved to be wrong, so that the place was left alone and the war in the Pacific came uneventfully to an end, as did the war in the Arctic, where British ships had been patrolling in the White Sea and blockading Archangel.

The Crimean War was finally brought to a close by the Treaty of Paris signed on March 30th, 1856. The Turks obtained a small amount of territory at the mouth of the Danube; otherwise Allied gains in the Crimea were exchanged for Russian gains in the Caucasus, and things were much the same as before, except for the fact that Russia was once again compelled to agree not to maintain a fleet in the Black Sea.

CHAPTER X

THE FIRST TORPEDO WAR

1876–1877

ALTHOUGH there was to be no Russian Black Sea fleet in the future, no treaty limits were imposed on the Russian Baltic fleet, and almost as soon as the Crimean War was over a re-organisation and rebuilding of the Baltic fleet was begun by the Grand Duke Constantine, brother of Tsar Alexander II, and great-grandfather of Prince Philip, Duke of Edinburgh.

Constantine began work on the navy from two directions. There was a shipbuilding programme providing for ten screw line of battle ships, seventeen frigates and the inevitable coastal gunboats for the Baltic shallows; and there was also instituted a thoroughgoing scheme of naval education and training which affected everyone from flag officers to newly joined boys. The dreadful legacy to morale of the war passed by the Baltic fleet in harbour while the enemy steamed about the sea, blockading and bombarding, he sought to dispel by giving the fleet as much sea time as possible, when necessary outside the Baltic.

Constantine's chief helper at the Ministry of Marine was Likhavchev, a survivor of Sevastopol, who in 1859 went from the Ministry in St. Petersburg to the Far East to command the Russian force there when a crisis arose in Russo-Chinese relations. The outcome of the crisis was the cession by China to Russia of the Amur province and the site upon which was built the port of Vladivostock. At the same time, however, another valuable prize escaped the Russians, for Likhavchev annexed the island of Tsushima, the scene of the great Russian disaster in 1905, only to be disavowed by his Government, so that the island came under Japanese rule.

The year 1859 is of special significance in naval affairs because it was the last year in which the yardstick of naval strength between the powers was the number of wooden line-of-battle ships which they possessed. In the next year the first seagoing ironclads were ready and the old wooden battleships became obsolete so fast that within seven years the last of these units in the British fleet had been paid off.

It was appropriate, therefore, that at this stage the first book produced in English surveying the naval strength of the principal powers should have been published—the forerunner of the works of Brassey, Jane, Steevens, Bywater and the rest in England and of a stream of other writers abroad. This book was *The Navies of the World; Their Present State and Future Capabilities*, by Hans Busk, described as M.A. of Trinity College, Cambridge. It was a topical book because of the revolution in naval architecture and the tension between Britain and France—this was the year of Tennyson's 'Form, Form, Riflemen, Form'. It seems originally to have been sparked off by the report of a parliamentary committee which was appointed to inquire into the relative strengths of the British and French fleets and which reported that, built or building, Britain and France each had twenty-nine steamships of the line, while France had thirty-four large frigates against the British twenty-six. Of the first French ironclads the committee remarked that while their powers, 'plunged some people into deep distress . . . [they] were manifestly put forward to excite our foolish fears'.

After discussing the relative strengths and weaknesses of the British and French fleets, Busk's book went on to refer more briefly to the other principal fleets of the world. From this we learn that in 1859 the total strength of the Russian fleet was seven screw ships of the line, eleven screw frigates, twelve screw corvettes and smaller screw ships, in addition to twelve sailing ships of the line, seven frigates and seven corvettes—all obsolete.

It was upon this basis that Constantine began to build up the post-Crimean Russian navy. The first appearance of this force on the international scene came in 1863, with the outbreak of yet another insurrection in Russian Poland. There was danger of war with the West and the Russians sent two small squadrons into the Atlantic and Pacific—one to New York and one to San Francisco. The object of this move was twofold: first, if war came with Britain and France effective commerce raiding forces would be available on the high seas and the entire Russian fleet would not be shut up in home waters, as had happened in the Baltic and the Black Sea during the Crimean War; second, the United States had recently been within measurable distance of war with both Britain and France over the *Trent* affair and the French expedition to Mexico. Accordingly the visits of the Russian squadrons were to be interpreted as part of a plan to obtain a Russo-American alliance in case of necessity.

Nothing, of course, happened; the Russian officers in their green military-style tunics and caps were much admired by the American crowds and the Tsarist historians established a legend that Russian seapower had moved in such strength to the defence of the Northern side in the American Civil War, which was then in progress, that the British and French were compelled to give up their plans of intervention on the side of the South. Accordingly, they say, Russia can be regarded as the saviour for all time of the United States.

A further attempt to improve Russo-American relations was made in 1867 when Alaska, then Russian, was sold to the United States for 7,000,000 dollars. The reason for this was once again Russian fear of a war with Britain; in that case the Russians would have had little chance of retaining Alaska in the face of British seapower. It will be recalled that it was the same fear of British seapower that caused Napoleon to sell Louisiana to the United States in 1803. A certain amount of irony may be derived from the fact that two of the greatest territorial gains by the United States derived from fear of British seapower.

In the meantime the international naval building race, which endured in one form or another until the end of World War II, when it recommenced in another form, had begun. Great wooden fleets built up over the years were useless and all the principal types of warships had been rendered obsolete by the coming of the ironclad, so that all the nations were able to start from scratch.

In this race the British and the French got off the mark together. By 1868 the former had twenty-nine armoured ships afloat and the latter twenty-six. It was only the Franco-German War two years later, which, calling for all-out concentration by the French on their army, enabled the British to forge ahead and gain the position of numerical superiority which they maintained until the 1920s.

The 1870s had also seen the beginning of the new Russian navy with the laying down of battery ships, a fashionable type in those days. These vessels had their guns firing from ports on both sides of the hull, but were unable to use more than half their armament on one beam or the other. These were either built of iron or were wooden ships with iron armour along their sides. They were followed by turret ships, whose many fewer but much heavier guns could be trained on either beam. The origin of these turret ships had been a raft of barrels designed and built by Captain Coles, R.N., for use in the Sea of Azov during the Crimean War, on which a single gun was mounted which could be turned in any direction. This raft had drawn only twenty inches of water.

Two of the Russian ships of those days which had extraordinarily long lives were the *Petr Veliki* and the *General Admiral*. The former lasted from 1872 until after World War I, while the *General Admiral* survived even World War II in a subsidiary capacity.

The new Russian ships were essentially designed for the Baltic; the Black Sea remained out of bounds for Russian warships until the Franco-German War and the big cruisers, for commerce raiding on the oceans, came later. Once the discomfiture of the French in 1870 was clear, the Russians denounced the relevant clauses of the Treaty of Paris. The only two guarantors interested in its maintenance were France and Britain; the former was too busy with the Germans to do more than protest, while Britain was not prepared to act alone in defence of the treaty.

After the treaty had been denounced the first big warships built by the Russians in the Black Sea were the two famous circular *'Popovkas'*, named after their creator Admiral Popov. Their hulls were completely round—and 121 feet in diameter. The theory of this was that the curvature of their hulls and armour would cause shells to glance off the sides of the ship, which was theoretically true, but what proved not to be just theoretical but terribly practical was the fact that, caught in a current, they spun round and round like a saucer floating in a sink.

Accordingly these ships were retained merely as floating forts and no effort was made to use them as seagoing warships during the Russo-Turkish War, although, on paper at least, they were the only real warships which the Russians had in the Black Sea at the outbreak of war. Instead, in order to challenge Turkish command of the sea the Russians resorted to a very considerable feat of improvisation. They took over some nineteen of the fastest merchant vessels under the Russian flag in the Black Sea—ships of about 1,000–1,500 tons, the fastest capable of about fifteen knots—and equipped a number of them to carry torpedo boats, which were steam launches brought down from the Baltic by rail and armed with different types of the primitive torpedoes of those days. The first of these was the spar torpedo, which was an explosive charge on the end of a long pole in the bow of the torpedo boat. This charge was exploded by coming alongside the enemy, lowering the end of the spar and detonating when it struck the enemy's hull under water. Another type of torpedo was towed by a launch which was supposed to drag it across the bows of an approaching enemy. Finally there were the 'fish torpedoes', true ancestors of the torpedoes of today, which were driven by their own power—usually compressed air—and fired from torpedo tubes, or dropped over the side. In addition, there were a number of other odd torpedo ideas current in those days—notably the German boat which was filled forward with explosives and steered towards the enemy, whereupon the crew of the torpedo boat jumped overboard.

If the boat missed the enemy they were supposed to swim after it, climb on board, aim it at the enemy once again and once again jump overboard. The tubes for launching the first fish torpedoes which the Russians used were attached to the bottoms of the torpedo boats outside the hull because there was not room for them inside the tiny craft.

Primitive though all this was the Russo-Turkish War can be described as the first torpedo war in our sense of the phrase, for the torpedoes used in the Crimean War and the American Civil War were really either moored mines (in both wars) or explosive charges on spars (in the American Civil War).

Opposing this scratch Russian fleet of armed merchantmen and torpedo launches the Turks had one of the strongest fleets numerically in the world at that time—fifteen modern ironclads, the largest of which, the 9,000-ton *Messudieh*, survived to be sunk by a British submarine in the Dardanelles in 1914.

The commander-in-chief of the Turkish fleet was a former British officer, the Honourable Augustus Charles Hobart-Hampden, son of the 6th Earl of Buckinghamshire and the last, probably, of the 'sailors of fortune'. Born in 1822, he served in the Royal Navy for over thirty years, seeing service against the slavers in the South Atlantic and against the Russians in the Baltic during the Crimean War, but despite his family connections and an appointment to the royal yacht, he failed to receive rapid promotion and, when the American Civil War broke out, became an extremely competent blockade runner under what was literally the *nom de guerre* of Captain Roberts. His cargo on his first successful run into the Confederate port of Wilmington, N.C., through the Northern blockading forces, included 1,000 corsets, 500 boxes of Cockles pills and toothbrushes. Outward bound for Europe the cargo, of course, was always cotton.

When the Civil War was over Hobart-Hampden, generally known as 'Hobart Pasha', succeeded Sir Adolphus Slade as commander-in-chief of the Turkish navy. His first active service was to put down a rising in Crete by cutting off the supplies which the rebels were receiving from their sympathisers in Greece. Twice his name was removed from the British navy list and twice restored. Shortly before the outbreak of the Russo-Turkish War, while at home in England, he began experiments with torpedoes on a pond at Upottery in Devonshire, with the assistance of the village blacksmith.

The Russo-Turkish War of 1877–8 presented the usual features of the struggles between these two countries. The Russians advanced to the Danube and then nearly to Constantinople, while in the Caucasus, in horrible weather and in horrible country, the two toughest armies in the world fought each other. The lack of a Russian Black Sea fleet meant that the supplies for these campaigns had to be carried overland, and in Europe there was only one railway line leading from Russian territory down to the Danube at Galatz. At the same time Turkish command of the sea meant that the Russian attacks against Constantinople and in the Caucasus had both to be made overland. There was no possibility of a landing, for example, at the entrance to the Bosphorus, in an attempt to avoid the 300-mile slog southward overland, marked by fierce fighting at Plevna and elsewhere.

The first naval action took place on the Danube on May 11th, 1877, when one of the Turkish ironclads, *Lutfi Djelil* (2,500 tons), was blown up. On May 25th came the first torpedo attack, at Braila. Four of the Russian torpedo boats, under Lieutenant Dubasov, came down the river at night against the Turks in the midst of pouring rain. Dubasov led in the *Tsarevitch*, with a crew of fifteen and the *Xenia* with a crew of nine. Suddenly the *Tsarevitch* had to stop to raise additional steam. This happened four times in an hour and a half, by which time the Russians had covered eight miles. Finally, by three o'clock the *Tsarevitch* was within sight of the nearest of the enemy— the *Seifez* of 328 tons and some monitors.

From a distance of 135 yards Dubasov started his run in; half-way to his goal a Turkish challenge rang out. Dubasov muddled his reply and the alarm was given. A sentry fired a rifle, the *Seifez* switched on her lights and her crew went to action stations. By now the *Tsarevitch* was so close alongside the enemy that her people could hear the click as the lanyards on the triggers of the Turkish guns were pulled—three clicks, three misfires. Dubasov came alongside the *Seifez* aft and his spar torpedo struck the enemy just forward of her stern; Dubasov fired. There was a great explosion, a column of water 120 feet high crashed down on the Russians, accompanied by a shower of debris. The water half swamped the little craft and Dubasov prepared to abandon ship. Then, when he saw that the hull of the *Tsarevitch* was undamaged, he gave orders to bail her out and began to go astern as the Turks opened fire with rifles from the decks of their sinking ship.

They also opened fire with their twelve-ton turret guns, but the range was too short, and the shells passed harmlessly over the Russians' heads. Dubasov then ordered the *Xenia*, his second boat, commanded by Lieutenant Tchestakov, to attack. The *Xenia*'s torpedo was also exploded against the enemy, jamming his turret, but also putting the *Xenia* out of action, for she fouled some wreckage, her screw would not work and she had to be separated from her enemy by her crew fending her off from the Turk's side with boat-hooks. A third Russian boat, the *Djigit*, was damaged and had to be run aground as the flotilla withdrew. She was got off at daybreak and fled up the river in full view of the enemy. The last glimpse the Russians had of the *Seifez* was as she sank.

A fortnight later, on June 10th, another torpedo attack was made on the Turkish Danube flotilla, this time from the sea instead of from upstream. The *Veliki Kniaz Constantine*, one of the fast passenger steamers—1,400 tons and fifteen knots—converted to carry six torpedo boats, escorted by a similar ship, the *Vladimir*, appeared off the Sulina mouths of the Danube. Here a squadron of four Turkish ironclads was reported to be lying, protected by an early form of boom defence consisting of ropes running from one guard boat to the next. The leader of this expedition was Lieutenant Makarov, of whom much more will be heard later. A few days earlier he had tried unsuccessfully to attack an enemy ship off Batum (then a Turkish port) with towed torpedoes, but had found it impossible to bring them into contact with the enemy.

Now, however, spar torpedoes were available for five of the six boats. All boats were lowered into the water and headed in towards Sulina. The second of them was commanded by Lieutenant Rozhestvensky, of whom also much more will be heard later. Rozhestvensky seems to have been the first into the attack, but his target, the *Idjilalieh* (2,000 tons), was protected by obstructions against which he in vain fired his torpedo, so that he achieved nothing beyond damaging the bow of his boat in collision with the anti-torpedo defences. According to a contemporary account the boat was only able to get steam up by burning oakum and salt—however, she did get safely away, together with all of her sisters, except one sunk by an enemy shell after having been in collision with the boom.

Up the Danube at Nikopol, 240 miles away, two more torpedo boats were launched against a Turkish monitor on June 23rd, but the Turk was well defended by torpedo nets and a very vigorous captain, said to have been an Englishman, who steered towards the boats and tried to pin them against the bank while he waved his hat in reply to their small arms fire.

The object of this Russian activity, together with the laying of mines and the sinking of blockships designed to stop the navigation of the Danube by the Turks, was to provide protection for the Russian troops when they were finally ready to cross the river and proceed to the liberation of Bulgaria at the end of June. However, there was always a danger of an attack by Turkish ships up the river so long as they were in possession of Sulina, and the Russians therefore decided to try to take this place by an attack from seaward. The attacking force was a very scratch collection of three gunboats, a barge, two tugs, and seven torpedo boats, one a gift from the Odessa Yacht Club. These ships brought with them ninety torpedoes, seventy-five rockets and two torpedo tubes for firing Whitehead 'fish torpedoes'.

The flotilla first ascended the Kilia mouth of the Danube to Tulcea, where the Danube splits into its three mouths—Kilia, Sulina and St. George—and then came down by the Sulina mouth, taking the Turks in the rear and attempting, on November 8th, to mine them in. The Turks, led by a tug and the gunboat *Sulina*, steamed up the river to attack the Russians over the Russian minefield—the draft of the tug was sufficiently shallow to permit it doing this in safety, but the *Sulina* struck a mine and sank, her funnel and upperworks remaining above the surface. This discouraged the other Turks from attacking that night, and they contented themselves with driving off the Russians with shell fire from behind the minefields. The Russian shallow-draft mortar boats attacked over the mines next day and forced the Turks to take shelter behind a breakwater. This ended fighting on the Danube.

At the other end of the Black Sea, Batum was the principal Turkish port for the support of the Caucasus front, and its open roadstead made it an admirable target for torpedo attacks by the boats of *Veliki Kniaz Constantine*, all painted seagreen as a form of camouflage. An added means of concealment was the use by the *Constantine* of the best Welsh steam coal, which was almost smokeless, while the Turks used soft coal whose smoke could be seen from miles away, thus giving plenty of warning of their presence. The first Russian attack on Batum was made on May 11th, nothing being achieved because of the failure of the towed torpedo.

The next attack on this coast was made against Sukkum Kale, 100 miles north-west of Batum, on the night of August 23rd/24th during an eclipse of the moon. Makarov in the *Constantine* was in charge of the attack with the usual four torpedo boats. When the moon was nearly eclipsed Lieutenant Zatzarennyi in the *Tchesma* led in. He found a huge fire burning on the beach, lighting up the whole harbour, including groups of Turkish troops and a battery on the shore as well as the *Assar-i-Chevket*, a central battery ship of about 2,000 tons. The torpedo boats *Sinope* and *Navarin* attacked with towing torpedoes. Refusing to stop when challenged, they exploded one of their torpedoes under the Turkish vessel, but this had no effect except to shake a great deal of coaldust and soot off the ship on to the surface of the sea. The *Sinope* was attacked by a small boat from the *Assar-i-Chevket*; a Turkish seaman caught Lieutenant Pifarevsky, the *Sinope*'s captain, with a boat-hook and had nearly pulled him into the sea when one of the *Sinope*'s crew shot the Turk and Pifarevsky was able to scramble back on board his own craft, which then withdrew.

The *Tchesma* had been searching the harbour for another target than the *Assar-i-Chevket*, found nothing worth while, and came back alongside the Turkish ironclad just as the *Sinope* and *Navarin* fired their torpedoes; these did the Turk no damage, but made her roll so much that she struck the *Tchesma* and forced her bow under water. The Turks fired off great quantities of small arms ammunition without hitting anything and the Russian escaped to join her consorts alongside the *Constantine*, only to find that the *Torpedoist*, the last of the four torpedo boats, was missing. She turned up just as the *Constantine* sighted a large Turkish ironclad, the *Osmanieh* (6,000 tons), much more powerfully armed and a knot faster than Makarov's ship. However, the Turks' look-out was poor, the torpedo boats were got on board within seven minutes and Makarov made off.

After this he was promoted to captain, and on the night of December 27th was back again with the *Constantine* and four torpedo boats off Batum. The *Tchesma* and *Sulina* had now been fitted with torpedo tubes; *Tchesma*'s was lashed under the keel, the lashing being cut when the torpedo had been fired; *Sulina*'s tube was on a raft lashed alongside her. *Tchesma*'s 'fish torpedo' was the second ever fired in action—the first had been that fired by the British battleship *Shah* against the Peruvian rebel ironclad *Huascar* on May 2nd in the same year (1877).

Batum was now well blacked out by the Turks and it took the Russians some time to find the place; when they had done so the *Tchesma* and *Sulina* attacked the largest ship that they could find but without success. On the way back, owing to a mistake in identification, they nearly attacked the *Constantine*.

A final attack on Batum was made on the night of January 25th/26th, 1878, when the *Tchesma* and *Sulina*, with the same captains as previously, Zatzarennyi and Stchelinski, crept into the harbour with bright moonlight shining on the water and on the snow-covered foothills of the Caucasus. From a distance of eighty yards they torpedoed and sank the guardship *Intikbah*, a vessel of about 2,000 tons, which sank within two minutes.

During this war only once did surface ships fight each other on the high seas when the *Assar-i-Chevket* sighted and pursued the armed merchant cruiser *Vesta* on July 23rd. After a long stern chase, the Turk had very nearly come up with the Russian ship when at the last moment the Turk was disabled by a lucky hit and fell astern.

'The credit due to the Russians is immense,' wrote F. T. Jane, founder of *Fighting Ships* and also a naval historian, commenting on the events of the war. He went on to say:[1]

> They had no fleet to start with, and they used an almost unknown weapon. We can not judge Makarov's exploits by the light of present day knowledge: he had to invent his tactics . . . Nor, because their loss of life was small and insignificant, can this be held to detract from the individual bravery of the Russian torpedoists; on going into action there were absolutely no reasonable prospects of such an extraordinary survival.

[1] *The Imperial Russian Navy*, p. 200, W. Thacker & Co., London, 1904.

CHAPTER XI

COURSE FOR PORT ARTHUR
1904

B Y the Treaty of Berlin, Russia failed to obtain what she thought to be the legitimate reward for her victory over Turkey, and it seemed to the Russians and to many other people that it had been the power of the British Government and the British navy which had prevented them from doing so.

Britain, at this time, adhered to a policy of checking Russian aggrandisement by threat of war, if necessary. Russia, though determined upon expansion, after the Crimea never pressed her claims hard enough to bring about war with Britain. The upshot was that Britain consented to comparatively small gains by Russia and denied her the big ones which, in the case of the Russo-Turkish War of 1877 and the Treaty of Berlin, would have meant the destruction of Turkey and the Russian capture of Constantinople. Later, as will be seen, Britain and France were to offer Constantinople to Russia for the taking.

After the lesson in the importance of seapower taught by Britain's effective opposition to their ambitions the Russian Government produced in 1882 the first detailed and systematic plan for a wholesale increase in the navy of their country. The twenty-year plan of that date provided for the building of fifteen battleships, ten cruisers and eleven gunboats—a plan afterwards expanded to comprise twenty battleships and twenty-four cruisers. At the time when this plan came into force the Russian navy included only four efficient battleships; in 1885, when the plan was being carried out, the United Kingdom had twenty-seven battleships and France fifteen, so that the Russian plan was well on the way to giving St. Petersburg something like a naval balance of power. It was never the Russian object to build a fleet big enough to challenge alone the British navy; what was planned was a fleet which, in alliance with that of France or some other ally sufficiently strong, might topple the British.

The danger that this might happen seemed very real, and many imaginative accounts of 'the next naval war' written in the 1880s and 1890s by European authors described a tremendous struggle between the British navy, usually caught off its guard by a surprise attack by the combined fleets of France and Russia, while the fleets of Italy and Germany played a minor role or none at all, according to the whim of the author, who also adjusted the outcome of the war to suit the lesson he was trying to teach or the sales for his book which he hoped to obtain.

Bit by bit fear of Germany caused France and Russia to build up an alliance of the type originally envisaged against Britain. However, the idea of naval war against Britain and perhaps against Germany as well continued to inform Russian and French naval thought for very many years—right up to the time of the *Entente Cordiale*.

As far as the Russian navy was concerned, in the 'seventies the emphasis had been laid on the construction of fast and powerful raiding cruisers. It was not until the programme of 1882 that the building of battleships was resumed, and even then commerce-raiding cruisers were in the forefront of Russian naval imagination, and they have continued to be there up to the present day.

The first reflection of this preoccupation was the publication, in the middle 'eighties, of a book by a Russian naval officer called *Russia's Hope*. This book described how Britain's trade in Eastern waters could be destroyed by the operations of a force of eighteen medium-sized fast cruisers of the same type as the *Admiral Kornilov*, which had then just been laid down in a French yard. This was a ship with a displacement of 5,000 tons, an armament of two eight-inch and fourteen six-inch guns and a speed, very high for those days, of 18.5 knots.

Russia's Hope was translated into many languages and became a kind of textbook of cruiser warfare with, it is believed, very strange fruit some thirty years later. One of the operations attributed to the *Admiral Kornilov* in *Russia's Hope* was an attack on the shipping in Bombay harbour, which was destroyed by using a ship carrying oil as a kind of fireship—oil tankers were a novelty then—and by spreading oil on the surface of the sea.

In 1914 the German cruiser *Emden* was in the Indian Ocean, trying to do to British merchant shipping exactly what the *Admiral Kornilov* and her sister ships had been described as doing in *Russia's Hope*. It is generally believed that the *Emden*'s captain, the famous von Müller, had read this book and that it gave him the idea of the attacks which he carried out on the ports of Madras and Penang. At Madras he was particularly successful in setting fire to the oil tanks in the port.

There was another indication of the shape of things to come in naval warfare in the Russian naval programmes of the 'eighties, for the Russian navy obtained, albeit only briefly, its first submarine.

This was a boat of 243 tons, designed by the Swedish engineer Nordenfelt and built by Vickers, Barrow. She was 123 feet long, and had a circular hull with a diameter of 12 feet amidships, while fore and aft the hull came to a point. The boat carried two torpedo tubes and four torpedoes and in that way she was considerably ahead of her generation. But she had no periscope, for the 'optical tube' had not yet been invented, and she had no engines for submerged propulsion. The place of the periscope was taken by two conning towers a couple of feet in height, with heavy glass windows, through the foremost of which the torpedoes could be aimed, while the captain conned the boat from the after window. Communication between the fore and aft ends of the boat was by means of a narrow passageway through which a man could travel on all fours over the boiler.

This boiler supplied steam for propulsion on the surface; when the boat was dived the boiler was shut down, but sufficient head of steam could be built up to permit the boat to run some twenty miles under water. To protect her on the surface she carried two Nordenfelt quick-firing guns. In this respect she was also well ahead of her time; some twenty-five years were to elapse before guns were regularly mounted in submarines.

This precursor of the gigantic Russian submarine fleet of today had a very short life, for she was lost off the coast of Denmark on her way to Russia just after she had been completed. During the 'nineties there were rumours that Russia was building a huge submarine fleet of 300 boats of the French Goubet type, but no attempt to build up a submarine force for the Russian navy was actually made until the Russo-Japanese War. The rumours of the building of these 300 boats years before that date is an example of how Russian naval construction has always been covered in great clouds of secrecy. At the beginning of the 'nineties another series of rumours as to Russian naval construction had spread through Europe. On this occasion they had concerned a huge new cruiser, fast enough to escape from any ship stronger than she was herself, and powerful enough to sink any possible enemy that could catch her. This ship was the *Rurik* and she caused as much of a stir as did the German 'pocket-battleships' just before the Second World War.

The *Rurik* appeared such a menace that, before her details were accurately known, the British navy built two other armoured cruisers even bigger, more powerful and faster than the *Rurik* had been reported to be. After giving years of anxiety, the *Rurik* made her first public appearance at the naval review held to mark the opening of the Kiel Canal in 1893, and it was seen, to the astonishment of everyone, that she was a full-rigged three-masted ship, complete with yards and sails, that is to say about twenty years out of date, although just completed. The other principal naval powers had long since abandoned the practice of equipping their steel-hulled, steam-propelled ships with the masts and yards of sailing ships.

Ever since that date Russian naval architecture and its products have been looked at suspiciously by foreigners, and it has certainly often been true that the best Russian ships have been built to British, American, French, Italian and German designs, even down to the present day.

The *Rurik* had been built with an eye to the raiding of British commerce, but soon after she was completed the whole European and Asiatic political scene changed, and it was against another enemy of Russia that the *Rurik* was to fight.

At the beginning of the 1890s the vast Chinese Empire seemed about to collapse. The Russians were looking at Manchuria and the Japanese watching the ramshackle Empire of Korea, where their interests ran across those of China, while the French were thinking of following up their conquests in Indo-China by the occupation of the province of Yunnan. Britain would not have refused Chinese territory had it been necessary to take it to prevent any other power getting it, but her great interest was the liberty to trade where she wanted. In this the British found themselves joined by the Americans, whose strong support of 'The Open Door' in China marked one of the very first breaks with their traditional policy of isolation.

War between China and Japan followed in 1894 and, to the surprise of most people, the small but efficient Japanese navy defeated the Chinese fleet. Korea for a while was freed from Chinese influence, but it was soon clear that the Russians hoped to succeed the Chinese as virtual overlords of the country. This policy alarmed the Japanese as much as the corresponding policy of China had already done. An early indication of Russian designs came during the peace conference at Shimonoseki in 1895, which ended the war between China and Japan. The Japanese had captured the ice-free Chinese naval base of Port Arthur and announced their intention of keeping it, under the terms of the peace treaty, whereupon Germany, France and Russia 'advised' her to return the base to China. The language of the 'advice' was unheard of in those days, when diplomacy was not carried on in public by denunciation, démenti and demand. It was, however, to be heard again within the next twenty years, for, when the Japanese demanded the surrender of the German base at Tsingtao in August

1914, they copied word for word the 'advice' which the Germans, and their temporary allies the French, and the Russians had tendered them in 1895.

Three years after the Japanese had been forced to return Port Arthur to the Chinese the Russians occupied it as a naval base. Up to that time their chief naval base had been Vladivostock. Not only was that place far from ice-free in winter, but the islands of the Japanese Empire lay across its communications with the Pacific and with the China and Yellow Seas, command of which was essential for operations against China and Korea.

In 1898, the same year that Port Arthur was seized, a new Russian naval programme was introduced, calling for the construction of eight battleships, seventeen cruisers and fifty destroyers and torpedo boats. It was these ships of the 1898 programme which formed the backbone of the Russian navy in the war with Japan which began in February 1904.

It was also from 1898 onward that the Russians began to keep a powerful battle fleet in the Far East, which was built up until, in 1904, it was roughly the same size as the entire Japanese navy, although the Japanese had countered these moves with a naval building programme of their own and by securing Britain as an ally.

The great increase in the German navy had alarmed the British and they began to look for what support they could get. Eventually it was to lead to the *Entente Cordiale* with France and alliance with Russia, but the first step was to reach an agreement with Japan. This agreement laid down that, if Britain was at war with two or more countries, Japan would come to her assistance. Similarly, if Japan was at war with more than one country Britain would join her.

The first practical result of this treaty was that the British, counting on Japanese aid, were able to withdraw their battleships from the Far East and concentrate them in home waters against Germany; the second result was that, when Russia and Japan went to war, it was known to all that if any country went to Russia's assistance that country would be attacked by Britain.

The Russo-Japanese crisis, which led to war in February 1904, was one of those long grumbling affairs with which we have become so familiar in the course of this century. The Russians spread through the Manchurian provinces of China and seeped into Korea; the Japanese worried and prepared their fleet. Seemingly endless diplomatic negotiations between the two countries in St. Petersburg followed.

They had been started on the initiative of the Japanese in June 1903, and the Japanese had then suggested a division of Korea along the 39th parallel, the northern area going to Russia and the southern to Japan. The 39th parallel was the dividing line fixed in 1945 between the Russian and United States zones of Korea, and re-established after the Korean war in 1953 as the boundary between North and South Korea.

In February of 1904 the negotiations were still going on in what seemed a timeless way. After a delay in the talks a little longer than usual, while the Russian foreign ministry was very slowly composing an answer to the latest Japanese note, Kurino, the Japanese Minister in St. Petersburg, suddenly asked for his passports on February 5th. Two days earlier the Russian First Pacific Squadron at Port Arthur had assumed a preliminary degree of readiness and gone to sea, for the Russian war plan included a fleet action as soon as possible. The Russians saw no sign of the enemy and they returned to port. However, they anchored outside the entrance to Port Arthur in the road-stead, because the shallowness of the entrance to the harbour made it impossible for the fleet to enter or leave at certain stages of the tide and the Russians were afraid of being caught in Port Arthur, unable to get out.

Two destroyers were ordered to patrol offshore; but, if the fleet was more or less ready for war, the garrison was not and the guns of the shore batteries were still in the tarpaulins and grease used to protect them in winter. Admiral Alexiev, the Russian governor-general of Siberia and commander-in-chief, together with Vice-Admiral Stark, the admiral commanding the fleet, both believed that breaking off diplomatic relations was not the equivalent of a declaration of war and waited for the situation to be cleared up in a formal manner.

The night of February 8th was calm and cold. Just before moon-rise the Russian warships, lying at the entrance to Port Arthur fully illuminated, saw destroyers approaching, but took no action, for they thought that they were the two patrolling Russians. These ships had been under orders, upon sighting anything suspicious, to return to harbour at once to report, but not to open fire under any circum-stances.

Without warning torpedoes began to explode amidst the Russian ships and, within a few minutes, two of the total force of seven Russian battleships and one of the Russian light cruisers were out of action.

Three days before, during the middle watch on February 5th, the Japanese Combined Squadrons under the command of Vice-Admiral Heihachiro Togo had been lying in their base at Sasebo. Orders came for the Japanese captains to repair on board the flagship *Mikasa*, where they were shown down to the admiral's quarters. On the desk before Togo rested a plain black unlacquered tray and on the tray a short naked sword, the *seppuku*, used by the Samurai for suicide in case of disgrace. The significance of this was clear to the Japanese officers; it was almost needless for Togo to say: 'We sail tomorrow and the enemy flies the Russian flag.'

Then he went on to give them their orders. Destroyers, with heavy ships in support, were to attack Port Arthur; a cruiser force was to go to Chemulpo (now called Inchon) in Korea, deal with a couple of Russian warships known to be there and secure the port for the landing of Japanese troops, as General MacArthur secured it for the landing of his troops in 1950; another division of destroyers was sent to search for a possible detached Russian force which, in fact, was not at sea at all.

The Japanese ships cleared Sasebo. As the main fleet headed towards Port Arthur the cruiser *Takachiho* hit a whale and killed it, so that the Japanese ships sailed on through a sea stained with blood.

During the evening of the 8th the destroyer captains were summoned on board the *Mikasa*; Togo spoke briefly and simply and the captains knew what they had to do. There was a quick burst of cheering, an exchange of toasts between the admiral and his young officers in champagne, and they went back to their ships, which soon disappeared ahead of the fleet in the falling twilight.

There were ten of these destroyers and they were making history on a grand scale. Ahead of them was the defeat of Russia and the victory of Japan, with the Russian revolution and the Japanese victories at Pearl Harbor and Singapore and the scene in 1945 on board U.S.S. *Missouri* in Tokio Bay.

The ten destroyers, small ships of about 300 tons, steamed into the night, corkscrewing through the sea at half speed in order that bow and stern waves should not be too visible in the dark. They were a new type of ship in those days; this was to be their first trial in war. The ten attacked in three divisions—four, three and three boats— *Shirakumo, Asashio, Kasumi, Akatsuki, Ikazuchi, Oboro, Inazuma, Usugomo, Shinonome, Sazanami*—White Cloud, Morning Tide, Mist of Flowers, Morning Twilight, Thunder, Moon through the Mist, Lightning, Feathery Cloud, Daybreak and Rippling Wave.

As the Japanese approached the entrance to the harbour the two Russian destroyers on patrol passed between the first and second divisions. This threw both the second and third divisions into a confusion from which they could not recover. All three hits on Russian ships were scored by the first division. Later other torpedoes could be seen, glistening in the light of the Russian searchlights, caught in the net defences. The Japanese torpedoes had been fitted with net cutters on their warheads, but none worked, and the torpedoes which did hit their targets and explode seem to have been fired from angles on the bow or stern of the target not covered by the nets which were draped from the sides of the ships on long booms.

In comparison with what was at stake and what was determined that night outside Port Arthur the damage done by the Japanese to the Russians when they attacked seems small. Eighteen torpedoes were fired—out of twenty carried by the ten boats. Fifteen missed or were caught in the net defences; of the other three, one hit the battleship *Retvisan*, one the battleship *Tsarevitch* and one the light cruiser *Pallada*. All three ships were put out of action, but none were sunk. Torpedoes were still primitive, as were torpedo tactics and destroyers themselves; this accounts, in part at least, for results which might have seemed disappointing to the Japanese in view of the advantage of surprise which they had had. But, in fact, the three torpedo hits decided the course of the war. The Russian fleet was out of action and the Japanese troops landed unchecked in Korea. Russian morale was abysmal, Japanese morale was high; Japan's allies rejoiced and Russia's allies wondered what awful disease had smitten her.

Across the Yellow Sea, at Chemulpo, a strong Japanese cruiser force had met the Russian cruiser *Variag* and the gunboat *Korietz*. The Russians had no chance and, after a brave resistance, the *Variag* scuttled herself.

The memory of this action is still preserved in the Red navy; one of the Russian cruisers of the 1950s was called *Variag*, and *Variag*'s fate is still recalled by ordinary Russian civilians, one of whom, fresh from Moscow on a Soviet Government mission recently explained the outcome of the affair to a British journalist in English which, while shaky, was touching, 'She was hopeless, so she opened her key hole and drowned herself.'

On the morning after the destroyers' attack at Port Arthur, Togo appeared off the port with his battleships and began a somewhat half-hearted bombardment. He could almost certainly have destroyed the Russian fleet then and there, but he knew that he had to keep looking over his shoulder to where the Russians had another fleet in the Baltic, as big as that already at Port Arthur, which could in its turn be sent to the Far East. In addition, there was a third fleet of about the same size in the Black Sea—although this, for diplomatic reasons, was unlikely to take part in the fighting. Accordingly Togo had to fight the war in such a way as to keep his own fleet intact while being able to sink at least two and possibly three fleets, each as strong as his own. There would be no chance of the Japanese replacing their losses during the war, for the primitive state of their shipbuilding industry and the international laws governing neutrality both made it impossible.

The sudden attacks on Port Arthur and Pearl Harbor are not the only parallel that can be drawn between the war that started in 1904 and that which started in 1941. Just as the Japanese in 1941 and 1942 dared not exploit to the full their successes in the Pacific and the Indian Ocean for fear of weakening themselves elsewhere, so in 1904 they could never risk all on a single battle. Their strategy in both wars was to seize by surprise as much territory as they could and pause to consolidate their gains, hoping that they would be in so strong a position that their enemy would not be willing to pay the price of driving them out. In 1904–5 they were right in their calculations, though the outcome was more closely run than was sometimes thought by people confused by the pro-Japanese sentiment and propaganda which operated particularly in Britain and the United States.

If the fundamental problem for Japan was how to overcome total Russian forces much stronger than her own, the Russians' problem was how to concentrate these forces in the Far Eastern theatre of war. The Black Sea fleet, under the terms of the Treaty of Berlin, was forbidden to pass the Bosphorus; and Russian diplomacy failed to persuade the powers principally interested—Turkey and Britain—to waive the relevant clauses of the treaty.

However, so far as the fleet in the Baltic was concerned, there was no doubt in St. Petersburg as to what should be done. The Russian army in Manchuria was to stand on the defensive, waiting the arrival of reinforcements by the Trans-Siberian railway, then almost completed. Port Arthur was to hold out, even though besieged, defended by its garrison and by its fleet—henceforward known as the First Pacific Squadron. The Second Pacific Squadron—the Baltic fleet—would then be sent round the world to the Far East under the command of Vice-Admiral Rozhestvensky, the successful torpedo-boat captain of the Russo-Turkish War. Once it had arrived, the combined First and Second Squadrons would defeat Togo's force and cut the communications of the Japanese army with the home country. Japan would surrender and, in anticipation of this event, plans had been prepared for the military occupation of the defeated country.

In the meanwhile the Russians thought that there was a chance of buying some useful second-hand warships, and a mission was sent abroad for this purpose. It met, however, with no success, either because the countries chiefly concerned—Argentina, Brazil and Chile —declined to behave in an unneutral manner or the Russians refused to pay the prices asked.

At the same time a Russian diplomatic offensive was begun for the opening of the Dardanelles, which ended as fruitlessly as had the financial offensive in Latin America. The fact that Britain was allied to Japan was certainly very much in the minds of all to whom it was suggested that they might be of assistance to Russia.

Meanwhile, in Port Arthur the immediate problem was to get the First Pacific Squadron into a seaworthy condition once more. First, the three torpedoed ships had to be repaired, in a port where there was only one dry dock and that too small to take a battleship. Even more important was the task of steadying the morale of the officers and men of the luckless First Squadron and convincing them that the war had not already been lost and that they, their fleet and Port Arthur were not doomed. This morale had been still further lowered by two additional losses, the minelayer *Yenissei* and the light cruiser *Boyarin*, which had both been sunk after striking their own mines.

In this crisis the Admiralty in St. Petersburg took, belatedly, it is true, almost the one sound step which marked their conduct of the war. As commander-in-chief of the First Squadron they appointed Admiral Stephen Ossipovitch Makarov. This was the officer who, it will be remembered, had greatly distinguished himself as a torpedo-boat commander in the war against the Turks. But there was much more to Makarov than just a capacity for 'Death or Glory' leadership.

In the first place he was one of the very few senior officers of the forces of Tsarist Russia to have emerged from the ranks of the people; both his grandfathers were non-commissioned officers, in the days when the period of military service was twenty-five years.

Makarov himself went to a naval school in Siberia at the age of ten and soon began to show his talents, scientific and technical. He invented a collision mat to be placed over a hole in a ship's side below the waterline; he invented an armour-piercing shell and a cofferdam,[1] so that damaged ships could be repaired without having to go into dry dock. When he arrived at Port Arthur to take command he found his cofferdam being used to repair the ships which had been torpedoed on the first night of the war.

[1] A cofferdam is a steel box-like structure which can be fitted over the damaged side of a ship below the waterline, and then pumped out, so that repairs may be tackled.

Makarov thought and planned continuously for war—'You must feel at home at sea' was his slogan. To get that state of mind was not easy in the Russian Baltic and Black Sea fleets, which spent only three months each year in full commission exercising, while the other nine months of the year were spent in harbour with only one-quarter of the normal complement on board.

But probably Makarov's greatest pleasure was in Arctic exploration and in hydrographic work. His cruise round the world, in command of the surveying ship *Vitiaz*, not only added greatly to the world's knowledge of oceanography but enabled him to train a number of young officers in the way that he thought they should go. He designed one of the first ice-breakers, *Ermak*, built on the Tyne, and he wished to take her to the North Pole. This ambition he never realised, but his work on the development of ice-breakers made possible the opening of many of the northern waterways of Siberia, hitherto closed for most of the year.

When war came he was serving as Port Admiral at Kronstadt. On his staff at the time was Commander Vladimir Semenov, who wrote:

> It was no easy matter serving under Makarov. Often there was no time either for eating or sleeping; but for all that it was a splendid life. What was especially characteristic of Makarov was his horror of all 'routine', and his hatred of the old office custom of devolving everything on others, of avoiding any and every responsibility, and therefore of never coming to an independent decision, but of passing on every paper to someone else 'to be dealt with'. Whenever such an attempt at shirking a decision or allowing a question to drag on came to light, then it was that, in my opinion, the Admiral, for once in a way, lost all control over himself. Then he often ran to the telephone himself, censured and gave orders to the persons concerned in the sharpest manner possible, and threatened to call them to account for their misdeeds.[1]

In appearance Makarov was striking, with a high-domed, bald forehead and a long forked fair beard, the ends of which hung low down on his chest. Even in an era of great Russian beards he was known as 'Beardy'.

A month passed between the outbreak of war and the arrival of Makarov to take command at Port Arthur. During that time the Japanese tried to remove the threat which the Russian fleet still presented to the lines of communication of the Japanese army by bottling up the Russian ships within the harbour of Port Arthur.

Three attempts in all to do this were made, on February 24th,

[1] *Rasplata* (The Reckoning), chap. I, p. 2, John Murray, London, 1909.

March 27th and May 3rd, and some seventeen vessels were expended, in vain, as blockships. All were sunk by the Russians before they could get into a position in which, by scuttling themselves, they would close the harbour. An operation similar to this had been attempted by the Americans during the Spanish-American war, when Admiral Sampson had tried to shut up the Spanish fleet within the harbour of Santiago in Cuba by sinking a blockship in the entrance to the harbour. This had proved unsuccessful; the operation was to be tried again by the British in the First World War at Zeebrugge and Ostend and was also unsuccessful.

Even before the arrival at Port Arthur of Makarov, Russian cruisers and destroyers put to sea frequently to drive off Japanese patrols, while the *Retvisan*, still hard aground at the entrance to the harbour, after having been torpedoed on the first night of the war, was constantly engaged. She was finally refloated and moved into the harbour for repairs on the day that Makarov arrived. The new admiral at once hoisted his flag in the five-funnelled cruiser *Askold*, while the luckless Stark was left flying his flag in the battleship *Petropavlovsk*. Two days later, on March 10th, Makarov was in action.

Two Russian destroyers on patrol, *Rechitelni* and *Stereguchi*, were engaged off the entrance to Port Arthur by four Japanese destroyers, *Usugomo*, *Shinonome*, *Sazanami* and *Akebono*. *Rechitelni* got clear, but *Stereguchi* was stopped by a hit in her engine room and her stern wrecked. Dead in the water and surrounded by the enemy, she kept her forecastle gun in action.

As soon as the news of this action was reported to Makarov by the signal station on Golden Hill, he ordered *Askold* and a smaller, faster ship, the light cruiser *Novik*, to the rescue. *Novik* led out, flying Makarov's flag. The sight of the Admiral leading the rescue party caused tremendous enthusiasm amongst the Russian fleet, but it could not save the *Stereguchi*. All her officers and most of the crew were killed and there was no one on deck to offer resistance when a Japanese destroyer went alongside to take possession of the drifting ship; but there were still two ratings below, who refused the Japanese summons to surrender and who scuttled the ship, perishing with her.

Immediately after this the Japanese battle fleet appeared and began a long-range bombardment of the Russian base, to which the Russians were unable to reply. Makarov, in his barge, went around his ships as shells were falling in the harbour, to encourage them as best he could during their ordeal; their guns could not bear and they could not leave the port to attack the enemy until high water—by which time the Japanese had withdrawn.

After this exasperating day, Makarov organised a system of in-direct fire control so that the guns of the ships in the harbour could be controlled from observation posts ashore. He made the fleet prac-tise entering and leaving harbour in an emergency. This was very necessary and highly successful. Originally it had taken twenty-four hours to get a fleet of twenty ships clear of the harbour, but Makarov's training brought the time down to two and a half hours.

Makarov next decided to exercise the fleet, with dreadful results, for three of the battleships collided with each other. However, no great damage was done.

On March 22nd the Japanese fleet began another bombardment of Port Arthur, but by now Makarov's efforts had borne fruit and the Japanese ships were driven off without obtaining any success.

As the Japanese withdrew the Russian fleet left harbour—five battleships strong—*Petropavlovsk*, flying the flag of Makarov, *Poltava*, *Sevastopol*, *Pobieda* and *Peresviet*. They remained under cover of the shore batteries, for the time had not come for them to try their strength against Togo, especially as the *Retvisan* and *Tsarevitch* were still under repair.

However, this sortie of Makarov's showed Togo the danger which the Russian fleet might once again be to the Japanese lines of com-munication, and he thereupon ordered the second unsuccessful attempt to block Port Arthur.

Makarov next turned his attention to a shake-up amongst his captains, and from that process there emerged two men who were to make history. Commander Essen, who had been captain of *Novik*, went as captain of the battleship *Sevastopol*—an unheard-of appoint-ment for a commander. With Makarov, Essen was to become one of the two great Russian admirals of the age of steam and steel. Also chosen at this time for a special appointment was Lieutenant Kolchak, who was selected to command the destroyer *Serditi*, attached to the flagship, and was to end his life before a Bolshevik firing squad in Siberia, after having been commander-in-chief of the Black Sea fleet during the First World War and leader of the last hope of the Russian anti-Communists.

These two appointments and a number of others were the occasion of considerable strife between Makarov and Alexiev and between both of them and the Admiralty in St. Petersburg, but finally things were settled as Makarov wished and by the end of the first week in April he had his fleet in hand. The conclusion of this phase of the naval war coincided with further rumours from Russia that the Baltic fleet was to be sent to the Pacific. While it was clear that the task of taking the Baltic fleet to the Far East would be probably the most difficult logistical operation since Hannibal tried to take his elephants across the Alps it might be possible, and Togo had to redouble his efforts to dispose of Makarov and the Port Arthur fleet before help could reach them from Europe.

The first Japanese measure was to plan the final attempt to block the entrance to Port Arthur. Then the auxiliary minelayer *Koryu Maru*, with an escort of torpedo boats was sent to lay mines off Port Arthur. The lay took place under cover of mist, rain and darkness on the night of April 11th–12th. On the next evening the weather was much the same; eight Russian destroyers were sent to reconnoitre the Japanese base in the Elliot Islands, about 100 miles to the north-east, where Togo had established a base among the Islands, very similar to Scapa Flow in the Orkneys.

One of the Russian destroyers on this sortie, the *Strashni*, lost her next ahead in the fog and, when dawn came, found four Japanese destroyers between her and Port Arthur. These had no difficulty in sinking her, but were then driven off by the armoured cruiser, *Bayan*, which lowered boats and started to pick up Russian survivors. Two Japanese armoured cruisers, the *Tokiwa* and *Asama*, and four light cruisers, *Chitose*, *Takasago*, *Kasagi* and *Yoshino*, then came up and started to engage the *Bayan* at a range of about 8,000 yards. The Russian, having been able to pick up only five survivors of the *Strashni*, turned back to Port Arthur, but soon met Makarov coming to her rescue in the *Petropavlovsk*, with the battleship *Poltava* and the cruisers *Askold*, *Diana* and *Novik* in company. This force was, in turn, much superior to the Japanese cruisers, who slowly withdrew, trying to lure Makarov farther out to sea towards Togo, approaching at full speed.

Very soon the Japanese battle fleet was within sight of the *Petropavlovsk*—six Japanese battleships and eight cruisers against two Russian battleships and four cruisers. By now visibility was good and the three other seaworthy Russian battleships were also at sea. Togo began cruising slowly off Port Arthur, at a distance of between twelve and fifteen miles, watching.

What he saw was a series of huge explosions; the *Petropavlovsk* had struck one of the Japanese mines laid the night before: almost immediately her own mines blew up, her boilers exploded and her magazines exploded as well. She sank within two minutes.

Commander Semenov, then executive officer of the *Diana*, wrote afterwards:

An explosion, with a dull rolling sound shook the whole ship as if a 12-inch gun had gone off quite close. I looked round vaguely. A second explosion even more violent! What was happening? Suddenly cries of horror arose: 'The *Petropavlovsk*! The *Petropavlosk*!'

Dreading the worst I rushed to the side. I saw a huge cloud of brown smoke. 'That is pyroxiline, therefore a torpedo,' passed through my mind. In this cloud I saw the ship's foremast. It was slanting, helpless, not as if it were falling but as if it were suspended in the air. To the left of this cloud I saw the battleship's stern. It looked as always, as if the awful happenings in the forepart were none of its concern. A third explosion! White steam now began to mix with the brown cloud. The boilers had burst. Suddenly the stern of the battleship rose straight in the air. This happened so rapidly that it did not look as if the bow had gone down but as if the ship had broken in half amidships. For a moment I saw the screws whirling round in the air. Was there a further explosion? I don't know.

It appeared to me as if the after-part of the *Petropavlovsk* (all that was visible of her) suddenly opened out and belched forth fire and flames, like a volcano. It seemed even as if flames came out of the sea, long after it had closed over the wreck.

When I saw the explosion, I mechanically looked at my watch, and then wrote in my note book:

'9.43—explosion on board *Petropavlovsk*.

'9.44—all over.'

Seven officers and seventy-three men were saved out of a complement of 715. There was no trace of Makarov. His body was seen by one of the survivors, the Grand Duke Cyril, lying on the bridge, which was covered with dead and wounded; the ship's forecastle, around the forward turret, was split open. The Grand Duke Cyril had been the heir of the Tsar until the birth of the Tsarevitch in the preceding year; he lived to become the pretender to the Russian throne after the execution of the Imperial family in the cellar at Ekaterinburg. The famous Russian painter of battle pieces, Verestchagin, invited aboard by Makarov as his guest, was also amongst those killed in this disaster.

As soon as he could see what had happened the second in command of the fleet, Rear-admiral Prince Ukhtomsky, in the *Peresviet*, assumed command and began to lead the fleet back to its base. Half an hour after the *Petropavlovsk* had sunk the *Pobieda*, following her, struck a mine in her turn and began listing to starboard.

Up to that moment discipline in the Russian fleet had been perfectly maintained, but now guns' crews began to open fire in all directions without orders, and men, grabbing up hammocks or lifebelts, prepared to jump overboard from undamaged ships, shouting that submarines were upon them.

The ships were soon firing at each other and officers had to use brute force to tear the crews away from their guns to stop them firing. The fleet, including the damaged *Pobieda*, returned to harbour and Togo withdrew, leaving a small force on watch.

It was about noon that the terrible events of this day ended. That one battleship had been lost and another damaged hardly mattered compared with the death of Makarov. There could be no replacing him, the remaining flag officers in Port Arthur were of poor quality and better men sent from Russia did not arrive before the siege cut off the fortress from the outside world.

Togo was again much criticised for not pressing home an attack against the Russians when they were in a state of disorganisation, but, as usual, he was haunted by fear of losing any of his big ships.

Just what risks he had to run in any case to keep the seas open for the Japanese expeditionary force was shown on May 15th, a month after Makarov's death, when two of Togo's six battleships, the *Hatsuse* and *Yashima*, struck mines and sank; on the same day the cruisers *Yoshino* and *Kasuga* were in collision off Port Arthur and the *Yoshino* sank. In addition, on this day the Japanese lost a destroyer and a gunboat while two gunboats were damaged in accidents. Of the battleships, the *Hatsuse* sank at once, but the *Yashima* was taken in tow. With these disasters just behind him it is not surprising that another possible opportunity to destroy the Russian fleet was refused by Togo on June 23rd; if he could not risk a decisive action with six battleships there was no possibility of his doing so with only four, especially as all six remaining Russian big ships were again ready for sea.

The Russian sortie of June 23rd had been ordered by Alexiev, after a meeting had been held by Vitgeft and his captains to discuss what the fleet should do now that all six battleships were approaching readiness. Vitgeft had been appointed to command the fleet at Port Arthur after the death of Makarov by Alexiev. Ukhtomsky, who had assumed leadership when the *Petropavlovsk* was sunk, commanded the battleships. Two admirals senior to Vitgeft had been appointed, Vice-Admiral Skrydlov in command of all naval forces in the Far East and Rear-Admiral Bezobrazov to command the fleet at Port Arthur. Both these officers, however, went to Vladivostock and, making no attempt to reach Port Arthur, hoisted their flags in the cruisers of the Vladivostock force. There were thus three admirals in the three ships which composed the Vladivostock force—the third admiral being Yessen, who had been appointed its commander originally. Vitgeft asked his subordinate admirals and the captains of his big ships, one after another, whether the squadron should remain in Port Arthur to the end or whether it should try to escape to Vladivostock.

Matussevitch, the chief of staff, and Essen, were in favour of leaving for Vladivostock and continuing the fight as a fleet. All the other captains and rear-admirals—nine of them—were in favour of staying at Port Arthur so that the guns and crews of the fleet could be used ashore for the defence of the place. Then the generals took a hand, urging that the fleet should go to sea and try to interrupt the flow of Japanese reinforcements and supplies which were daily reaching the front. The sortie of June 23rd was decided upon, with the object of attacking either the Japanese fleet or ships carrying supplies for the Japanese army.

A few days before, on June 12th, the Vladivostock squadron had also sailed to raid the Japanese lines of communication. This they had done with effect, sinking three transports containing eighteen eleven-inch howitzers (the original Big Berthas made by Krupp) needed for the siege of Port Arthur and also valuable locomotives and rolling stock. In addition, some 1,300 Japanese soldiers were drowned, having refused to surrender. This attack had caused Togo to send his cruiser admiral, Kamimura, with five armoured cruisers, away from Port Arthur into the Sea of Japan. Kamimura failed to find the raiders and was still away from Port Arthur when the Russian squadron finally came out. This meant that Togo had four battleships and three armoured cruisers with which to face six Russian battleships and one armoured cruiser.

There could have been no question of the Russians escaping before their absence was spotted by the enemy; they had lost the habit, which Makarov had taught them, of leaving the harbour quickly. Once more it took hours to get to sea and then it was necessary to wait for a channel to be swept clear of mines.

By the time this had been done the Japanese were ready and waiting, so that Vitgeft decided to put back to harbour, seeing that surprise had been lost, although never before or after were odds so favourable to the Russians. Japanese destroyers attacked before the Russians were safely in the harbour, without success. However, the *Sevastopol* struck a mine, which caused a panic on board, vigorously repressed by Essen; aboard the *Diana* during this attack the anti-torpedo armament was engaged on one side of the ship while on the disengaged side of the same ship the exhausted men slept peacefully by their guns.

Within the next few weeks the Japanese army closed in upon Port

Arthur and by August 7th—a Sunday—while the Russians were holding a special service to pray for victory, the first Japanese shells from the land fell into the port. Now if the Russian fleet remained in Port Arthur it was only a question of time before it was destroyed by the guns of the Japanese army. Accordingly, on August, 10th, the fleet sailed, this time with definite orders to make for Vladivostock. The cruisers from Vladivostock were ordered to sea once more to compel Togo to divide his forces by sending Kamimura and his armoured cruisers back into the Sea of Japan.

CHAPTER XII

COURSE FOR VLADIVOSTOCK
1905

O F the battle of August 10th—also called the Battle of Shantung and the Battle of the Yellow Sea—Captain William
Pakenham, R.N., the British observer with the Japanese fleet,
wrote afterwards:

> The fleet from Port Arthur held the day in suspense for more than five
> anxious hours.

It began as a stokers' battle. Togo's fleet was much quicker than it
had been on June 23rd to get into position and was soon in pursuit of
the enemy. The Japanese did not follow immediately in the wake of
the Russians, but steamed to the south of them on a course which was
more or less parallel. In the first place Togo feared that if he engaged
in a conventional stern chase a moment might come when one or two
of his leading ships would be exposed to the combined fire of all the
Russian battleships, while the rest of his ships, inevitably strung out in
a chase, were not yet within range.

In addition, Togo hoped to use his superior speed to get ahead of
his enemy and get between them and Vladivostock. The success of
both fleets depended on their stokers; these were days in which
stokers were stokers, not neat young men in clean overalls controlling
with a flick of the wrist the supply of oil and air to the boilers, but
men of enormous physical strength working in abominable heat,
bringing coal from the bunkers and shovelling it into the roaring
furnaces.

In addition to the men, there were the machines; ship for ship
most of the big Japanese vessels whether built in the United Kingdom,
France, Germany, Italy or the United States proved better than the
Russian ships whether built in Russia, France, Germany or the
United States. The Japanese ships had been better maintained—
partly because of the difficulties of getting repairs done at Port Arthur
—and their crews were better trained and more used to dealing with
unforseen emergencies. It was this that was to decide the action, but
only after those 'anxious hours' of which Captain Pakenham wrote.

In the first stage of action the Russian gunnery, though slower than the Japanese, was better aimed and the Japanese line of battle began to suffer. Through accidents and direct hits five out of the sixteen twelve-inch guns, which were the principal armament of the Japanese fleet, were out of action by the end of the engagement.

In the chase Togo was gaining on the enemy, but he was hardly gaining on the setting sun. Darkness might mean the escape of his enemy, for in those days there was no known way of fighting a night action between big ships. At 5.45 Togo decided it was now or never, and turned in to open fire. By this time he was well ahead of the Russians.

This is what Admiral Ballard, in his book *The Influence of the Sea on the Political History of Japan*, calls 'the most critical minute of the war'.

A twelve-inch shell hit the flagship *Tsarevitch* on the starboard side of the conning tower and jammed her helm so that she began to turn in a great circle to starboard, towards the Japanese line. At almost the identical moment another shell hit the bridge, killed Vitgeft, and disabled all the members of his staff and the captain and navigator of his ship. For a while there was no one at the con of the ship and she turned around helplessly, still heading towards the enemy, followed by her next astern, *Retvisan*, whose captain thought that he was conforming to the movements of his commander-in-chief in the *Tsarevitch*. That ship, her helm still jammed, continued her turn so that she headed back to the Russian battle line and then passed through it, narrowly missing both the *Peresviet* and *Sevastopol*, who had to alter course to avoid her. In this way they finished the process of throwing all the Russian battleships into complete and most dangerous confusion.

The senior unwounded officer of the *Tsarevitch* was found at his action station below decks and told what had happened. He came as quickly as he could to what remained of the bridge and signalled to the second flagship, *Peresviet*, in which Ukhtomsky was flying his flag, telling him that he was now in command of the fleet. But the signal halliards of the *Peresviet* had been shot away, so that she had no means of signalling to the rest of the fleet either the orders of the new commander or an explanation of what had happened to the *Tsarevitch*.

Finally, however, Ukhtomsky got the main part of the fleet under control and formed it up to steam back towards Port Arthur. Once again Togo had a chance to give the badly beaten Russian fleet the final blow and once again decided not to risk it; but some of the Russian ships were already out of the war for good.

The *Tsarevitch* got separated from the other Russians during the night and went to the German base of Tsingtao, where she was interned in accordance with international law. The *Novik*, probably the best ship in the whole Russian navy, succeeded in coaling at Tsingtao and getting away to the northward, intending to go north about around the main islands of the Japanese archipelago on her way to Vladivostock. She was caught by two bigger Japanese cruisers, *Chitose* and *Tsushima*, and was driven ashore in the La Perouse Straits, between the Russian island of Sakhalin and the Japanese island of Hokkaido. Two other cruisers were also interned, having been cut off from Port Arthur—the *Askold*, which went to Shanghai, and the *Diana*, which got as far as Saigon in what was then French Indo-China. Five destroyers were also interned, while one destroyer, *Rechitelni*, was captured after taking refuge in the Chinese port of Chefoo. She was the only ship lost, but for all the good that the First Pacific Squadron could now do it might just as well have been at the bottom of the sea, where it was destined to end four months later.

Meanwhile, far away to the north, in the Sea of Japan, were the Vladivostock cruisers under Yessen, which had come out to meet the Port Arthur ships. There also were Kamimura's cruisers looking for them, and finding them, on the morning of August 14th, in the Korea Strait just north of Tsushima. Of the three Russian cruisers the two largest, the *Rossia* and *Gromoboi*, escaped, badly damaged, back to Vladivostock, while the third, the oldest and slowest, the *Rurik*, which had only ten years before caused great apprehension to the admiralties of the world by her size and power as a commerce raider, was sunk after a gallant defence. Kamimura's six cruisers ought to have been able to finish off the Russians, but at a critical moment in the battle it was reported to Kamimura that most of his ammunition was exhausted and he decided to use what was left to destroy the *Rurik*. Afterwards he found out that he had been misinformed and that a great deal of ammunition was still available, but by then it was too late.

After the two surviving Russian cruisers had returned to Vladivostock the *Gromoboi* stranded badly and could not be repaired before the end of the war; this is worth noting as an indication of the extremely poor resources of Vladivostock as a base, and is also an indication of the value that it might have been to Rozhestvensky's squadron had it ever reached there.

The damage to the *Gromoboi* left only the *Rossia* effective, for the fourth cruiser of the squadron, the *Bogatyr*, had already been put out of action by accidental stranding. The *Rossia* was not deemed fit to carry out commerce raiding by herself, and the activities of the Vladivostock squadron came to an end.

It would seem that these cruisers ought to have been able to accomplish a good deal more than they actually did. Though weakly protected and weakly armed, they were big fast ships, and their radius of action was, nominally at least, about 13,000 miles. Despite this, their activities were confined to a series of nine short sorties varying in length from one to thirteen days. In the thirteen-day cruise, from July 18th to 30th, the only one in which they left the Sea of Japan, they passed through the twelve-mile-wide Tsugaru Strait, between the Japanese islands of Hokkaido and Hondo, and cruised in the Pacific off the east coast of Japan, seeking a liner which was known to be bringing about 20,000,000 gold yen (about £2,000,000) for the Japanese Government from San Francisco. The steamer with the gold escaped them and the sinking of the transport *Hitachi Maru* on June 15th on its way from Japan to the mainland with guns and troops on board for the siege of Port Arthur remained their one and only real success. In all, during these raids, only eighteen Japanese merchant ships were captured or sunk.

One other attempt was made to carry on commerce raiding in the Pacific, by the armed merchant cruiser *Lena*. However, sabotage took place on board and the ship went to San Francisco and was disarmed.

More and better manned armed merchant cruisers would have proved themselves greatly superior as commerce raiders to the big cruisers. The construction of the *Rurik* and the rest of these ships had been a great mistake by the Russians, but most other navies made the same mistake as well. Had the money spent on the cruisers by the Russians been used to build three battleships of the same size and cost, the situation in the Far East at the outbreak of the war would have been very different. But the failure of these ships in the Russo-Japanese War did not bring to an end the vogue for very large cruisers. These eventually developed into the battle cruisers of the First World War, which suffered so heavily at Jutland and afterwards. The final lines in that chapter of naval history were written when the *Hood* was sunk by the *Bismarck*.

With the First Pacific Squadron driven back to Port Arthur and the Vladivostock cruisers out of action, the war at sea came very nearly to an end, while the siege of Port Arthur entered its closing stages, supervised by the Japanese fleet, which continued to maintain a close blockade of the harbour.

As for the Russian ships inside Port Arthur, it was decided that their crews and, as far as possible, their armament should be used ashore. Altogether 284 guns were landed. There was no longer question of the fleet being a fighting force, but Alexiev, still viceroy and commander-in-chief, smuggled orders in a Chinese junk into Port Arthur instructing the battleships, with the *Bayan* and *Pallada*, to break out and go to Vladivostock.

The leader of this enterprise was to be Rear-Admiral Viren, who had been captain of the *Bayan*, but he refused to go, saying that if he sailed his ships they would run a very grave risk of being sunk, whereas if they could be preserved they would be a priceless reinforcement for the Second Pacific Squadron which was still in the process of being formed in the Baltic.

It was just at this time—the first week of September—that the Battle of Laioyang was fought ashore; the Russian army which had been hoping to relieve Port Arthur by an advance from the north was defeated, and it was clear that there could be no relief for the besieged fortress.

In this last phase of the siege an attempt was made, inside Port Arthur, to operate a tiny submarine, the *Petr Kochka*. For this sortie her original motive power, two pairs of bicycle pedals, were replaced by the engine of a motor car, but to no purpose. Another naval officer endeavoured to construct himself a balloon, to aid in spotting for the guns of the fleet, but without success.

At this stage, with Port Arthur exposed every day to intense bombardment which soon began to pick off the ships of the First Pacific Squadron, the Second Pacific Squadron sailed from the Baltic.

Although the war had started in February it had not been until September that the Second Squadron had gone to sea to carry out gunnery practice; the results of this first exercise were that two cruisers ran aground, while the battleships were continually in grave danger of colliding with each other. Even at this stage Rozhestvensky had plenty of scope for his famous rages with which he used to reduce his chief of staff—Captain Clapier de Colongue—to tears.

The squadron finally sailed from Libau on October 15th, heavily laden with stores of all sorts and accompanied by a number of supply ships—which were to go all the way to Port Arthur, or to Vladivostock if necessary, as there were not sufficient stocks for the fleet at either place and it was appreciated that the Trans-Siberian railway would be so busy trying to supply the army that there would be no room for supplies for the fleet. So packed with stores were the Russian ships that the decks and alleyways were covered with sacks of coal. One of the articles most urgently needed as replacements during the voyage which was just beginning was boots. Because of the coal on deck men could not go about barefoot, while the coal, bursting through the sacks, cut shoe leather to bits. There was not enough ammunition for practice firing and any practice firing which might have been possible would have tended to wear out the guns before there was a chance of firing them in anger. However, at the very beginning of the voyage these guns were in action, against the squadron's own ships and against British trawlers.

Rumours were current in the squadron, and ashore, that Japanese torpedo craft would intercept the Russian ships as they left the Baltic. No one in authority seems to have stopped to consider how it could be possible for these craft to reach western European waters without having touched neutral ports and having been reported.

On the night of October 21st–22nd the squadron passed through the British fishing fleets off the Dogger Bank; some of the small vessels were taken for enemy torpedo boats and fire was opened. One British trawler was sunk and six were damaged; in addition, the Russian cruiser *Avrora* was hit four times by Russian shells. In Britain there was an immediate outcry, in which anger and contempt were mixed. While questions of apology and compensation were being argued the British Channel, Home and Mediterranean fleets were disposed so that they would be able to attack the Russian squadron. For four days the Russians were constantly shadowed and the crews of the British ships were at action stations. The nearest British force, the Channel fleet, under Lord Charles Beresford, was much more powerful than the Russian, and the British admiral proposed, on grounds of chivalry, to attack it with only half of his available ships— an idea which upset the Board of Admiralty and provoked one of the conflicts which eventually led to Beresford's retirement.

There is a story about Rozhestvensky at this anxious time which must command admiration; off Tangier a British cruiser squadron was watching the Russians, manoeuvring impeccably as it did so. Rozhestvensky called for his officers, pointed to the British and said: 'Gentlemen, that is how it should be done.'

The crisis caused by the Dogger Bank incident began to abate on November 1st and Russia agreed soon afterwards to pay compensation. Meanwhile, Rozhestvensky and the main body of his Second Squadron steamed on towards the Cape of Good Hope, while a light force of cruisers and destroyers under Rear-Admiral Folkershamn headed for the Suez Canal. The two forces were to rendezvous in Madagascar.

For the time being the squadron's chief trouble was coaling at sea in the tropics, an operation that was performed for the most part from German colliers outside the three-mile limit of territorial waters laid down by international law. The colliers were provided on contract by the Hamburg-Amerika line, and it is worth noting that, while Germany on the one hand and Russia and France on the other were enemies in the cold war of those days, the Germans and the French both gave the Russians all the aid they could against the Japanese, who were the allies of Britain, who in turn was an ally of France.

Coaling in the Russian ships on this voyage could go on in a single ship for more than twenty-four hours at a stretch, in shade temperatures ranging from 100 to 115 degrees, with clouds of coaldust hiding the sun through the daylight hours and everyone from the captain downwards working ceaselessly in holds and bunkers at the hoists and winches, with wads of cotton waste between their teeth to help them to breathe. This work was done by crews few members of which had ever been outside the Baltic. One day, Rozhestvensky's flagship, the *Kniaz Suvarov*, by taking on 120 tons of coal in an hour, broke the world's record of 102 tons previously held by the British navy.

On its way round Africa, from Tangier the squadron went to Dakar and from Dakar to Great Fish Bay in Angola. Mechanical breakdowns in one ship or another were almost continuous. At Great Fish Bay a 300-ton Portuguese gunboat ordered the squadron out of territorial waters in the name of Portuguese neutrality, and the Russians went on to Angra Pequena in German South West Africa, where they were given the facilities which they required. From there to French hospitality, in defiance of international law, in Madagascar was a comparatively easy run, and the arrival there, at Ste. Marie on the north-east coast, took place on December 29th. The squadron, almost at once, moved on to Nossi Bé at the extreme north-western tip of the island; there it learned that Port Arthur had fallen, and all that was left of the First Squadron had been sunk.

The end of the story of the First Squadron had begun on December 5th, when the Japanese army, after fierce fighting, had taken 203-metre Hill, which commanded the harbour. Thenceforward it was easy for the eleven-inch howitzers in position to pick off, one after another, the big Russian ships. The very first round fired struck the *Poltava* and set fire to her; she finally sank in shallow water on an even keel, with her masts and superstructure remaining out of the water. On the next day the *Retvisan* and the *Peresviet* were both sunk, and on the day after that the *Pobieda* and the *Pallada*. Altogether, on the 6th and 7th, more than 500 rounds of eleven-inch ammunition were fired by the Japanese, and on the 8th the *Bayan*, the minelayer *Amur* and the gunboat *Giliak* were also sunk. The sole surviving big ship was now the *Sevastopol*, commanded by Essen and manned only by 100 men out of her normal complement of 700—all the rest had been landed to fight ashore.

Essen borrowed enough men to get his ship out of the harbour and lay out in the open sea, behind torpedo nets, protected from the Japanese guns ashore, but exposed to the torpedo attacks of the Japanese destroyers. On five successive nights the Japanese fired 150 torpedoes, of which two hit, putting the *Sevastopol* out of action altogether for good and all. The Japanese losses in these operations had been two torpedo boats sunk and fourteen damaged.

The resistance of Port Arthur was nearly at an end and the *Sevastopol* was sunk by Essen in deep water. She was the only one of the sunken ships which did not fall into Japanese hands when Port Arthur surrendered on January 2nd, 1905, after a resistance of seven months. Essen's sabotage of his ship had been too thorough.

No one had taken the same trouble to sabotage the ships sunk in the harbour, and the biggest of them were raised by the Japanese and commissioned under the Japanese flag—*Pobieda*, *Peresviet*, *Retvisan*, *Poltava*, *Pallada* and *Bayan*. The *Variag* had also been raised and repaired by the Japanese at Chemulpo, and the *Novik* from the La Perouse Straits. Oddly, the careers of the *Peresviet*, *Poltava* and *Variag* under the Russian flag were to be resumed some twelve years later.

On learning the news of the fall of Port Arthur, Rozhestvensky's first plan was to hasten to Far Eastern waters as quickly as possible, before the Japanese had had time to repair and refit their ships after their strenuous year of war. Accordingly, he hoped to leave Madagascar within a week of his arrival, but in fact he was there for three months. It was a very trying climate, hot and damp. The ships seemed almost to become absorbed by the jungle alongside which they were moored, while the crews, when they were allowed to go ashore in the appropriately named Hellville, gave themselves up to the traditional amusements of sailors with nothing to do and plenty of money to spend—facilities for their amusement appeared almost overnight in this remote corner of a remote island, amid the monkeys, the rats and the reptiles, scores of which were soon on board the ships as pets. As the crews settled down to dissipation tropical marine growths formed on the hulls of the ships, with a consequent reduction of their speed. Meanwhile Rozhestvensky waited, on orders from St. Petersburg, for reinforcements whose strength in no way compensated the squadron for what it lost by delay in waiting for them.

The fall of Port Arthur and the loss of the First Squadron had entirely changed the situation. There was little possibility that the

Second Squadron would be able to fight its way through the Japanese-controlled waters to Vladivostock, and even if it could do so it was still unlikely to exert any influence on the conduct of the war. Rozhestvensky asked to be relieved of his command and, his request refused, turned once more to trying to get his undisciplined crews in hand. At the same time he faced the increasing unwillingness of the neutral powers to offend Japan by facilitating his voyage. The Hamburg-Amerika line announced its intention of stopping delivery of coal, and only at the last moment agreed to resume the delivery at places up to the 12th parallel North latitude, but would do nothing north of that line.

Other misfortunes were falling upon the squadron; food and clothing were running out as well as boots. These were serious matters, for the bitter spring weather of the Sea of Japan would soon have to be faced. However, the latest and almost the heaviest charge upon Rozhestvensky's firmness of purpose was laid by a naval correspondent, named Captain Klado, whose sinister activities leave one at a loss to guess his motives. Klado had been an officer on Rozhestvensky's staff and had returned to Russia to give evidence before the international commission on the Dogger Bank incident, of which he himself had seen almost nothing. After participating in the commission's work, he began writing newspaper articles deploring the superiority of the Japanese fleet over the Second Squadron. This was true enough, but Klado's articles succeeded in severely depressing the morale of the Russian officers and ratings.

Even more serious, however, in its effect was the conclusion drawn by Klado. To make up the deficiencies of the Second Squadron he proposed the dispatch of a Third Squadron, made up of old coast defence vessels and obsolete cruisers which had been left behind when the Second Squadron had been formed as being likely to prove a hindrance rather than a help. Now, however, these ships were brought forward, manned with the lees of the recruiting depots, placed under the command of Rear-Admiral Nebogatov and dispatched to the Far East, despite Rozhestvensky's express pleadings, for he knew that the addition of these old slow ships to his squadron would mean loss of the speed which would be essential, either to avoid the Japanese or to fight a way through their main fleet. Why Klado was given official and decisive support is one of the myteries of human behaviour of which there are so many in the actions of the officials and politicians of Imperial Russia. The generally accepted explanation is that private contractors had done well out of equipping the Second Squadron and were accordingly anxious for the dispatch of a Third and even a Fourth Squadron.

There is evidence that Rozhestvensky endeavoured deliberately to miss Nebogatov, but it was in vain. He sailed from Madagascar on March 16th, setting off on a non-stop voyage of 4,700 miles to the coast of Indo-China. Mechanical breakdowns were frequent, and the long rollers of the Indian Ocean very nearly capsized the small and unseaworthy destroyers which were under tow. Nevertheless, the coaling of the squadron at sea went on—a feat unheard of then and one that has never been paralleled in the history of the sea. Similar replenishment operations at sea in the Pacific during World War II were carried out with oil fuel, and were therefore infinitely simpler.

Lost to the world for three weeks, Rozhestvensky reappeared off Singapore on April 8th. Here Nebogatov established contact with him, thanks to the zeal and endurance of a Russian seaman. Babushkin, a stoker petty officer from the *Bayan* at Port Arthur, had been allowed by the Japanese to return home after the capitulation on grounds of ill health—he had received eighteen splinter wounds from a bursting shell while serving ashore. On his way home Babushkin landed at Singapore and reported to the Russian Consul. Between them they planned to give Nebogatov the latest news of Rozhestvensky—which Rozhestvensky had withheld, presumably because he did not want the junction between the squadrons to take place.

In an open steam launch Babushkin and two other men cruised off Singapore for three days; food and water were exhausted, the two men with Babushkin tried to disobey him and take the launch back to port, but he overpowered them, despite the fact that some of his wounds had reopened, and hung on until Nebogatov arrived. He gave him the news, the junction of the two squadrons took place and the Russian disaster became even more terrible than it would otherwise have been had the Russian sailor Babushkin not been such a hero.

The junction of the two squadrons took place on May 9th, in an obscure harbour on the coast of Indo-China. Originally the Second Squadron had arrived on April 14th at Kamranh Bay, only to be told by the French a few days later that it must move on. It did so, to a less publicised part of the same coast where, at length, Nebogatov arrived.

Five days later the combined squadrons sailed north to the Straits of Tsushima, where the Japanese, repaired, restored and refitted, were waiting in their Korean anchorage for one of the decisive battles of history.

The course Rozhestvensky had chosen was the most direct and most obvious. There was a theoretical possibility that he might have taken a course to the eastward of the main islands of Japan, and tried to enter the Sea of Japan through the narrow Tsugaru Strait—used by the Vladivostock cruisers for their sortie into the Pacific of the previous July—or La Perouse Strait farther north, but either course would have added more than 1,000 miles to the distance steamed, and involved coaling at sea several times near the enemy coast. Moreover, Togo had the interior lines and would almost certainly have been able to interpose his fleet between Rozhestvensky and Vladivostock no matter which way the Russians had entered the Sea of Japan.

Rozhestvensky certainly handled the fleet on the last two days of its existence, May 27th and 28th, 1905, as if there was nothing to be done but to set a direct course for Vladivostock and steam on it, come what may. With a fleet that was slower than the enemy (about twelve knots to fifteen) and about half as powerful there could only be one outcome to that.

On board the battleship *Osliabia*, the second-in-command, Folkershamn, lay dead. For the sake of morale the rest of the fleet was not informed; even Nebogatov was not told and accordingly did not know that he would succeed to the command if anything happened to Rozhestvensky.

CHAPTER XIII

TSUSHIMA

1905

IN misty weather, on the night of May 26th–27th, the Russian squadron was steaming slowly through the Straits of Tsushima. Wireless and wireless direction finding were new then, but the Russians could hear Japanese transmitters ashore and afloat talking to each other and roughly judge their bearing. Traffic seemed quiet and normal. The moon began to break through the mist, threatening to give the Russians away. 'Against the mist, dimly whitened by its silver rays, the ship's funnels, masts and rigging were sharply outlined,' wrote Semenov.

Although everything depended on the Russians getting through unobserved, the two hospital ships, which were steaming in the rear of the fleet, were burning all their lights, and it was one of these ships which was first spotted by the Japanese on the morning of May 27th.

It was a North Sea kind of dawn, grey and damp, with a sort of half mist, half drizzle. By and by through the mist the Japanese ships began to appear to the Russians, steaming along on a parallel course, watching them for a few minutes and then disappearing once more into the mist.

First the armed merchant cruiser *Shinano Maru* showed up on the beam, then four Japanese light cruisers astern, then the armoured cruiser *Idzumo*—a big ship this and her presence was a clear sign that the Japanese battle fleet was near at hand. Then she disappeared and her place as shadower was taken by an obsolete battleship and a light cruiser, and finally by three armoured cruisers.

While this was going on the Russian fleet was slowly passing the island of Tsushima and then steadying on a north-easterly course— N.23 E.—for Vladivostock.

The day was the anniversary of the Coronation of the Tsar and Tsarina, and Thanksgiving Services were held on board the big Russian ships. Afterwards, the officers not on watch went below to drink champagne already set out by stewards on tables in the wardroom in honour of the occasion, but at that moment action stations were sounded. The Japanese were closing in and the *Orel* opened fire without orders. The other ships joined in, and the Japanese disappeared again. Rozhestvensky signalled 'Don't waste ammunition' and hands were sent to dinner.

Once the Russians were reported to have left the waters of Indo-China an anxious time had begun for Togo. The main Japanese fleet was lying in Sylvia Basin at the southern tip of Korea, waiting for the reports of its scouts. It seemed almost inevitable that the Russians would have to come through the Straits of Tsushima, but nobody could be sure. There was the possibility already mentioned that the Russians might try and pass outside the barrier of the Japanese islands and come in from the north-east. In theory they would be spotted and Togo would have plenty of time in which to get between them and Vladivostock, but again no one could be sure, and Togo worried. During daylight on May 26th seemed to be the last possible moment on which the Russians, however slowly they were steaming, could try to break into the Sea of Japan, and when the day passed and no news came it began to look, after all, as though the Russians had headed out into the Pacific and would try to break through from the north-east. Togo's staff got ready to execute the changes of plan which would be necessary.

Then came the radio message from the *Shinano Maru* at 4.45, just as it was getting light: 'Enemy squadron square 203.'

The numeral coincidence of square 203 and 203-metre Hill which had been the key to the capture of Port Arthur struck the Japanese auspiciously as Togo put to sea.

First Togo steamed south-eastward from his Korean base almost to the coast of Japan, passing well ahead of the Russians and out of their sight. He then turned westward and at about 1.40 in the afternoon the Russians saw him, six ships in line ahead, the same six ships of the Japanese First Division which had barred the way of the First Pacific Squadron on August 10th and which were now barring the way, nine months later, to the Second and Third Squadrons.

The *Mikasa* was leading and flying Togo's signal, 'The fate of our Empire hangs on this one action; you will all exert yourselves and do your utmost.' Then came the *Shikishima*, *Fuji*, *Asahi*, all battleships, the *Shikishima* being clearly distinguishable by her three funnels, while the other three had only two each, and then the two Italian-built cruisers, *Nisshin* and *Kasuga*, each with two big funnels far apart and a single mast half-way between them.

Togo ordered, 'Open fire.' The flag used for this signal was preserved and was flown by the *Akagi*, the Japanese carrier flagship, during the attack on Pearl Harbor in 1941.

The Japanese steamed on across the bows of the Russians and then suddenly turned. One after the other they reversed their course so that instead of steaming in line from east to west led by the *Mikasa* they were, still following *Mikasa*, steaming from west to east. The turn, which took fourteen minutes, was a very tricky business, for everyone turned, one after the other, on the same spot and all the Russians had to do was to concentrate their salvoes upon that single spot. Togo's reason for doing this risky thing is believed to have been his determination to lead the line himself, while if he had not turned the Russians might have been able to pass astern of him and escape northward to safety.

Once the Japanese turn was completed their line of battle was joined by the six armoured cruisers of Kamimura—*Idzumo, Yakumo, Asama, Adzuma, Tokiwa,* and *Iwate,* which then took station astern of battleships, so that the line was now twelve ships long, steaming on a collision course at right-angles to the Russians.

This was the famous manoeuvre of 'Crossing the T'. The Japanese were aiming to steam across the head of the Russian line, concentrating all their fire on the *Suvarov,* which would be the only ship in a position to reply, for she would be masking the fire of all those astern of her. To prevent this happening Rozhestvensky was forced to order his fleet to turn to the eastward and away from Vladivostock. Round One had gone to the Japanese, but, despite this, it was a Japanese ship that fell out of line first. Captain Yatsushiro of the *Asama* had gone into action on his bridge playing a flute. Now he had laid down his flute and his damage-control parties were struggling up to their waists in icy water, working on the mess decks, lit only by the misty daylight leaking in through the holes made in the sides by shells and splinters, to save their ship.

The two fleets were now on a nearly parallel course, steaming east at a gradually diminishing distance of about 7,000 yards. Commander Akiyama, one of Togo's staff, wrote afterwards about this period of the battle:

The enemy opened fire at 2.08 p.m. and our First Division bore it for a few minutes and replied at about 2.11. The number of enemy shells fired during these few minutes exceeded three hundred and the *Mikasa* was damaged and had casualties before she had fired a shot. About a half hour later the enemy's battle formation was entirely out of order, so that the fate of our Empire was really settled within this first half hour. The *Mikasa* and the eleven others of the main force had taken years of labour to design and build, and yet they were used for only half an hour of decisive battle. We, too, studied the art of war and trained ourselves in it, but it was put to use only for that short period. Though the decisive battle took such a short time, it required ten years of preparation. In this sense the battle may be said to have continued for ten years.

There were by now about 500 Japanese guns in action and their principal targets were the first and second Russian flagships, the *Suvarov* and, fifth ship in the line, the *Osliabia*, which, in trying to turn away from the Japanese, had got out of station and come closer than she had intended to the enemy. She was thus brought under the combined fire of seven of the Japanese line—*Shikishima, Fuji, Kasuga, Nisshin, Idzumo, Tokiwa* and *Yakumo*—but it was the twelve-inch guns of the *Shikishima* and *Fuji* that did the damage. The *Osliabia*'s forward turret was put out of action and then three shells hit her in the bows at almost the same place on the waterline. She stopped and began to heel over. The white-clad Russian sailors could be seen jumping into the water as she rapidly turned right over. After floating for a while bottom up she finally sank; on her quarter deck had been Folkershamn's coffin and this floated clear, saving the life of a drowning Russian sailor who clambered on to it.

The *Suvarov*, too, was soon in a bad way, heavily on fire with her bridge burning and flames coming out of scuttles and hatches, virtually out of action.

At the end of an hour's fighting the Russian fleet had lost all cohesion, and individually and in little groups its ships sought to evade the enemy fire and to escape.

A first chance of escape presented itself, just after the *Suvarov* had been knocked out, to her next astern, the *Imperator Alexander III*, Captain Bukhvostov.

As the Japanese headed eastward across the bows of the Russians, the latter had been compelled to turn eastward, too. But the Japanese were steaming at fifteen knots while the Russians were making only eight. In this way the Japanese drew ahead and thus left the Russians a chance of doubling back across the enemy's stern and once more heading for Vladivostock. This Bukhvostov attempted to do.

Togo replied by turning back again at 1506 westward and, with his superior speed and fire-power, he was once more able to compel the Russians to conform to his movements and to turn away in a hopeless circle to the south.

The crippled *Suvarov* was now in the middle of the battlefield; both her masts and both her funnels had been shot away, but, 'always the flagship', as the Japanese Official History comments, she kept on firing with everything that she had left.

During the *Alexander III*'s attempt to escape across the stern of the

149

Japanese the range had dropped to about 2,500 yards. The ship was hidden in yellowy smoke, lit from within by flames and the flashes of explosions; behind her came the *Borodino*, which seemed ablaze from stem to stern. As the smoke thickened over the battle zone and the two fleets got nearer to each other the Russians had to check fire for fear of hitting their own ships, so confused and clouded had everything become. Only the curious luminous pinkish yellow colour of the funnels of the Russian big ships, when they were still standing, showed their identity.

To finish off the *Suvarov* with torpedoes, first the cruiser *Yakumo* and then the torpedo gunboat *Chihaya* with the four boats of the Fifth Destroyer Division came in, some to less than 400 yards, and then withdrew without scoring a single from their fifteen torpedo tubes.

By now Rozhestvensky had been badly wounded twice and was unconscious; his skull had been fractured when he was thrown against the side of the conning tower by a bursting shell and he had been wounded in the leg.

A Russian destroyer, *Buiny*, came alongside and the admiral was half lowered and half thrown down the side of the *Suvarov*. The *Buiny* made off in search of another battleship to which she might transfer the flag. Now Rozhestvensky was, for the first time, given a proper medical examination, and it was clear that he was so gravely wounded that there could be no question of his resuming command.

It was about 4.30 and the Russian battleships were still heading southward, away from all hope of safety. The line was ragged, with ships falling out from time to time to make repairs, fight fires, clear away wreckage and stop up holes, but the ships that fell out always came back again, except for the *Suvarov*, dead in water, but keeping up a steady aimed fire with one twelve-pounder, all that was left fightable of her armament of sixty-four guns, from twelve-inch to one-pounders.

At about five o'clock the Russian battleships once more turned northward towards Vladivostock, the Japanese conforming and firing at any target they could see through the mist and the smoke. Meanwhile the smaller Japanese cruisers under Vice-Admiral Dewa were having a minor battle of their own with the Russian cruisers and the small coast-defence vessels of Nebogatov's squadron, astern of the Russian main body. In this the Japanese *Kasagi* was temporarily knocked out and other Japanese ships damaged, without any effect on the battle, and Togo left the sorting out of this situation to the remaining cruisers. He himself was after the battleships, and about 6.30 he found them again, with an hour to go before sunset. The *Imperator*

Alexander III was once again driven out of line, this time for good. She stopped and drifted away and was lost to sight for some time; Kamimura an hour later, in the *Idzumo*, came across her in the twilight mist, but before he could attack her he saw her capsize and sink.

Togo had decided, when planning the battle weeks before, that he would draw off at sunset and leave the field to the destroyers, for no one knew anything about a night action in the conditions of those days and all sorts of confusion would almost certainly arise. But, just before the Japanese hauled off, the *Fuji* hit the *Borodino* with a single twelve-inch shell, which exploded in the Russian's magazine. She fired once more from her forward turret and then blew up. Only one officer of a complement of 740 officers and men was saved from the ship.

About the same time, away to the south, the *Suvarov* finally sank, finished off by nine Japanese torpedoes, with her single remaining gun still in action until the moment when she turned over in a thick cloud of yellow smoke. She floated for a few minutes bottom up and then slid below the surface, with her hull standing vertically out of the water for a few instants before she finally disappeared. For a few moments a cloud hung over the spot and then drifted away. H. W. Wilson, the British naval historian, described her fight as one of the hardest ever fought by a warship. He was writing in the light of the First World War; with yet another world war behind us we are bound to concur in his judgement.

When darkness came the Japanese battle fleet steamed away to the northward, to rendezvous at dawn next morning off the island of Matsushima, 200 miles to the north of Tsushima, ready to begin the action again. In the meantime the scene of the first part of the battle was left to the Japanese torpedo craft, whose task it was to harry the remainder of the enemy fleet. In Togo's big ships men fell out from action stations and came on deck to get some fresh air, while the carpenters busied themselves with the making of coffins.

The torpedo craft swept the seas for what was left of the Russian fleet, already a completely beaten force, with five out of her six big battleships already sunk. One group of the Russian cruisers, those under Enkvist, had given up the struggle after making no very serious effort to break through, and had steamed as fast as they could southward to safety and internment by the Americans at Manila. These ships were the *Oleg*, *Avrora* and *Jemtchug*. They all survived to fight another day—*Jemtchug* being sunk in World War I, *Oleg* during the Russian Civil War, while *Avrora* remains to this day, preserved as a trophy at Leningrad in recognition of her services to the Bolshevik cause during the October revolution of 1917. But there is no doubt that they were wasted in the war against Japan and the poverty of their showing contrasts strangely with the desperate courage of the battleships. Admittedly no attempt was made to use them as scouts for the battle fleet and that must have been discouraging. Instead they were pinned down as escorts to the supply ships when, instead, they might have been used as commerce raiders and to create diversions which would have made it necessary for Togo to split his forces as he had divided them before, when the Russians were working simultaneously from Port Arthur and Vladivostock.

The Japanese destroyers swept across the battlefield, coming in from almost all quarters of the horizon. Only to the south-west was there a gap and the Russians automatically turned in that direction. What remained of the Russian fleet was now, nominally, under the command of Nebogatov, although this he did not know.

In the night fighting which followed, the *Admiral Nakhimov* and *Navarin* were sunk, together with three Japanese torpedo boats, the only losses sustained by the Japanese in the battle. As dawn came on May 28th the *Vladimir Monomakh*, dead in the water, scuttled herself, after having tried to defend herself with rifle fire against the enemy as they came in close to finish her off. At about ten o'clock that morning the *Sissoi Veliki* also sank, after having been badly damaged. The *Admiral Ushakov* also scuttled herself, and then the remnants of the Russian fleet were the *Orel*, the only modern battleship left, a sister ship of the *Suvarov*, together with the obsolete *Imperator Nikolai I*, the *General Admiral Apraxin* and the *Admiral Seniavin*, both ancient coast-defence vessels as well as the modern light cruiser *Izumrud*.

Just after 10 a.m. the Japanese found them. Steaming in detached groups across the bows and the sterns of the Russians, they opened fire. There was no escape for any except the fast *Izumrud*. Nebogatov ordered the ships still in company with him to surrender. He himself hoisted the white flag and then went over the side in full dress uniform to surrender his ships, leaving behind his officers.

On board the *Orel* officers were horrified at the surrender order, for three out of their four twelve-inch guns were still in service and she could still steam sixteen knots. Some went below to try to scuttle her as the Japanese prize crew came on board; the Japanese hunted them through the ship, dragged them up on deck and shot them.

One by one the remaining Russian ships were sunk—only the armed yacht *Almaz* and two destroyers reached Vladivostock. Two cruisers nearly got away—the *Izumrud*, with only ten tons of coal left, ran aground 100 miles to the north of Vladivostock and was blown up to prevent her falling into Japanese hands, while at dawn on May 29th the *Dmitri Donskoi* was also scuttled off Matsushima, having exhausted all her ammunition in a running fight with two Japanese cruisers, an armed merchant cruiser and seven destroyers. The last ship to be accounted for was the destroyer *Bodry*, discovered a week after the battle by a British freighter, stopped, having used all her fuel and having burned all the woodwork which she had on board. She was towed to Shanghai and interned.

But the greatest sensation of the closing stages of the battle was the capture of Rozhestvensky and his staff. They had been moved from the *Buiny* to her sister ship *Bedovy* because the former was running out of fuel. However, a few hours later, at about one o'clock on the afternoon of the 28th, the *Bedovy* was intercepted by two Japanese destroyers and at once surrendered without any attempt at resistance or escape. Rozhestvensky was still unconscious and his staff decided that his life should be saved at any price. It is hard to believe that Rozhestvensky ever felt any gratitude for this. The last four years of his life, which ended in 1909, were miserable in the extreme, for with Nebogatov and a number of others he was tried by court martial on his return from his Japanese prison camp. He endeavoured to take all the blame upon himself, but he was acquitted, and Nebogatov and the others sentenced to death. Their sentences were, however, commuted to life imprisonment and one of them, Lichin, the captain of the *Apraxin*, survived to fight as a private soldier in the war of 1914–18. He was pardoned by the Tsar and restored to his rank and estates shortly before the outbreak of the revolution.

Tsushima took place nearly sixty years ago: since then we have been through two world wars, in which things occurred much more horrible than anything that could have been imagined in those days when the Japanese were driving the Russians across the plains of Manchuria and sweeping them from off the China Seas, and we live under the shadow of a final catastrophe. Nevertheless the story of the voyage of the Second and Third Pacific Squadrons around the world and of their final destruction still to this day must move to pity and horror all who read it.

The only coherent element in the story was Rozhestvensky's determination to get his fleet to the Far East; everything else is disparate. Some ships were good and some were bad, some crews were good and some were bad and so were some officers. But mostly the officers and men were people who knew how to die but not how to fight. Money had been poured into the construction of a battle fleet, but through corruption or economy shells had been made of cast iron instead of steel, so that they broke up on contact and, incidentally, were one of the prime causes of the reverses which the British fleet came to suffer at Jutland. The Japanese had equipped their fleet with high-explosive shells, which burst on contact, doing great external damage to the unarmoured parts of ships, but rarely penetrating the main armour belts. The Russians, on the other hand, had selected armour-piercing shells, of less bursting power but designed to force a way through the heaviest armour before bursting inside a ship, within its vitals.

After Tsushima the Russian defeat seemed to prove that the Japanese had been right, and the British navy adhered faithfully to high-explosive shells, not realising that the failure of the Russian armour-piercing shells was due to their poor quality of construction and not to the principle upon which that construction was based.

After Rozhestvensky had displayed the most extraordinary abilities both to lead and to drive his men, there followed the final incongruity of his conduct when the time came for him to lead his fleet into action.

'No commander-in-chief can ever have led his forces into battle with such calm irresolution,' comments Mr. Richard Hough in his book *The Fleet That Had To Die*,[1] but Rozhestvensky's leadership of the fleet up to that moment had been neither calm nor irresolute. His tempers and his rages were famous, but through them all his resolution was indomitable. However, when he had brought his fleet to the threshold of battle he gave up real leadership and contented himself with steaming straight for the enemy, without any attempt to avoid a head-on collision which was bound to cost the Russians heavy casualties, at a time when it was essential that they should get to Vladivostock with as few losses as possible.

Every effort that had been put into the voyage of the Second and Third Squadrons was bound to be wasted if they were sailed straight past Tsushima. All that had been done became quite useless, worse than useless; if Rozhestvensky had been a little less energetic and a little less successful his fleet would never have got to the Far East at all and there would have been no Tsushima.

As it was, Tsushima ended the last possible hope that the Russians had of defeating the Japanese and, shortly afterwards, with British blessing and active American good offices, negotiations for a treaty of peace were begun. The British interest in peace was very real. The Japanese were their allies, while the Russians were the allies of their

[1] Hamish Hamilton, 1958.

allies, the French. With the German menace, growing greater year by year it was urgent that nations who might possibly be friendly to Britain should be restrained from tearing each other apart.

In the end, by the terms of the treaty signed at Portsmouth, New Hampshire, in August 1905, the Japanese gained Port Arthur, control of Korea and of the southern part of Manchuria—which, though nominally Chinese territory, had been the scene of most of the land fighting of the war. In addition, they also gained the southern half of the island of Sakhalin.

All these places were to change hands again several times within the half-century that followed the Treaty of Portsmouth. Port Arthur was Japanese until the Russians regained it at the end of World War II and then returned it to China in 1954. South Sakhalin also became Russian again in 1945 and remains so to this day. Manchuria remained nominally Chinese, but under the divided control of the Russians and Japanese until the Russian revolution, when the Japanese extended to the whole province a fairly loose control which in 1931 they made firm, subsequently creating the puppet Empire of Manchukuo. This, in turn, was swallowed up after the war, first by Nationalist and then by Communist China. Korea, after having been part of the Japanese Empire until 1945, now lies in two bits, divided between Communists and non-Communists.

CHAPTER XIV

'THE OLD CORRUPTIVE INFLUENCES'

1905–1914

D ISASTROUS though the Russo-Japanese War had been to the Tsar's Empire, even before it was over there were clear indications that an even greater disaster threatened to destroy the whole gigantic, crazy structure.

Already in January 1905, when Rozhestvensky and the Second Squadron were in the waters of Madagascar, riots and strikes had broken out in Russia and been repressed with bloodshed. Then, in June 1905, came the *Potemkin* mutiny in the Black Sea fleet. The brilliant but violently partisan film of Eisenstein has given the story of the *Potemkin* world-wide fame, but the truth will never be known.

At the end of the war morale in the Black Sea fleet was extremely low; the other two Russian fleets had been destroyed while it had never had a chance to fight at all. At the same time its best officers and ratings had been withdrawn and sent to the Pacific squadrons, while the Black Sea fleet found its sea time cut to a couple of months in the year, and was manned by the rawest of crews. A month after Tsushima, on June 27th, when the ship, whose full name was *Kniaz Potemkin Tavricheski*—Prince Potemkin of Taurida—was at Tendra carrying out firing trials, trouble started following complaints about the quality of the food on board. Food has always been a fruitful source of grievance whenever there has been discontent on board ship. Messing in a warship is never luxurious and was much less so before the introduction of refrigeration.

There was plenty of material upon which the *Potemkin*'s malcontents could work in order to bring about a mutiny, given the general inefficiency of the Russian navy at this time and a system which operated entirely on a basis of privilege. Under the circumstances in which the war with Japan was fought it is very surprising that serious flare-ups never occurred amongst men who were actually doing the fighting, but only amongst men who had no fighting to do and who, for the most part, had only a few months before been called up for service.

What happened exactly was not clear and now never will be. As

Mr. Hough points out in his book The 'Potemkin' Mutiny,[1] there now
exist two completely different versions of the affair, one the official
Communist line and one the story of the surviving officers of the ship.
Meat, said by men to be bad, was brought on board to be made into
borscht. The men said that they would refuse to eat it.

According to the Communist version, which is, of course, that
adopted by Eisenstein, when the refusal to eat the soup became
definite, Commander Giliarovsky, the executive officer of the ship,
ordered that a number of men should be selected at random from the
ship's company, covered with a tarpaulin and shot in accordance
with an old Russian naval custom. The firing squad refused to obey
orders and all the ship's company were then in an uproar. In an
effort to quell them Giliarovsky drew a revolver and killed one man, a
rating named Vakulinchuk.

The officers' version of the affair makes no mention of the tarpaulin
and the firing squad and simply says that Vakulinchuk tendered a
written protest to the commander, who threw it overboard. Vakulinchuk made a gesture of resentment which Giliarovsky interpreted to
mean that he was about to be attacked. He lost his head and shot
Vakulinchuk.

It seems clear that after that the crew attacked Giliarovsky and
killed him, the captain, the chaplain and four other officers and threw
their bodies overboard. Other officers, to save themselves, jumped
into the sea and swam to a torpedo boat N 267, lying nearby. This
little ship was content to watch events, afraid to try to escape for fear
of the guns of the battleship, which was now under the operational
command of one of her sub-lieutenants, supervised by a kind of forerunner of a Soviet, made up of the ringleaders of discontent in the ship.

However, having seized the ship, the mutineers had no real idea of
what they wanted to do. They finally decided to make for Odessa,
where the workers were known to have been restless and on the verge
of rioting ever since the previous January. N 267 went meekly with
her.

When the Potemkin arrived at Odessa on June 28th the body of
Vakulinchuk was taken ashore and placed on exhibition. Rioting
broke out and fires started in the port and through the town.

Somewhere between 5,000 and 6,000 people are believed to have
lost their lives when the authorities tried to suppress these troubles,
and there took place the famous charge of the mounted Cossacks
down the Richelieu steps, driving the crowd before them, which
provided the most sensational sequence in Eisenstein's film.

[1] Hamish Hamilton, 1960.

Meanwhile, the *Potemkin* herself had fired two rounds into the town, which had started a panic at the railway station as thousands tried to escape into the countryside.

When news of these doings reached Sevastopol three battleships, *Georgi Pobiedonosetz, Dvienadsat Apostolov* and *Tri Sviatitelia*, were sent to Odessa to deal with the mutinous ship. When, however, the *Potemkin* sighted them, the mutineers got steam up and put to sea, somewhat tentatively. The other three battleships, so far loyal to the Imperial Government, then steamed off and the *Potemkin* went back to Odessa.

Within the past eighteen months the Russian navy had lost thirteen battleships at the hands of the Japanese. All the Russian battleships that remained were the eight ships of the Black Sea fleet, so that there was a natural unwillingness by the Tsarist authorities to sink one of them, even though its crew was in a state of mutiny.

The mutineers considered that this encounter had been a great victory for them and it raised their hopes of the whole fleet coming over to their side. Within a few hours two more battleships, the *Rostislav* and *Sinob*, the former flying the flag of Vice-Admiral Krieger, the commander-in-chief, arrived off Odessa to join the three, so far, loyal ships.

The *Potemkin* headed out to sea again for the second time that day and steamed past the five hostile ships at close range. All hands were at action stations on both sides and remained there until the *Potemkin* passed the *Georgi Pobiedonosetz*, when, according to the film, the latter's crew left their posts in scores and rushed on deck, cheering and waving their caps. That this ever happened is denied to this day by Tsarist naval officers.

Certainly, however, a number of curious things were happening that day, and the next occurred when the *Pobiedonosetz* turned around and followed the *Potemkin* back to Odessa, while the other battleships returned to Sevastopol. Once there, forty young naval officers volunteered to 'crew' the destroyer *Stremitelny* and go to Odessa to sink the rebel battleships.

The *Pobiedonosetz*, not knowing of this, then stated that she was going home, apparently having repented of her mutinous action. She started to steam out of the roadstead, but *Potemkin* trained her guns upon her and she started back to her berth, only to run smartly hard aground, where she stuck for the remainder of the operation.

Discouraged, the *Potemkin* left, for what her crew hoped would be asylum at Constanza in Rumania. The Rumanians offered to buy the ship; the Russian mutineers replied to what they thought an insult by offering to buy the flagship of the Rumanian navy, an ancient cruiser

—for although they were short of rations, they had no shortage of money. Finally the *Potemkin* left Rumanian waters and steamed to Theodosia, at the other end of the Black Sea, with the avenging *Stremitelny* in hot but disorganised pursuit.

Once arrived at Theodosia, on July 5th, the *Potemkin* demanded food, coal and fresh water, which she now needed badly; the Mayor of Theodosia offered food, but could supply neither coal nor fresh water. A sailor named Matushenko, who by now was running the ship, threatened to bombard the town if fresh water was not forthcoming, whereupon the population of Theodisia took to the hills, unimpressed by the *Potemkin*'s measures taken to show goodwill—such as dressing the ship overall with flags and putting the crew in their best white uniforms. The *Potemkin*'s men then tried to seize some lighters, filled with coal, lying in the harbour. Fighting broke out and the mutineers were driven off by loyal soldiers. Miserably the ship went back to Constanza, where she scuttled herself in shallow water. She was soon raised and refitted, but the bullet-marks in the cabin where the captain was killed were simply whitewashed over and remained until the ship was broken up after World War I.

The *Potemkin* affair was over, but things in the Black Sea fleet were still in a very bad way; already, just prior to the *Potemkin* mutiny there had been troubles at Nicolaiev, the principal dockyard in the Black Sea.

Later, in November, the *Potemkin* was in trouble again at Sevastopol. Renamed *Panteleimon*, after a saint in the calendar of the Greek Orthodox Church, and after a sailing ship of the line, she was at that place when one of the infantry regiments ashore mutinied, together with the cruiser *Otchakov* and four destroyers. In charge of this was a naval officer called Schmidt, who had been put in prison for subversive activities. He was released by the rioters, went on board the *Otchakov*, hoisted an admiral's flag and signalled: 'I command the fleet Schmidt.' He then telegraphed the Tsar, calling for the convocation of a constituent assembly.

Loyal troops took possession of the town and, after a brief interval, the warships surrendered, Schmidt afterwards being executed.

In addition to the changing of the name of *Potemkin*, two other important ships also had their names changed as a mark of disapproval of their crews' behaviour during the troubles; the *Otchakov* in the Black Sea became the *Kagul* and the *Pamiat Azova* in the Baltic became the *Dvina*, This last ship also lost the right to fly a special ensign of her own, bestowed in recognition of the services of her namesake at Navarino (see p. 95), which consisted of the usual blue cross of

St. Andrew on a white ground defaced by the insignia of St. George; she was to prove another of these long-lived Russian ships which we will meet again.

The internal troubles of Russia abated after 1905, but it was on a very uncertain foundation that a beginning was made with the reconstruction of the Russian navy. The country's first very tentative steps towards democracy were taken with the creation of a parliament, called the Duma. Its powers were extremely limited, but they did include control of the naval estimates and it was a hard fight to get the necessary credits passed for the building of new ships.

However, a beginning was made on a large scale with a programme, in 1909, which included the construction of four dreadnought battleships, nearly twice as large as anything that had fought on either side in the Russo-Japanese War. These ships, called *Gangut*, *Petropavlovsk*, *Sevastopol* and *Poltava*, were of 23,000 tons, armed with twelve twelve-inch guns and built to an Italian design which, modified by various Russian ideas, resulted in a poor type of ship. Impressed by what had happened to the unarmoured parts of the big ships at Tsushima, the Russians decided their ships were to be armoured over all that part of their hull which was above the waterline and, in addition, to add strength to the hull for navigation in the Baltic ice, there were no scuttles in their sides. In the days before air conditioning this meant that the ships were very uncomfortable and insanitary.

Following the *Ganguts* came a much bigger and more sophisticated programme in 1912. In this can be seen the genesis of types of ships not, at that time, known in any other navy, but which were to be the backbone of the navies which entered the Second World War.

First came four 32,000-ton capital ships—*Borodino*, *Kinburn*, *Ismail* and *Navarin*, which combined the speed of battle cruisers with the protection and armament of battleships—a combination which, just after World War I, Sir Winston Churchill from his experience described as the ideal one for the future. It was, however, not adopted by anybody except the Russians for many years. In the same year there were also laid down four light cruisers of 7,000 tons. This, again, was a type which had to wait until the experience gained in World War I caused its adoption in other navies. Thirty-six destroyers of a new type included in this programme were also years ahead of the destroyers of any other navy in speed, gun-power and, above all, in torpedo-power. While British destroyers were carrying only two tubes apiece, the new Russian destroyers were being designed to carry as many as fifteen. The prototype of these boats was the bearer of a name made famous by the war with Japan—*Novik*—and until the British V and W destroyers came into service in 1917 and 1918 these Russian ships were probably the best destroyers that anybody had.

When this programme, which was for the Baltic, had been begun, the turn came for the Black Sea fleet, which was to have four battleships of an improved *Gangut* class, four cruisers similar to those of the Baltic fleet, as well as twelve *Novik*-type destroyers. One novelty of this date, which is an example of how far-seeing the Russian naval architects could be, was the world's first minelaying submarine, *Krab*. The other side of the medal as regards Russian warship design and building at this time is the fact that, although the *Krab* was laid down six years before any other minelaying submarine, she took seven years to build, and by the time she was ready there were a number of minelaying boats in service in both the British and German navies.

Russian preoccupation with minelaying, natural after the events of the Russo-Japanese War and the need to deny Russian coastal waters to the greatly superior German fleet, resulted in the manufacture of an extremely efficient type of mine, which the British navy was not able to equal until 1917. With this improved Russian mine a well-developed doctrine of minelaying grew up.

These big building programmes put a great strain on the Russian yards and factories, so that the very curious step was taken of ordering a great deal of material in Germany, although it was clear at that time that it would be against Germany that the new navy would most probably be used. Nevertheless, the engines and boilers of the *Navarin*, one of the big battleships, and four of the destroyers were ordered in Germany, as well as two light cruisers for service as training ships in the Pacific.

None of this material came into Russian hands. *Navarin*'s machinery was cut in half in 1915 and used to equip two very fast German minelaying cruisers, which were later to secure a major success against a British convoy on the Scandinavian run. The destroyer machinery was similarly used in some German hulls and the two light cruisers were taken over for the German navy.

One was torpedoed and sunk by a British destroyer at Jutland, while the other, in 1920, was handed over as a prize of war to the Italians and served in the Italian navy until just before the Second World War.

Shortage of industrial resources did not inhibit Russian naval architects in their determination to make the biggest possible warships. The ships which were to have been laid down in 1916, had there been no war, would have been monsters, larger and more powerful than anything thought of when they were designed for the British, United States or German navies. They were to have an armament of twelve sixteen-inch guns, equal in power to the armament of nine eighteen-inch guns, which was the main armament of the biggest and most powerful battleships ever built, the Japanese giants *Yamato* and *Musashi*, which were laid down twenty years after the Russian ships were designed and which closed the long series of iron and steel battleships which began with the British *Warrior* in 1860.

In addition to the ships already mentioned the programmes current in 1914 provided for twelve submarines in the Baltic and a few more in the Black Sea, but the building of all these new ships was held up for years by delays due to the backward state of Russian industry. The first battleships took four or five years to build, when similar ships were built in Britain or Germany in two and a half years. The *Borodino* class ships laid down in 1912 were still uncompleted five years later when the Revolution broke out, and the same was true of the eight light cruisers.[1] Twenty-six of the thirty-six destroyers, however, had been completed by 1917 and there were eighteen new submarines in commission. Approximately seventy submarines were on the stocks, including some of 2,000 tons, then the largest in the world. In the Black Sea ten boats of the new programme had been completed and six were still under construction.

But none of these ships were available in 1914 except for the *Novik*. Apart from this ship the Russian Baltic fleet in 1914 was made up exclusively of semi-obsolete ships, for the rapid development which had followed the completion of the *Dreadnought* in 1907 had made obsolete even the best of the ships designed before 1905, however good their design had been at the time when they were completed. Typical of this was the fleet flagship, the armoured cruiser *Rurik*, built by Vickers, Barrow, in 1905–8. When completed she had been the beau ideal of the armoured cruiser, but within a few months she was outclassed by the British and German battle cruisers.

Two semi-dreadnoughts, *Andrei Pervosvanni* and *Imperator Pavel I*, had similarly been overtaken by events, while the other two battleships were smaller still. One was the *Tsarevitch*, released from internment by the Germans at the end of the Russo-Japanese War, and the other was the *Slava*, a ship of the *Kniaz Suvarov* class four units of which had been lost at Tsushima, but not herself ready in time for the end of the war.

---

[1] The machinery of one of the *Borodinos* was manufactured in the United Kingdom, sent by ship to North Russia and then by canal from the White Sea to the Baltic.

The cruisers, armoured and protected, were nearly all veterans of the Pacific. There were the *Gromoboi, Rossia* and *Bogatyr* from the Vladivostock squadron, with the *Oleg* and *Avrora* from Rozhestvensky's fleet, and the *Diana* which had been interned after August 10th, 1904. The twenty-eight destroyers of the Baltic fleet except the *Novik* were primitive, together with thirty-four torpedo boats, while the eight submarines were just about useless, being small and obsolete. In addition were three sisters of the *Bayan* which had been sunk at Port Arthur—a new *Bayan*, a new *Pallada* and the *Admiral Makarov*, completed between 1908 and 1910.

In theory this handful of outclassed ships was faced by the whole might of the German navy with its seventeen modern dreadnought and battle cruisers, the second largest navy in the world. In practice, however, threatened as they were with a fleet action against the largest navy in the world, there was little which the Germans could spare for the Baltic.

So it was that at the beginning of August 1914 the Germans had opposing the Russians only seven light cruisers (five of which were obsolete) three very old and small U-boats and eleven destroyers and torpedo boats, also mostly obsolete.

The German Baltic commander was Gross-Admiral Prinz Heinrich von Preussen, the brother of the Kaiser, whose position was a sad trial to the other senior German naval officers, since he outranked them all, including the commander-in-chief of the High Sea Fleet, upon whose shoulders fell the principal burden of the war at sea.

To command the Russian navy, to re-form it and train it from scratch, two of the most distinguished captains of the Russo-Japanese War had been placed in high position. Essen, who had been captain of the *Novik* and then of the *Sevastopol*, was appointed to command the Baltic fleet, while Kolchak commanded the destroyers and torpedo boats in the same force. Essen was in the Makarov tradition, but, like Makarov, there was no one to replace him when he died, exhausted, in the first winter of the war.

But if the two best leaders were chosen for the new Baltic fleet, the Russian High Command still had no idea of combined naval and military operations and the navy was placed under the direct orders of the general commanding the northern Russian army, where, of course, the fleet commander had just about as much freedom of action as any of the army corps on that front.

But worse than this silly system of command, and worse than the delays in the construction of new ships, was the state of morale of the crews and the disgusting state of naval administration. Commander

The Russians at Sea

H. G. Grenfell, R.N., the British Naval Attaché in St. Petersburg, wrote, on March 19th, 1914, a few months before war broke out:[1]

In connection with . . . the present apparent decision of the Russian government to proclaim to the world its complete confidence as to the satisfactory condition, now and hereafter, of Russian armed forces, more especially with regard to the particular date of 1917. I must beg to be allowed to represent to Your Excellency that it is impossible for me to share this optimistic estimate, at any rate so far as the naval situation is concerned.

There is small chance of the new naval programme being completed by 1917, but if even by some miracle this should prove to be the case, it does not at all follow that Germany intends to be seriously alarmed. I happen to be upon extremely good personal terms with my German colleague, and have a fair idea of the sense in which he is reporting to his Government concerning the value of Russia's naval developments in the Baltic. He, as a seaman, equally with myself, had recognised the fundamental mistake of the Russian Admiralty in devoting its energy and money principally to increase of purely material strength rather than to the far more urgent problem of building up a system of honest administration and the creation of a well-trained, capable, well-paid and contented personnel. Germany's older type battleships will amply suffice to mask any strength by sea that this country is likely to possess before the year 1918.

The shattering revelations of the Japanese War discovered, not only to us, but to the whole world, the feet of clay of this lumbering colossus; is it, therefore, reasonable to imagine that within the subsequent period of less than ten years, politically marked as they have been, not so much by progress as by reaction, the old corruptive influences formerly at work have already ceased to propagate their evil fruit?

[1] *British Documents Relating to the Outbreak of the Great War*, vol. X, part 2, pp. 771–2, H.M.S.O., London.

CHAPTER XV

THE BALTIC AND THE BLACK SEA

1914–1917

IT is hardly ever possible in the 250-year history of the Russian navy to say that that service enjoyed good fortune. Nevertheless, within a month of the outbreak of the First World War the Russian fleet achieved a success for the Allied cause which was to have an important effect on the conduct of the war at sea.

The war between Russia and Germany had begun on August 1st, 1914. On that day two German light cruisers, *Augsburg* and *Magdeburg*, then the only modern vessels available in the Baltic, began a series of bombardments of Russian coastal towns by an attack on Libau, combined with a minelaying operation. Libau, then the southernmost Russian Baltic port, had been selected in the 'nineties for development as a big naval base, but the destruction of the Baltic fleet in 1905 and the immense growth of the German navy gave the Russians little hope of holding a position so far forward. Accordingly, on the outbreak of war in 1914 their first concern was to make useless the port before it fell into German hands, and there was no immediate Russian reaction to the attack of August 1st.

The *Augsburg* and *Magdeburg* then began to press on farther northward with their attacks and on August 26th appeared at the entrance to the Gulf of Finland. The weather was foggy and the handsome four-funnelled *Magdeburg* grounded broadside on to the island of Odensholm. After trying every measure within their power to get her free the Germans blew up her forepart and most of the crew were taken off by a destroyer. The captain of the *Magdeburg*, Captain Habenicht, with five officers and men, remained behind and were still on board when two Russian destroyers, *Lieutenant Burakov* and *Riany*, arrived. They were under the command of the energetic and able Captain Nepenin, who was officially in charge of communications and intelligence for the Baltic fleet ashore.

However, when Nepenin heard that the German light cruisers were in the neighbourhood he decided that he would go and see for himself what was happening. When he arrived where the *Magdeburg* lay he sent a lieutenant named Hamilton with a boat's crew to the German ship. The surprised Hamilton was greeted by the German captain, who tendered his sword. The Russian officer explained that he was not sufficiently senior to accept it, ordered the German flag to be hauled down and replaced it with the Cross of St. Andrew. Hamilton also began a search of the ship for confidential books, which resulted in the discovery of the German secret signal book, lying haphazardly on the upper deck amidst a confusion of stores, clothes and papers. A little while later the Russians sent divers down to see whether it would be possible to refloat the stranded ship. These divers found the body of a German warrant officer, which had on it another copy of the same priceless signal book. One of these copies was sent at once to the British Admiralty and it was invaluable for the reading of German signals by that remarkable organisation which has become known as '40 O B'.

The Germans modified and developed their codes and cyphers throughout the war, but the fact that we were so often able to keep up with them stems, in the first place, largely from the capture of the books from the *Magdeburg*. In fact, Russian Naval Intelligence had already succeeded in obtaining a copy of this book in Germany, but this they never revealed to their Allies.

While things had been happening around the stranded cruiser Russian and German cruisers and small craft had been playing blind man's buff steaming in and out of fog and mist, without, in those pre-radar days, being able to do each other any real damage. This was to be typical of most of the surface action in the Baltic during that war and any serious damage to ships on either side was nearly always to be done by underwater weapons. The Russians laid mines off German ports and the Germans used submarines whenever they could spare them, while towards the end of 1914 British submarines began to enter the Baltic to co-operate with the Russians, whose fleet comprised no modern submarines. However, before this undersea war of attrition got started units of the German High Sea Fleet intervened in the second month of the war.

The Russian advance into East Prussia had been checked at Tannenberg by the end of August, but the Russian advance in Galicia was still going strong and it was decided to send a squadron of six obsolete battleships[1] into the central Baltic to make a demonstration which would, it was hoped, result in a switch of Russian pressure away from the Austrian front. The demonstration took place on September 29th, without any special effect on the fighting, 500 miles away. A sortie in the following month was interrupted

[1] Fourth Battle Squadron, two *Braunschweig* and four *Wittelsbach* class.

by the incorrect report that the British Grand Fleet was about to attack the German coast.

After these demonstrations the torpedo and mine war began to claim casualties. The Germans scored first when, on October 11th, 1914, the armoured cruiser *Pallada* was torpedoed and sunk by *U-26*. All that remained of her and her crew of 600 was her ikon floating on the sea. Next month the Russians had their revenge. November 17th was one of the feast days of the navy, when, by tradition since the reign of the Empress Anne, the fleet was provided by the ruler with roast goose for all. On this day news came that the enemy cruiser *Friedrich Carl* had sunk after striking a Russian mine off Brüster Ort in East Prussia. The German ship had been covering a force on its way to Libau to block the entrance to the harbour, which, however, had already been made useless by the Russians in anticipation of their evacuation of the place.

This German expedition Libau-bound passed a Russian force made up of the cruisers *Rurik*, *Bogatyr* and *Oleg* and the minelayer *Amur*, which went as far west as Stolp Bank and Bornholm to lay mines. Neither force sighted the other; later other Russian ships went as far west as Cape Arcona and the island of Rügen.

The pattern of the naval war in the Baltic was now set. The fact that this pattern was superficially fairly uneventful did not diminish the importance of what was going on. We have already seen how limited were the resources on both sides—the Russian ships did not exist, the German ships were needed to face the British in the North Sea—but control of the Baltic was vital to the Germans, their armament industry being dependent on iron ore brought by sea from Sweden. To attack this traffic and any German warships that might be encountered the White Ensign entered the Baltic for the first time, during hostilities, since the Crimean struggle sixty years earlier. In reply to Russian appeals for help two British submarines arrived in the Baltic in October 1914 (*E 1* and *E 9*), while four more were sent the next year (*E 8, E 13, E 18, E 19*, of which *E 13* was lost on passage).

Naturally there was some feeling, both in Britain and Russia, during the first winter of the war that two submarines were not, in fact, a very large direct contribution by the British navy to make to the war in the Baltic, and schemes were considered for a possible break into the Baltic by the British Grand Fleet in one form or another. This idea was the basis of the enormous scheme inspired by Lord Fisher, the British First Sea Lord, for building a special force of over 600 warships and landing craft of all types to enter the Baltic, pick up a Russian army and land it on the Pomeranian coast. The

Germans appreciated that such an operation might be possible, but only after the British Grand Fleet had destroyed the German High Sea Fleet in the North Sea and after the Russian army had won a great victory on land. Such a combination of events they considered very remote.

With the coming of winter weather minelaying became almost impossible for the obsolete little Russian destroyers, and the only ships available were the cruisers. On her way to one of these expeditions on February 13th the *Rurik* grounded in a heavy snowstorm on an unmarked sandbank off the northern tip of Gotland. In a short time she had taken on board 2,700 tons of water, which flooded two out of three of her boiler rooms and increased her draft by about five feet. With her guns unable to bear and her maximum speed two knots, she made her way to Reval through fresh ice, grounding several times owing to her increased draft, now eight feet greater than normal, the passage taking three days. The snow and fog which had caused the accident continued and hid the helpless ship from the Germans who were in the neighbourhood.

When she got to Reval she was met by Essen, who ordered her to continue, after a temporary patching, to Kronstadt, where there was the only dry dock suitable for a thorough refit. In theory the passage from Reval to Kronstadt was impossible because of ice at this time of year, but Essen decided that it should be attempted. The alternative was to waste two months waiting for the ice to melt. Thanks to Essen's insistence and the work of two ice-breakers the passage was made and repairs were begun. Just as they were being completed the Russian navy suffered what seemed then its greatest imaginable disaster, for Essen died at the age of fifty-four. His successor, Vice-Admiral Kanin, was a much less energetic officer.

By the end of April the ice in the Gulf of Finland had melted and the 1915 minelaying season began. This continued on the lines of the previous year's work, while the British submarines resumed their attacks on the merchant ships engaged in the iron-ore trade, and the emphasis of the surface ships' war shifted to the battle for Riga. The German successes on land had rolled back the Russian front on a huge scale, with withdrawals of up to 250 miles, and on the Baltic coast the principal object of the German army was now Riga, a most valuable base for an attack on Petrograd, as St. Petersburg had become on the outbreak of war.

In June, German ships began to appear at the entrance to the Gulf of Riga, soon accompanied by two aircraft which dropped the first bombs to be seen in this theatre of war. These bombs made a considerable impression upon the Russians, for, although the Germans failed to make a direct hit, their aim was disconcertingly good and the Russians had nothing in the way of anti-aircraft weapons except rifles and machine-guns.

To distract German attention from Riga five cruisers, the *Admiral Makarov*, flying the flag of Rear-Admiral Bakhirev, *Bayan*, *Rurik*, *Bogatyr* and *Oleg*, with attendant destroyers, were sent south to bombard Memel.

On the night of June 30th–July 1st in patchy fog the Russian formation broke up, the *Rurik* and *Novik* losing touch with the other cruisers and destroyers, who, continuing on their course, met the German minelayer *Albatros* next morning, attacked her and drove her ashore in neutral waters off Gotland. There, despite a counter-attack with torpedoes by three destroyers, the Germans had to leave her. The bombardment of Memel was cancelled.

The Russians were watching the Swedes rescue the crew of the stranded minelayer when two German cruisers, *Roon* and *Lübeck*, arrived. The Russians were the stronger force on paper, but, after their action with *Albatros*, were running short of ammunition, so that the two oldest battleships of the Baltic fleet, *Tsarevitch* and *Slava*, were ordered to their rescue. However, the two German ships, not knowing of the Russian weakness, drew off, only to meet the *Rurik* trying to rejoin her squadron mates. Again there was an exchange of salvoes at longish range, with gunnery much hampered by mist. The *Rurik* was hit once by an eight-inch shell from the *Roon*, which burst just aft of the bridge, destroying the admiral's sea cabin. At about the same time one of the *Rurik*'s forward ten-inch guns broke down. The turret was filled with gas and the other gun in it also put out of action, so that the *Rurik* turned away to use her after turret, which immediately scored a hit on the *Roon* and started a fire on the upper deck abeam of her fourth funnel. After having been hit several times more the *Roon*, with the *Rurik* in hot pursuit, steamed off, but the Russian soon had to give up the chase because of reported U-boat sightings.

During these operations the German cruiser *Prinz Adalbert* was detached to the rescue of the *Roon*, but on her way was torpedoed and badly damaged by the British submarine *E 9*. At the time *E 9*'s captain Horton thought the ship which he had attacked was probably the battleship *Pommern*. She disappeared in the mist immediately after being hit and was later claimed by the Allies as having been sunk. In fact, both the *Prinz Adalbert* and *Pommern* lived to be sunk another day.

At the beginning of August a big German fleet under Vice-Admiral Schmidt attempted to enter the Gulf of Riga through the Irben Strait —eleven battleships, twelve cruisers, with destroyers and minesweepers. The core of the Russian defence was provided by the *Slava*, a pair of gunboats, *Sivutch* and *Koreetz*, and very little else, except the British submarines. On August 8th the German attack began. There was a long-range bombardment of the *Slava* by the Germans, who were too far away for the Russians to be able to answer back; the light cruiser *Thetis* and three torpedo boats were damaged.

The Germans withdrew, but returned again on August 16th, when their big ships once again gave cover to their minesweepers— trawlers and old torpedo boats—which the *Slava*, single-handed, did what she could to stop. Bit by bit the Germans worked their way into the Gulf and the Russians prepared to withdraw towards the northern exit, Moon Sound, between the island of Ösel and the mainland.

The gunboat *Sivutch* was set on fire by an overwhelming German force, but fought back, so thoroughly ablaze fore and aft, that her plates glowed red-hot and began to explode her own ammunition.

During this action the sister ship of the *Sivutch*, *Korietz*, lost her way and, running aground, was wrecked.

The Germans, pressing their advantage, sent two big destroyers, *V 99* and *V 100*, into Moon Sound after the *Slava* on the night of August 17th–18th. On their way in they met the *Novik*, who, although outnumbered two to one, attacked at once, sank *V 99* and drove off and damaged *V 100*. The next day the German big ships came in as well and so did the British submarine *E 1* (Commander Noel Laurence). The *E 1* torpedoed the battle cruiser *Moltke*, who withdrew for repairs, accompanied by the whole fleet. This ended, for over two years, the German attempts to force Moon Sound. The torpedoing of the *Moltke* was followed on October 22nd by the sinking of the *Prinz Adalbert* by *E 8*, with the result that the obsolete German heavy ships were withdrawn from the Baltic and paid off, a step taken in part also to provide officers and crews for the new U-boats.

The light cruisers left behind also suffered. *E 19* sank the *Undine* between Sassnitz and Trelleborg on November 7th, the *Bremen* was sunk by a mine on December 17th, and by the end of the year, with the *Lübeck* badly damaged, the *Augsburg* was the only operational German ship in the Baltic bigger than a destroyer.

The Russian navy could clearly claim to have won at least one round in the struggle for the Baltic, especially as the British submarines, now five in number, were working against the German iron-ore trade with Sweden.

But coming events were casting their shadows before. At the beginning of November a sortie by the big battleships was planned, when a mutiny broke out on board one of them—the *Gangut*—the crew protesting against being given a kind of buckwheat porridge for supper instead of macaroni. Their complaints were followed by the demand that the ship's commander should be sent ashore, together with all officers bearing foreign names. Fifty of the leaders of the mutiny were arrested and imprisoned, but a few days later there was a similar outbreak on board the *Imperator Pavel I*, one of the leaders of which was a seaman called P. E. Dybenko who attained a high place in the Soviet scheme of things, until he was purged in 1937.

Nevertheless a little later the *Gangut* and the *Petropavlovsk* did leave the Gulf of Finland, for almost the only time during the war, and appeared in the Central Baltic as far south as Gotland, without, however, meeting any enemy. Advantage was taken of these sorties further to freshen the minefields of the Gulf of Riga. Ever since August 19th Kolchak, then Director of Naval Operations, had been in charge of the defences of the Gulf, and his energy and intelligence served to consolidate the success that the Russians had won.

With Moon Sound assured, there was a more important job for Kolchak, and on January 5th, 1916, he was appointed commander of all the Baltic fleet destroyers. Apart from damage to the *Zabiaka*, one of the brand-new big Russian destroyers, by mines, after which she was towed home by the *Novik*, this was the last important event of the year in the Baltic. Winter set in, ice once again brought all navigation to an end, and the next three months were devoted as usual to repairs and refits while, in addition, some of the ships, notably the old cruisers, had their armaments increased and were rearmed with modern guns.

New destroyers and submarines were completed; some of the latter were Russian built, others had been built in pieces in Canada, sent across the Pacific and then, by Trans-Siberian railway in packing-cases, to the Baltic and the Black Sea, where a beginning was made with their reassembly—six boats in the Baltic and six more in the Black Sea.

The spring of 1916 went forward without the threat of an intervention by the High Sea Fleet, for the newly appointed and very energetic and able commander of that force, Scheer, had great plans for action in the North Sea which resulted in Jutland. The sequel to this battle made it impossible for him to spare heavy ships for the Baltic. Nevertheless Moon Sound was still a threatened sector of the Russian seaward defences, and it was there that Kanin and Kolchak began to build up their strength as soon as they could move ships through the melting ice.

The backbone of the defences of the Sound was once more the *Slava*, which, on April 27th, had the unwished-for distinction of being the first capital ship in history to be hit by bombs from an aircraft. Five men were killed, two wounded, and the ship was sufficiently badly damaged to need a force of forty dredgers to make a passage for her out of Moon Sound. This new passage also made it possible for other big ships to enter the Gulf of Riga from the Gulf of Finland without having to make the much longer passage through the open sea.

Minelaying and submarine operations were continued, the latter being reinforced by four semi-obsolete British boats of the C class (*C 26, C 27, C 32, C 35*) which had been towed up to Archangel and then brought down, aboard barges, by river and canal to Petrograd. Unfortunately, to lighten them for their journey their batteries had been removed and placed on board a merchant ship which made the trip from Britain to Archangel independently. She was sunk by a U-boat on her way and it was therefore necessary for the boats to wait for another consignment of batteries before they could go to work.

The season for submarines had, however, hardly begun when the British *E 18* was lost the day after she had torpedoed the *V 100*, blowing her bow off but not sinking her. By this time the successes of the British submarines had forced the Germans to adopt the convoy system for their Baltic trade, with the help of seventy escort craft, torpedo boats, trawlers and the like. As a result British successes came to an end, but the German Official History says that the diversion of the seventy escort vessels from the North Sea to the Baltic resulted in considerably reducing the freedom of action of the High Sea Fleet. Convoys of ships, creeping up the Swedish coast and passing within a reasonable distance of Russian bases were tempting targets for Russian destroyers, and a couple of these attacks were undertaken by Kolchak. These were the last operations carried out under his orders before he was appointed, on July 17th, vice-admiral and commander-in-chief of the Black Sea fleet at the age of forty-one. Two months later Kanin was succeeded as commander-in-chief in the Baltic by Nepenin, formerly the Fleet Intelligence officer who had been largely responsible for the *coup* of the *Magdeburg*'s confidential books in 1914.

The new commander-in-chief was a much more enterprising officer than his predecessor, but there were only three months more to go to the end of the season and only six months to the Revolution, and he had no opportunity to make his mark. However, he began by strengthening his position in the Gulf of Riga, bringing in through the new channel the *Tsarevitch, Diana* and *Admiral Makarov* to reinforce the *Slava*.

Russian minelaying continued as the season neared its end, one field off Baltic Port having an especial success. On the night of November 9th–10th eleven German destroyers of the Tenth Flotilla entered the mouth of the Gulf of Finland to bombard Baltic Port. The flotilla, however, entangled itself in a series of minefields and two boats were lost before the bombardment began; five more were lost on the way home, so that in all seven were sunk out of a total of eleven.

This was the last serious blow that the Germans suffered during the war at the hands of the Baltic fleet. As some compensation in the following week the *Rurik* struck a mine off Hogland, but managed to reach Kronstadt.

At the end of December once more ice shut down the Baltic war and when the ice melted in the spring the Russian navy and the Russian empire melted with it.

The Black Sea

For nearly three months after the outbreak of war in August 1914 the Black Sea was in a state of uneasy peace. Turkey, after having spent decades relying on British support to protect her against Russia, had seen the two powers draw together in an alliance against the German menace. This was an obvious opportunity for German diplomacy of which full advantage was taken, and Germany began to replace Britain as Turkey's protector. The Germans started by trying to resuscitate the Turkish army, with very little success. Even the superb toughness of the ordinary Turkish soldier and the skill of the German instructors could not prevent the defeat of the Turks at the hands of the Italians, Greeks, Serbs, Bulgarians and Montenegrins during the years 1911 and 1912.

Revenge for these defeats seemed essential to the group of ambitious men—literally 'The Young Turks'—who had seized power in 1908. They had been a familiar phenomenon at the outset of their career, a phenomenon perhaps even more familiar now than half a century ago. Disgusted with the corruption and beastliness of the time-dishonoured Turkish régime, they had formed a conspiracy, risen, deposed the Sultan, Abdul Hamid the Damned, and set up an administration designed for reform. This soon found itself being run by a Triumvirate of greedy men, who swallowed up the idealists and the idealism by which they had risen to power and became just another Turkish Government of the worst sort, and, as far as the waging of war was concerned, an extremely inefficient one as well.

In 1913, the Treaty of Bucharest having concluded the Second Balkan War, the Triumvirate began to consider the third one, and it would seem possible that it would have come some time in 1914–15 even if it had not been for Sarajevo. As it was, however, the two streams of war soon flowed together and the narrow fast-moving rapids of Balkan disputes were soon swallowed in the broad-rolling all-destroying stream of the First World War.

When the First World War did break out the British Government tried to secure Turkish support or at least neutrality, but everything was against it. There was first the absence of the British Ambassador from his post, the competence of the German Ambassador, the action of the British Government in taking over two brand-new Turkish battleships then fitting out in British yards. These had been intended by the Turks to turn the tables on the Greeks, who had had command of the sea during the First Balkan War.

On August 4th a formal alliance between Germany and Turkey followed, but there was no immediate declaration of war by Turkey. Two German warships, the battle cruiser *Goeben* and the light cruiser *Breslau*, arrived before the Dardanelles on August 10th. The two ships sought and obtained permission to enter Turkish waters in order to avoid attack by British vessels.

Both German ships became nominally Turkish and began peacefully working up for war. Suddenly, on October 28th, when the German admiral Souchon was ready, without a word to any Turk except probably to the pro-German Minister of War Enver Pasha, he took his ships to sea and, still flying the Turkish flag, began a bombardment of Sevastopol by the *Goeben* and Novorossisk by the *Breslau*. On the same day Turkish destroyers shelled Odessa and the Turkish cruiser *Hamidieh* Theodosia.

Henceforward, of course, there was war in the Black Sea as well. This war was not as one-sided as that in the Baltic. The backbone of the Russian Black Sea fleet were five pre-dreadnought battleships, with three cruisers, seventeen destroyers and four submarines, all obsolete. Although the combined fire-power of the battleships was more than twice as great as that of the *Goeben*, the German ship's speed was in turn twice that of the Russian battleships, so that the chance of a decisive encounter was very small.

However, the ships of the Black Sea fleet were much better equipped and trained than those of the Baltic. The affair of the *Potemkin* appears to have been followed by a really big attempt to put the fleet in order, carried out under the command of Vice-Admiral A. A. Eberhardt. One of Eberhardt's refinements, of which the Black Sea fleet was very proud, was the introduction of very short-wave radio-telegraphy within the battleships themselves to signal the range and bearing of the enemy, as well as firing orders, to the main armament from a central control position by the bridge. This, of course, was the basis of the system of director-controlled firing which was then just being introduced into the British and German navies, although in those navies the communication between the fire-control position and the guns was maintained more conventionally by ordinary electrical wiring.

The German and Turkish attacks of October 29th, 1914, did very little immediate damage, but they ruined Russia. There could be now no chance of opening the Dardanelles by diplomacy; only a large-scale military operation could do that and, if it were not done, there was no communication between Russia and the Allies except by the 6,000 miles of the Trans-Siberian railway or an unfinished railway between the Arctic port of Murmansk, and, 650 miles to the south, Petrograd. Both these routes were, of course, useless for large movements of supplies, and very soon the question of a big military operation to open the Dardanelles became urgent.

In the meanwhile Eberhardt began a mine war of his own, very similar to that being waged in the Baltic, and also a blockade of the coast of Anatolia. At this stage the only coal available for Constantinople, and therefore the Turco-German fleet and the Turkish war effort, came from the Anatolian port of Zonguldak. There was no railway, so that the coal had to be brought to Constantinople by ship, and the Russians set themselves to interfere with this traffic. This they did with considerable success, their efforts including the fitting out of a couple of small fast passenger steamers, similar to Cross-Channel packets, as seaplane carriers, whose planes carried out some of the very earliest bombing attacks from the air.

While the Russian big ships were interrupting as best they could the traffic along the Anatolian coast, obsolete Russian destroyers—there were no others—were harrying the left flank of the Turkish army on the Caucasus front. To divert them from this the *Breslau* appeared off Poti on November 2nd and shelled the place without any direct results. The Russian battle fleet, however, put to sea to intercept her on her way home and, in doing so, met the *Goeben*, who had come out to protect the *Breslau*. The two German ships met and then were discovered by the *Almaz*—the fugitive from Tsushima— some thirty miles south of Cape Saritch. The day was one of fog patches, but there was enough visibility for the five Russian battleships—*Evstafi* (flying Eberhardt's flag), *Ioann Zlatoust, Panteleimon, Tri Sviatitelia* and *Rostislav*—to open fire in line ahead, at 8,000 yards; the action only lasted ten minutes before the *Goeben* disappeared in the fog, having hit the *Evstafi* once in her forward starboard six-inch battery, killing four officers and thirty men.

Another attempt to put Zonguldak out of action was made later; the intention was to sink four blockships off the port, but in very bad weather the Russian force was intercepted by the *Goeben* and *Breslau*, two blockships sunk and the others driven off. On her return from this expedition the *Goeben* struck two Russian mines before the fascinated gaze of the Russian officer who had laid them and who found himself a prisoner on board the German battle cruiser, his blockship having been sunk beneath him. This same officer, from his Turkish prisoner-of-war camp, succeeded in smuggling back to Russia information as to the course taken by the *Goeben* and *Breslau* on their return to the Bosphorus and these routes were then mined.

To coincide with the Anglo-French attack upon Krithia on the Gallipoli peninsula another bombardment of the Bosphorus forts took place on May 9th, but it was interrupted by the appearance of the *Goeben* from Constantinople. Although there was no dry dock big enough to hold her at Constantinople the *Goeben* had had her underwater damage repaired by the use of cofferdams, similar to those employed at Port Arthur during the Russo-Japanese war.

The German ship fired more than 200 rounds from her main armament before the Russian battleships, which had been dispersed to bombard different targets along the coast, concentrated and drove her back into the Bosphorus.

The Russian blockade of the Anatolian coast also prevented the dispatch of Turkish troops and stores to the Caucasus front by sea at a time when the situation there was threatening to the Russians. When this pressure had become especially menacing the Russians had asked, on January 2nd, 1915, for an Allied move against Turkey. The Allies had agreed and the Dardanelles scheme had been born, although, within a few days of the request having been made, the Russians won a great victory at Sarikamish and the Turkish army was no longer an immediate threat.

At the same time as the attack on the Dardanelles the Russian battleships shelled the entrance of the Bosphorus and an invasion force was prepared for landing there, but there was endless delay and finally the great German-Austrian break-through in Galicia in May 1915 meant that all the Russian forces were needed to plug the gap and the idea of landing, if it was ever seriously intended, was abandoned. Although the British and French had promised that Constantinople, if taken, would be ceded to the Russians, and although success at the Dardanelles was vital if the Russian Empire was to survive, the Russian Government regarded the Allied attack with misgiving and jealousy. Only if Russia herself took Constantinople did they believe that the city would be Russian at the end of the war, and they were far from wishing their allies well. Captain B. H. Liddell Hart has written:[1]

> Russia would not help even in helping to clear her own windpipe. She preferred to choke rather than disgorge a morsel of her amibition. And in the end she was choked—the verdict should be *felo de se*.

During the summer of 1915 the Russian superiority in surface ships was greatly increased by the completion of the first of the new dreadnought battleships *Imperatritza Maria* and *Imperatritza Ekaterina II*, ships of 22,000 tons. They mounted twelve twelve-inch guns each, but unhappily had only twenty-three knots speed, so that they had no chance of catching the *Goeben*. Both these great ships were fated to have very short, unhappy lives.

When the *Imperatritza Maria* was being commissioned a very old man of over eighty presented himself to her commander and announced that he had come to join. It was his right, he said, for he had served in the last *Imperatritza Maria* at Sinope in the Crimean War—sixty-two years previously. In support of his claim he produced a letter from the Tsar appointing him to the new *Imperatritza Maria* and proceeded to settle down happily on board. It was not quite clear what could be done with this extremely ancient mariner, but then someone discovered that for over forty years he had been the concierge of a block of flats in St. Petersburg and he was given the task of watching while the ship was in port to see that no one unauthorised came on board. Just before the *Imperatritza Maria*'s story came to an end the old man received his commission as an officer.

At New Year 1916, the *Goeben* was out again and on January 8th met the *Imperatritza Ekaterina II*. As usual the weather was misty, the Russian ship had barely finished her trials and when she opened fire on the German and started in chase her turrets began to break down. Nevertheless her gunnery was not undistinguished, for she opened fire at 20,000 yards with a salvo which straddled the enemy and continued firing up to 24,000 yards, a long range for those days, altogether getting off ninety-six rounds.

[1] *The Real War*, Faber and Faber, London, 1930.

What the *Imperatritza Ekaterina II* had been doing on this occasion was covering yet another attack on Turkish coastwise shipping; these attacks eventually achieved such a degree of success that the activity of the *Goeben* and *Breslau* was reduced very nearly to zero because of the shortage of coal. At the same time the Russians were able to make increasingly free use of the Black Sea fleet support of their army, which had now fought its way from the Caucasus into Anatolia. In April 1916 a force of forty transports, protected by the entire Black Sea fleet, sailed from Novorossisk to help in the capture of Trebizond.

Eberhardt had certainly had one of the most successful careers as a commander-in-chief in recent years in the Tsarist navy, but in July 1916 he was succeeded by Kolchak, of whom even greater things were hoped. Apart from continuing to exercise the large measure of command of the Black Sea which the Russian fleet already possessed, the new commander-in-chief had ideas of his own on the subject of the offensive and brought with him to Sevastopol plans for another great attack against Constantinople, this time from the Bosphorus.

To cover the landing of Russian troops on the Black Sea coast of Thrace it was Kolchak's intention to pour thousands of tons of oil on to the sea at the entrance to the Bosphorus, and set it on fire. The current would then carry it down to Constantinople. Experiments and rehearsals for this operation were begun.

In the meantime the entry of Rumania into the war on the side of the Allies on August 27th, 1916, and the virtual overrunning of that country within a few weeks by a victorious army of Germans and their allies under Mackensen, had opened a new front for naval operations or semi-naval operations amongst the islands, swamps, streams and pools of the Danube delta.

The greatest material disaster to the Russian navy of the whole war took place at Sevastopol on October 27th, 1916, when an explosion occurred in the forward secondary armament magazine of the *Imperatritza Maria*. A fire followed; Kolchak went on board at (nce to superintend fire-fighting operations, but it soon was clear that the ship would blow up in a few minutes, with the certainty of great damage to the port and to the ships of the fleet lying in it. Kolchak first ordered one of the pre-dreadnoughts to fire on the *Imperatritza Maria* to sink her, but a slight miscalculation of aim might have caused the very explosion it was intended to prevent. Accordingly Kolchak gave orders for the seacocks of the blazing ship to be opened and was the last to leave her as her bows dipped below the surface and she began slowly to heel over, while an enormous, long, black scarf of smoke was blown by the wind across the harbour, where it hung in the air as a giant token of mourning.

At the beginning of the war there still existed in the Far East a pale shadow of the old Pacific squadrons which had been sunk in the Russo-Japanese War—two semi-obsolete cruisers, veterans of that war—*Askold* and *Jemtchug*, as well as some very small obsolete destroyers and submarines intended for the local defence of Vladivostock.

The two cruisers took part in the hunt for Spee's squadron and the other German surface raiders and the *Jemtchug* was at Penang on October 28th, 1914, when the *Emden* arrived in the roads disguised as a British cruiser, just before dawn, and torpedoed and sank her. Both the captain and executive officer of the *Jemtchug* were dismissed the service by court martial for having failed to keep a proper watch.

After the German raiders had been rounded up, the five-funnelled *Askold* went to the Mediterranean and served at the Dardanelles. By the time the Dardanelles campaign was over traffic to North Russia had been much developed as an alternative supply route to Russia, and the *Askold* was sent off to help protect it. At the same time to form a White Sea fleet the Russians had bought from the Japanese three ex-Russian ships which had fallen into their hands in 1905. These were the battleships *Tango* (ex *Poltava*) and *Sagami* (ex *Peresviet*) sunk at Port Arthur, and the cruiser *Soya* (ex *Variag*) which had been sunk at Chemulpo. *Sagami* and *Soya* received their old names, while the *Tango*, as there was by now a new *Poltava*, was renamed *Tchesma*.

The *Tchesma*, after having been briefly concerned in the demonstration made by the Allied Mediterranean fleets against the then King Constantine of Greece, safely reached the White Sea with *Variag*, *Askold* and half a dozen very old destroyers from Vladivostock. The *Peresviet* was delayed on her way from the Far East and was mined and sunk on January 9th, 1917, just off Port Said.

Ironically the *Tchesma* and the others had followed a course of their own devising leading through several suspicious areas, while the *Peresviet* was obediently following swept channels, believed safe.

CHAPTER XVI

THE REVOLUTION

1917–1921

I N March 1917 the biggest country in the world, with the largest army in the world, self-sufficient in food, generously supplied by its allies with money and in which great stocks of war materials lay ready for dispatch to the various fighting fronts was on the point of collapse. People in towns were hungry because food was not reaching them, and troops at the front were without weapons because weapons were not reaching them either. Two and a half years of war, 10,000,000 casualties, hunger, cold and a Government either inefficient or corrupt had broken the hearts of a people and made them very nearly ready to accept peace at any price.

Not only workers, peasants, soldiers, and sailors felt like this. Ever since the beginning of the war there had been close to that dim despot, the Tsar, a powerful party in favour of a separate peace with Germany. It had gathered strength from such miscellaneous elements as the monk Rasputin, genuinely war-weary members of the officers' corps and businessmen with an eye to their profits. They were complemented by left-wing extremists who believed that Communism could only be introduced in the country if the Tsar, the army and the navy were swept away and peace made with Germany. At the same time the Tsar's Government seemed so very disastrous that many patriotic liberal Russians and their Western Allies wished it away, because only thus did they think it possible for Russia to carry its share of the war to a victorious end.

Accordingly with the collapse no one stirred to defend the old order and, of the protagonists of the new orders who might have taken its place, only the Bolsheviks had the mixture of intelligence, cold-blooded nerve and luck needed for success.

The day the pre-revolutionary Russian world ended was March 12th, 1917. Once again transport had broken down, once again there was no bread for the crowds waiting in queues in a temperature below Fahrenheit zero. Angry and heartsick, the crowds began to demonstrate, workers joined them, police could not restore order and the soldiers, mostly new recruits and depot elements, not only would not restore order, but came over to the crowd.

Within four days the Tsar had abdicated, there was a Provisional Government of a sort which would have seemed mildly Liberal in contemporary England, there was a parliament—the Duma—restored to some authority and there were the Bolsheviks. In the middle there were the ordinary people, ignorant and leaderless.

When the first rioting broke out in Petrograd sailors in local shore establishments, mostly on courses or waiting for drafts, with little to do and no officers of whom they knew anything or who knew anything of them, demonstrated in bloody-minded fashion. Their discontent soon spread to the sailors and workers at Kronstadt. A mob of demonstrators poured on board the cruiser *Avrora*, lying in the Neva, and shot her captain dead when he tried to remonstrate with them.

Rumours and reports of all this reached Nepenin and the Baltic fleet at Helsingfors. So did an appeal from Rodzianko, President of the Duma, stating that the Tsar had abdicated in favour of the Provional Government and ordering Nepenin to place himself at its disposal. Similar telegrams had been sent to all other commanding officers and none had any real alternative but to obey. After all, the abdication of the Tsar and the transfer of power to the Provisional Government was perfectly legal and there was no other authority in Russia at all. Nevertheless, Nepenin has been blamed for obeying in much of the argument and bickering that has gone on ever since amongst Russian émigrés.

From the beginning Nepenin was faced with the problem of how to check, in his own fleet, the effects of the riots, risings, strikes and mutinies in Petrograd and Kronstadt. Ordinarily the standard treatment for a situation of this sort was to get every possible ship to sea, to give the crews something else to think about, to get them away from sources of infection and to split the squadrons up so that one bad ship or unit could not infect the others. In March 1917 this was quite impossible, for all the ships were frozen in and Nepenin could do nothing but wait.

Within a few days the troubles began. On March 15th Nepenin, in common with nearly all the commanders-in-chief, naval and military, accepted the authority of the Provisional Government, and on the next day followed the publication of the news of the Tsar's abdication. A hush fell on the fleet which lasted a couple of hours—then came the news that fighting had broken out on board the *Andrei Pervosvanni* and the *Imperator Pavel I*, in which a number of officers had been killed. These ships, semi-dreadnoughts and semi-obsolete, formed with the *Tsarevitch* and *Slava* the 2nd 'Battleship Brigade' which had a thoroughly bad reputation in the fleet, where its units were referred to as 'the convict ships'. On board the *Andrei Pervosvanni*, the flagship of the 'Brigade', the commander at nightfall reported to the captain and the admiral that the men were in a riotous mood. The admiral, Nebolsin, about to leave for the *Kretchet* to see the commander-in-chief, told his flag captain to arrange matters to suit himself and went over the side to carry out his planned visit.

The flag captain, Gadd, then discovered that some members of the crew had broken the locks on the rifle racks and had started shooting at some of the officers. He ran back to the wardroom, told the officers to get their revolvers and follow him. They dashed forward along the alleyway leading to the crew's quarters. The mutinous sailors disappeared, but soon gathered again, on deck, and began firing through the scuttles of the officers' cabins, where lights were burning; this was before the days of blackouts.

Putting out the lights, the officers barricaded themselves in their quarters, while the mutineers continued desultory firing, from which there were some casualties. As the firing continued Captain Gadd left shelter and went forward alone to reason with the mutineers. Some heard him fairly respectfully, while others tried to kill a couple of petty officers, and when Gadd tried to stop them he was himself attacked, and only saved at the last minute by some of the men who had been listening to him. For the time being an uneasy peace was established; in the meantime Nebolsin had been shot dead on the dockside.

On board the *Imperator Pavel*, however, matters went much worse, for her captain was overcome and simply sat in the wardroom telling his officers to do whatever they wanted; several were killed.

Mutinies were also reported amongst some of the destroyers and minesweepers. All the ships then started nominating spokesmen from the lower deck who eventually met on board the *Kretchet*, a former merchant ship, which served as Nepenin's flagship when he was in port.

Parties of men began roaming round the dockyard, rioting, shouting and, from time to time, killing officers they met, either by chance or because of some special grievance. Altogether some thirty-eight naval officers were killed at Helsingfors, including Nepenin himself. He was immediately succeeded by his second-in-command, Vice-Admiral Maximov, who figures largely in the black book of the Russian émigrés, for he is alleged to have first covered himself with red ribbons and then announced that he was 'The People's Admiral'.

While this was going on news came from Kronstadt that about

eighty officers had been killed there. The picture was much the same as at Helsingfors. Some had been deliberately killed because of their unpopularity, some were killed by accident—encounters with drunken bands and the like—and some were killed protecting their brother officers.

But, while the base at Kronstadt and the main body of the Baltic fleet at Helsingfors were riven by murder and mutiny, at the advanced base of the fleet, Reval, nothing at all was happening, and the cruisers and destroyers there got on with their winter routine of repairs, refits and training, but although some ships and men of the Baltic fleet were to show that they could still fight with the greatest bravery and some skill, the collection of Russian ships in the Baltic was never a fleet again and most of them were out of action for good and all.

In the swirl of revolutionary events, ships' soviets were created, officers' *épaulettes* disappeared, there were disputes over the flying of the Red flag and a beginning was made with renaming some of the ships. The *Imperator Pavel I* became the *Respublika*, the *Tsarevitch* became *Grajdanin*; off in the Black Sea the *Imperatritza Ekaterina II* became *Svobodnaya Rossia* and her new sister ship *Imperator Alexander III* the *Volya*. Ships which had been in the forefront of past mutinies were again renamed; the *Dvina*, which had been serving as the depot ship for the British submarines, assumed her old name of *Pamiat Azova* and with it the right to fly St. Andrew's Cross with the badge of the Order of St. George upon it, which the previous *Pamiat Azova* had won at Navarino, and the *Panteleimon* (ex-*Potemkin*) became *Boretz za Svobodu* (Standard Bearer of Liberty).

For the most part Kolchak was able to keep his Black Sea fleet pretty well under control during the first months of the Revolution. Some ships struck the Cross of St. Andrew and hoisted the national flag of white, blue and red horizontal stripes upside down so that the red stripe came uppermost, as an indication of their frame of mind, but otherwise there was, for the time being, little outward change except for the deletion of the word 'Tsar' from the inscription 'God Protect the Tsar' on the walls of Fort Constantine at the entrance to Sevastopol harbour.

Here, too, the crews of each ship elected their own committees. In the Baltic delegates from each of the committees made up the Centro-balt (the Central Committee of the Baltic), which fought bitter battles unceasingly with the officers and the various commanders-in-chief of the fleet. Of these there were three during the period of the Provisional Government; the first change of commander-in-chief in the

Baltic came in July when officers of the fleet persuaded Kerensky that there would be complete collapse if Maximov were not removed. He was accordingly summoned to Petrograd and Rear-Admiral Verderevsky appointed in his place, whereupon the *Petropavlovsk* mutinied and had to be restrained by Maximov himself.

Then the Bolsheviks rose unsuccessfully in Petrograd on July 16th. This rising was put down in three days, but it was a close-run business. The Provisional Government asked Verderevsky to send some trustworthy destroyers up the Neva to overawe the dissident soldiers and workmen of the capital, while, at the same time, the *Petropavlovsk* announced her intention of also going up the Neva. In the end the *Petropavlovsk* did not go, the destroyers did, and Verderevsky, arrested through a mixture of foolishness and false witness, was released and made Minister of Marine, being succeeded by Rear-Admiral Rasvozov, hitherto commanding the destroyers.

The left-wing Soviet rising against the Provisional Government was followed, on September 9th, by a right-wing rising led by Kornilov, the general commanding the Petrograd area. This was put down easily by Kerensky, and Kornilov arrested, but the affair fed all suspicion, genuine or otherwise, that existed among officers who felt that Kerensky would finally betray them to the Left. At the same time Republican elements of all sorts took the rising as proof of the basically reactionary nature of the officers.

The *Petropavlovsk* marked the event with yet another mutiny and the shooting of three of her officers, eighteen-year-old sub-lieutenants, who refused to sign a declaration, demanded of all officers, agreeing not to take part in any political movement.

During the first nine months of 1917 there had been a lull on the Russian land front, for the Germans and the Austrians hoped that Russia, if unprovoked, would gradually fade out of the war, although the Russian Government was pledged to continue fighting. However, the Russian soldiers wanted peace above all and this only the Bolsheviks promised them at once and unconditionally. On the Western Front the Allies were fighting desperate battles and hoping for American troops to come to their aid; the Germans were on the defensive, but were planning an all-out offensive for 1918 which would destroy the British and French before the Americans could arrive, and to do this they would need to transfer troops from the Eastern to the Western Front.

It was natural that the Allies should ask the Russians to put on yet another offensive to keep the Germans busy in the east, but an attempt at such an offensive finally brought down Kerensky and the Provisional Government. Whether it would have been possible to avoid the Bolshevik Revolution by treating the Russians as victims of shock who required rest and recuperation above everything else and who should not be expected to fight any more battles can never be told, but this policy never had a chance with the butcher's bills for the fighting in France and Flanders in 1917 coming in to the British and French people.

However, the lull continued during the summer, as it did on land, in both the Baltic and Black Sea, while crews rotted away and disorganisation in dockyards meant an end to the building and repair of ships. The circumstances under which some of the vessels were lost throws light on the state of the fleet at that time. The submarine *AG 15* was supposedly sunk because someone forgot to close a hatch when she dived. When the destroyer *Okhotnik* was mined her crew abandoned ship without orders, taking with them all available boats and life-rafts, leaving their officers behind, who were all drowned. Finally, the newly elected captain of the destroyer *Stroiny* ran his ship aground so firmly that she had to be abandoned.

Various torpedo craft were also sunk by mines during the period, and in September the Germans decided that the war on the Eastern Front was to be made hot again and Russia put out of the war for good and all. Riga was their first target and fell on September 4th; in the following month the Germans mounted their biggest amphibious operation of the war, against the islands of Dagö and Ösel. Twenty-five thousand men and 5,000 horses sailed from Libau, escorted by eleven of the biggest capital ships from the High Sea Fleet, with nine light cruisers, thirty-seven destroyers, seventy-two minesweepers, nineteen transports and twenty-one supply ships, the whole commanded by Vice-Admiral Ehrhard Schmidt, flying his flag in the *Moltke*, while the troops were commanded by General von Kathen.

The main body of the German fleet arrived off Tagga Bay on the north-west coast of Ösel at three o'clock on the morning of October 12th and began a bombardment during which one of the biggest, newest and most powerful ships in the German navy, the *Bayern*, struck a mine, as did another of the battleships, *Grosser Kurfüst*, but both ships were so well built they were able to carry on without interruption.

While the German main body was thus occupied with a direct attack on Ösel from the west, a smaller force went into the Gulf of Riga and attacked the island of Moon, between the east coast of Ösel and the mainland. Here the old *Slava* was on guard, but opposed to her were two much bigger German battleships, *König* and *Kronprinz*—twenty twelve-inch guns against four.

Kassar Bay, between Moon and Dagö, was the next scene of fighting. Here a force of four new Russian destroyers, supported by an ancient but valorous gunboat, the *Khrabri*, skirmished with the German forces. In the course of these operations the Russians lost the destroyer *Grom*. The *Khrabri* came alongside to take her in tow, whereupon her crew without orders abandoned ship. The *Grom* drifted off and was taken in tow by the Germans, but sank almost at once.

In preparation for the decisive attempt to force Moon Sound the Germans next turned their attention to a brand-new twelve-inch battery which had recently been installed at Zerel on the south tip of Ösel, and almost at once, on the 15th, the battery surrendered.

Two days later came the main German effort. The Russians, apart from destroyers which in the meantime had refused to carry out a torpedo attack against the German ships, had the *Slava*, *Grajdanin* (ex *Tsarevitch*), *Admiral Makarov* and *Bayan*, ships originally selected for service in Moon Sound and the Gulf of Riga because of their comparatively small size and consequent shallow draft.

At about noon the German battleships appeared in Moon Sound and began shelling the Russian ships at anchor in Kuivaast Roads, where their crews were just beginning their dinner. The Russians weighed at once, *Bayan*, the flagship of Rear-Admiral Bakhirev, signalling *Slava* to leave last, as she was already so badly damaged that it was feared that she might sink or ground in the channel and thus block it for everyone else. The *Bayan* herself was ablaze from an oil-fuel fire, but she and the *Grajdanin* got through. The *Slava*, however, struck a mine and finally sank at the entrance of the channel, listing at a heavy angle with her upper deck awash. Her flag, still the blue Cross of St. Andrew, was cut down by the Germans and taken to Berlin, where it was preserved in the Museum für Meereskunde, next to the flag taken from H.M.S. *Vindictive* after she had been scuttled as a blockship at the entrance to Ostend harbour. Both flags perished in the blitz on Berlin during World War II.

On November 6th the Bolshevik Revolution broke out and destroyers were sent by the Centrobalt to Petrograd to support the Soviet there against Kerensky and the Provisional Government. In some at least of these destroyers the original Tsarist captains and officers were still serving, and carrying out the orders of the Bolsheviks. In the middle of the brief and confused fighting the *Avrora* made her famous appearance on the revolutionary stage, when she fired a few rounds of blank ammunition to bring about the collapse of the forces of the legitimate Government.

There was now complete confusion in the Baltic and on November 17th Russia signed an armistice with Germany. The old Russian navy ceased to exist on January 2nd, 1918, and the Red fleet, together with the Red army, came officially into being. Eventually after a stormy peace conference at Brest Litovsk a treaty was signed, ceding vast areas of Russian territory to the central powers or their puppets, on March 3rd, 1918.

The affairs of one of these German puppets were the cause of the last naval operations in the Baltic prior to the Armistice of November 1918. The Bolshevik Russians had tried to set up a Communist Government in Finland; the bourgeois Finnish authorities appealed to the Germans to come to their help, and with great gusto the Germans announced their intention of so doing. An ultimatum to the Soviet Government demanded the withdrawal of all Russian ships from Finnish waters at once—the bulk of the Baltic fleet was still at Helsingfors.

The problem of getting away the Baltic fleet and as much assorted merchant shipping as possible was an extremely difficult one. In the hurly-burly of the Revolution little real work in the way of refitting and repair had been done on the ships for the past year, which their crews had spent in a state of semi-permanent mutiny. Now the ragtag and bobtail of these men had deserted, no great loss to anyone. The majority of the keener Bolsheviks had gone to fight ashore with the various Red naval parties, where they were to play a leading part in the Revolution over the next three years. All in all, the elements left behind were of a very dubious sort from everyone's point of view.

Rasvozov had been dismissed by a Commissar from Petrograd called Raskolnikov, a former reserve sub-lieutenant, and the senior Russian naval officer present at Helsingfors was Rear-Admiral A. M. Stchasny, of the commander-in-chief's staff; all the officers senior to him had been executed or murdered or disgraced or gone off in disgust to any safe or semi-safe refuge that they could find.

The alternative to moving the ships from Helsingfors would be their internment by the Germans and the Finns, so Stchasny set to work. The ice was still thick in the Gulf of Finland and in peacetime no one would have thought of trying to move a ship from Helsingfors to Kronstadt until the thaw had set in, when, ordinarily, the passage would have taken about ten hours. On this occasion some of the ships took as many days, many of them under tow. The temperature was —12°C., and, as the ships steamed on, accidents, groundings and collisions occurred and every now and again individual warships opened fire on the ice-breakers to spur on their labours. Finally the whole convoy of 170 ships was brought to safety, Stchasny in the *Kretchet*, coming last to make sure that no one was left behind. Immediately afterwards he was arrested on a charge of 'having made himself popular by performing an heroic deed with a view to using this popularity later against the power of the Soviets'. He was court martialled and shot. Even now, although we have become accustomed to a great deal of horror, the Stchasny affair has the look of having been murder—and not even a judicial one.

An indication of the cross-currents which at that time were influencing the Baltic fleet and its relations with Moscow, to which the Bolshevik Government had transferred itself, is given by a former officer of the Imperial Russian and British navies, D. Fedotoff-White, in his book *The Growth of the Red Army*.[1] The writer recalls having discussed with Stchasny on the ice in Helsingfors harbour in the early weeks of 1918 the situation before the Baltic fleet had been taken to safety. Stchasny said that in his opinion the Bolsheviks were German agents who wanted to hand over the fleet so that it might be used against the Allies. However, Stchasny went on, something would happen to stop them, and the Baltic fleet having made the Bolshevik Revolution possible would also bring Bolshevik power to an end.

Another officer of considerable ability, although much junior to Stchasny, who had the same views as his of the Bolsheviks' motives, was Lieutenant Lisanevitch, captain of the destroyer *Kapitan 2R Isilmetiev*, who secured the agreement of the officers and men of the Destroyer Division to a scheme whereby the Baltic fleet, to prevent the Bolsheviks handing it over to the Germans, should seize power and proclaim a dictatorship. The Destroyer Division sent emissaries to the Cruiser Division and the Battleship Division to obtain their support. They failed, and, of course, the authorities immediately tried to arrest Lisanevitch. A boarding party of Bolshevik sailors were sent on board the *Isilmetiev* and threatened her crew with live hand grenades at the ready if they would not say where Lisanevitch was. This the crew refused to do; the destroyer was searched thoroughly three times without success. Three days later Lisanevitch was able to leave his hide-out on board and make his way safely to Archangel and freedom.

Once the Baltic fleet had left Helsingfors the British submarines

[1] Princeton University Press, 1944.

there were scuttled, as were the four Russian submarines previously based at Hangö,

During February and March the German landings in Finland took place. At Helsingfors matters had been so well prepared in advance that, within half an hour of the German warships entering the harbour, the Finnish White Guard was organised and in possession of the key points of the capital. Towards the end of these operations, however, the German navy suffered its heaviest loss of the whole war in the Baltic when the battleship *Rheinland* ran aground on April 11th off Lagskär in the Åland Islands. She was eventually towed off and went back to Germany, but she was so badly damaged as not to be worth repair.

In the same way that the Germans were using the Russian collapse to consolidate their grip on the Baltic states which they had secured by the Treaty of Brest Litovsk, they also went ahead to take possession of the vast wheatfields and the nominally independent Republic of the Ukraine, as well as the naval bases of Sevastopol and Nicolaiev. By this time the decomposition of the Black Sea fleet, which had been staved off by Kolchak and some of his officers, seemed about to become complete. To get the ships away from the Germans the order was given by Moscow to sail them from Sevastopol to Novorossisk, and the need actually to do something gave Vice-Admiral N. P. Sablin, the nominal commander-in-chief, an opportunity to re-establish something of his authority in the same way that Stchasny had done in the Baltic. Happily Sablin was to avoid Stchasny's fate.

By April 3rd, as soon as it was clear that the only troops available to defend the Crimea against the Germans and the Ukrainians were a few hundred Red Guards, with groups of Chinese and Tartars, the move to Novorossisk began. In the face of the enemy Sablin was begged to resume command of the fleet. With hesitation he agreed, subject to the stipulation that his orders be obeyed. His first order pronounced that the fleet was henceforth Ukrainian and the big ships hoisted the Ukrainian flag—although others replied by hoisting the Red flag and yet others stuck to the Tsarist colours. But the Germans wanted Sablin and the fleet, so that its technical change of nationality did not cause them to halt their advance, and on April 12th their patrols were in the neighbourhood of Sevastopol. A day of argument and indecision followed, with the two big ships training their triple twelve-inch turrets on some of the destroyers to persuade them to prepare to leave harbour. Finally, at midnight, some with good grace and some with bad, fourteen destroyers left and four remained behind with the *Volya* and *Svobodnaya Rossia* and Sablin.

The destroyers that had left, after helping in the evacuation of the other Russian ports and the Russian-occupied parts of the Turkish coast, arrived at Novorossisk, and found that inland from that place were the first elements of the White Counter-Revolutionary army.

Negotiations about Sablin and the fleet went on for another month. Finally, learning on the night of May 14th that the German patrols were entering the northern part of Sevastopol, Sablin decided that the big ships would have to go. There was a last-minute hitch because the men in charge of the boom defence at the entrance to the harbour had disappeared and there was no one to open the gate to let the ships out. In the end a rear-admiral, a captain and various junior officers went down the harbour in the rear-admiral's private motor launch and worked the gate open.

The *Volya* and *Svobodnaya Rossia* immediately started down the harbour at the best speed they could make, while German artillery ashore opened fire on them. One destroyer, the *Gnievni*, ran aground on her way out of the harbour in the wake of the big ships and was sabotaged, as was another then in dockyard hands, the *Zavetny*.

The rest of the ships of the Black Sea fleet were also to have been put out of action, but the demolition parties told off for that work also disappeared, so that the old battleships and various lesser vessels, still flying the Ukrainian flag, fell intact into German hands. The situation in the Black Sea, and in Russia as a whole, was so confusing and so delicate that nothing was done about them for some weeks.

But at Novorossisk the situation was even more nightmarish. There was a Soviet Republic ashore, which anxiously asked the fleet if it would mind putting down the Red army which was in a state of mutiny; there were refugees from all along the Black Sea literally living on board ships in the harbour; there was the White volunteer army, though not much of it, inland and there was the fleet, which was a counter of enormous value in the hands of anyone who could get it—White, Red, Allied or German. In this way its situation resembled that of the French fleets in the Mediterranean in 1940–2.

But if the Black Sea fleet was the key to much in South Russia, it was at first a very rusty key. Its ships were short of fuel in the first place, while, although the battleships recognised Sablin as their admiral, the destroyers called for an election. However, this parti-cular difficulty was overcome by a unanimous vote of all ships for Sablin, a vote which included the support of the anarchist elements in the fleet.

The diversity of political opinions in the fleet was reflected in the

Volya by the fact that her big-gun turrets were painted different colours in accordance with the different political views of the men who manned them.

Sablin set the seal of his authority on the fleet with an order to all ships to rehoist once more the Cross of St. Andrew and this was done. At the same time it was announced that there would be no more elections. His first concern was to secure the landward defences of Novorossisk, vulnerable to Reds, Whites and Germans. There were no soldiers available, so the job fell to the sailors of the fleet, who next busied themselves successfully securing the liberation of a number of ex-Tsarist officers who had been in prison for several months without any charges having been made against them.

At about this stage the local Bolshevik Government thought it prudent to withdraw into the hinterland and this power vacuum was filled, more or less, by the fleet.

To obtain fuel, parties were sent as far afield as Tsaritsin, now Volgograd and formerly Stalingrad, and enough trainloads of oil were obtained to refuel the fleet before the local Soviet turned off the metaphorical tap. It is not clear whether this was done on the direct order of Lenin and Trotsky in Moscow or not, but certainly the position of the fleet was worrying them. Sablin refused to break with the Soviet Government as many of his officers urged him, but it was clear in Moscow that the fleet was a strong, well-organised force, which at any minute might turn out to be anti-Bolshevik. In the meantime German pressure grew for the internment of Sablin's fleet under their guard at Sevastopol.

As this pressure increased Lenin sent secret orders to Sablin telling him that he might shortly receive an *en clair* message to hand over the fleet to the Germans. If he received this message he was to sink his ships at once. This, of course, had the advantage of cheating the Germans and putting the fleet out of action as a political force, while Sablin got the blame.

It was not the Bolshevik intention, of course, that this plan of Lenin's was exactly what the Allies wanted to have happen. At this time the last of the great German offensives on the Western Front was in progress, but there was no way of telling that it was the last. In addition the battle against the U-boats in the Atlantic was not yet decisively won. Had the Germans received a reinforcement of the two big battleships of the Black Sea fleet, plus its destroyers and submarines, not only would capital ships have to be withdrawn from the Grand Fleet and sent to the Eastern Mediterranean to join those already there watching the *Goeben*, but additional anti-submarine vessels, urgently needed for convoy duty, would also have to be sent to look after them.

On the other hand, as far as the officers of the Black Sea fleet were concerned, there was a feeling that their ships might be the only organised Russian force in existence at the end of the war; it might be able to play an important, or even a decisive part, in determining the future government of Russia—on condition that it continued to exist. Thus a high proportion of these officers urged Sablin to permit the fleet to be interned, whatever the effect on Russia's former allies might be.

Representatives of the whole fleet, officers and ratings alike, held an all-night meeting on board the *Volya*, but nothing was decided. However, a delegate from the merchant ships in harbour made an appearance, criticised Sablin and began to build up a body of opinion which favoured carrying out the secret orders from Moscow. When it came to a vote the squadron was split three ways—450 for scuttling the ships, 900 for taking them to Sevastopol for internment, while there were about 1,000 abstentions. For the time being it was decided to leave Novorossisk and the funds of the squadron were so divided as to give everyone five months' pay in advance.

On the evening of June 28th the acting commander-in-chief, Captain Tikmeniev (Sablin had gone to Moscow), ordered all ships to have steam at one hour's notice from nine o'clock next morning. The two battleships and four destroyers obeyed, the rest of the ships continued to debate and argue and the men who had voted against a return to Sevastopol began to make their way ashore. Crowds gathered around the doubtful ships and urged them not to go. Numbers of men went to the *Volya* and were refused permission to come on board. The *Svobodnaya Rossia* had, however, left her gangway down and a howling crowd swarmed aboard. More meetings took place and, in the midst of it all, her engine-room complement announced that they would not take the ship to sea.

At one o'clock Tikmeniev ordered his ships to leave harbour and anchor in the roadstead. The *Volya* led the way, followed by five destroyers, *Bespokoini*, *Pospechni*, *Derski*, *Jivoi* and *Jarki*, with an armed merchant cruiser. They were pursued out of the harbour by small boats full of demonstrators who continued to harass the crews as best they could.

Finally, that night the *Volya* and the destroyers sailed for Sevastopol, leaving behind the *Svobodnaya Rossia* and nine other destroyers, which were then sunk—the destroyers scuttling themselves, while the *Svobodnaya Rossia* was torpedoed several times by the destroyer *Kertch* and finally sunk. When it arrived at Sevastopol the rest of the fleet was interned, with its old adversary the *Goeben* in attendance, for Sevastopol was a much better-equipped base than Constantinople or any other Turkish port. In the middle of the harbour now lay the *Imperatritza Maria*, afloat once more but upside down, her salvage having been abandoned for lack of technical resources.

The Germans took over immediately, for service in their own fleet, the cruiser *Pamiat Merkuria*, three destroyers and a submarine. Two months later, in September, when an Allied attack on the Dardanelles was thought to be imminent, the *Volya* and more destroyers and submarines were also seized, but they were not ready for sea by the time Germany and Turkey collapsed at the beginning of November. A few days later an Allied fleet, mostly British, at last steamed through the Dardanelles, past Constantinople and into the Black Sea, three years too late.

A little later, in November 1918, another British force entered the Baltic, and based on Reval set to work to protect the new Baltic republics of Estonia, Latvia and Lithuania from the Germans who had occupied them and the Bolsheviks who wished to do so. First blood in the naval part of this three-cornered struggle went to the Russians, for the British light cruiser *Cassandra* struck a mine and sank while bombarding the Russian positions at Narva on the night of December 4th–5th, 1918.

The Russians followed up this success by sending two destroyers, supported by the *Petropavlovsk*, to attack the Estonian positions from the sea. The two Bolshevik destroyers surrendered almost at once and the *Petropavlovsk* withdrew. The two destroyers were turned over to the new Estonian navy, where they served for many years before being sold to Peru. Their crews, on the other hand, were exchanged for a number of prisoners taken by the Soviet.

After this, part of the British squadron went to Helsingfors until the spring and the rest occupied itself with securing the withdrawal of the German forces behind the 1914 frontiers of the Reich, in collaboration with Paderewski, the great pianist, who was temporarily President of Poland. When the summer of 1919 came it was soon clear that the British Government had no intention of keeping a force in the Baltic indefinitely. The country was tired of war, men wanted to go home and the Labour Party and the trade-union movement were giving the Russian Communist movement powerful support on the British home front. When the British withdrew what was left of the Russian fleet would command the Gulf of Finland and be able to demolish the new Baltic states.

As a kind of reconnaissance in May the *Petropavlovsk*, much bigger than any Allied ships in the neighbourhood, came out from Kronstadt with the *Oleg*, but did not attempt to attack, and in the following month the *Oleg*, while on patrol, was attacked and sunk by a 55-feet-long British coastal motor boat (C.M.B.) commanded by Lieutenant A. W. S. Agar, R.N., who received the Victoria Cross for the action.

In order to neutralise the Russian ships a force of eight C.M.B.s was ordered to attack the Russian big ships in Kronstadt harbour. On the night of August 18th, just before the C.M.B.s were due to make their attack, British aircraft appeared over Kronstadt flying low —they thus attracted the attention upwards of the Russian defences, while at the same time the noise of the aircraft engines drowned the similar noise of the engines of the C.M.B.s. Under this cover three boats, dodging the destroyer *Gavryil* on patrol, broke into the harbour and torpedoed the *Pamiat Azova*, *Andrei Pervosvanni* and *Petropavlovsk*— three torpedoes, three hits. The only big Russian ship left undamaged was the *Rurik*, but the first three boats in were the only ones to get a chance to fire their torpedoes. The others were either sunk (three in all were lost) or broke down on their way to the target.

All three of the Russian ships hit sank in shallow water and were afterwards raised, but they were out of action for several months— some of them for years.

There were other losses by both sides. The British submarine *L 55* had been sunk by Russian destroyers on June 4th, while towards the end of the campaign the Russians lost the destroyer *Azard*, torpedoed, and the *Gavryil* and *Constantin*, mined. On the other hand, the British destroyer *Vittoria* was torpedoed and sunk by a Russian submarine on September 1st and her sister ship, the *Verulam*, was lost by mine on the night of September 3rd–4th.

Nine years later the *L 55* was salved by the Russians and, after being refitted, served in the Russian fleet for many years. On raising the submarine the Russians returned the bodies of her crew to Britain, an act of international courtesy rare in the Soviet-British relations of those days.

When the British fleet withdrew from the Baltic the White Russian army under General Yudenitch was almost in the suburbs of Petrograd and still advancing. Naturally the White Russians looked with dismay at the disappearance of the British and felt that they were being left in the lurch. It never seems to have been explained to any of the White Russian forces that the Allies were not in Russia to defeat the Bolsheviks, though they had no objection to the White Russians doing so; from this fact endless suffering and misunderstanding came, misunderstanding which is still alive amongst Russians, British, French and Americans to this day.

On October 22nd, 1919, the Red Army launched a counter-attack against Yudenitch and completely defeated him. Credit for this victory was given, by himself, to Stalin, who was particularly pleased with the way he ordered and carried out a landing in Yudenitch's rear, the Russian troops going ashore from a scratch collection of steamers and barges at Krasnaya Gorka, on the mainland south-west of Kronstadt. Stalin reported to Lenin:

> Have captured Krasnaya Gorka . . . naval specialists assert that the taking of Krasnaya Gorka from the sea amounts to tearing asunder all naval science. I can only bemoan the so-called science—in the future will act in same way.

That a landing from the sea behind an enemy flank did not seem an obvious thing to do, granted that material resources were available, goes to show a somewhat low level of the ideas at that time of both Stalin and his 'naval specialists'.

The spring of 1919 in the Black Sea saw a dashing Bolshevik advance on Odessa and Sevastopol. Sevastopol was saved for another twenty months, but Odessa fell briefly into Communist hands. During this period of alarm ten of the remaining submarines in the Black Sea were scuttled. This was done at the insistence of the British, who feared the possibility of having to conduct operations in the Black Sea in the face of hostile submarines. At the same time all the old pre-dreadnoughts and some other obsolete warships had their engines destroyed.

Of the modern ships, the *Volya* was taken over by the British with a couple of destroyers, while the French had the seaplane carrier *Alma* and two destroyers. The Italians and the Greeks each took one destroyer. The way in which these ships were taken over caused great offence to the White Russians, but they do not seem to have been able to provide Russian crews for them at that time.

The headlong advance of the Reds to the Black Sea was followed by an equally headlong retreat, so that by October 1919 the Whites under Deniken were at Orel, within 200 miles of Moscow. A Bolshevik counter-attack followed; there was another helter-skelter across the Ukraine, and by the spring of 1920 the White Russians, now commanded by Baron Wrangel, held little more than the Crimea.

At this stage the Bolsheviks turned aside to attempt the capture of Warsaw. This gave the White Russians a respite of which no advantage could be taken, partly because, in the summer of 1920, the

British Government told the White Russians that they would be unable to give them any more assistance.

Warsaw, however, resisted the Bolsheviks, who withdrew, cut their losses on the Polish front, rounded on Wrangel and, in December 1920, took the Crimea. Wrangel's followers, men, women and children, numbering 130,000, were crowded on board 126 ships including even lightships—and anything else that could float. The Black Sea fleet, which had been returned by the Allies, went off to Bizerta, where the ships were interned: *General Alexiev* (ex *Volya*), *Georgi Pobiedonosetz*, *General Kornilov*,[1] ten destroyers, *Cerigo*, *Stchaslivi*, *Gnevni*, *Derski*, *Kapitan Saken*, *Jarki*, *Zvonki*, *Zorki*, *Bespokoini* and *Pilki*, and five submarines, *Utka*, *Tulen*, *Gagara*, *Burevestnik* and *Orlan*.

On the charity of the French Government the squadron remained, with parts of its crews and refugees, at Bizerta until November 1924, short of money, food and clothes. Every so often rumours and wild hopes ran through the ships—once it was reported that the ships and everybody who wanted to go with them were being transferred to Yugoslavia. The wives and daughters immediately set to work sewing great Yugoslav flags—and then that bubble of hope burst.

Finally, when the French Government recognised the Soviet Union, the White Russians were ordered to leave their ships for good. The submarines ran their diesels at full power for the last time and the flag of St. Andrew—blue cross on a white field—was hauled down, for ever as far as we can see now nearly forty years later.

The ships were left to rot unattended for the next decade and then they began to be broken up. The last of them, the *General Alexiev* (ex-*Volya*, ex-*Imperator Alexander III*) was sold for scrap just a couple of years before the outbreak of World War II.

---

[1] As a reflection of the vicissitudes of the ships of the Russian navy during the first years of the present century there is the fact that the *General Kornilov* had had her name changed no fewer than five times, four of the changes having been due to political upheavals. She had begun life in 1902 as the *Kagul*; for no political reason that can be distinguished this was changed almost at once to *Otchakov*. In 1906 she was involved in the Black Sea mutinies and her name was changed back to *Kagul*. When the Revolution came the Red authorities gave her back the name under which she had mutinied, but naturally the White Russians undid this and called her *Kagul* again before renaming her *General Kornilov*, after the White general.

Finally therefore this ship ended up with the following style: *General Kornilov*, ex-*Kagul*, ex-*Otchakov*, ex-*Kagul*, ex-*Otchakov*, ex-*Kagul*.

Another ship which suffered nearly as many changes—and in addition flew five flags—was the destroyer *Spartak*, captured by the British in December 1918. She had been laid down for the Imperial Navy as *Kapitan 2 R Kingsbergen*, was renamed *Mikula Maklay* under Kerensky and *Spartak* by the Bolsheviks; she was then captured by the British, presented by them to the Estonians and named *Wambola*, finally being sold in 1933 to Peru, where she received her fifth name *Almirante Villar*.

CHAPTER XVII

LAUNCHING THE RED FLEET
1921–1941

AT the beginning of 1921 the Revolution and the Civil War were virtually over. The country was economically and physically in ruins, and millions were dying of hunger, but war, for the first time for seven years, seemed at an end. The Russians, who had been weary to death of war in 1917 and had then fought on for another three years against each other and against foreigners as well, at last seemed to reach the goal of peace, to obtain which they had destroyed the fabric of their country.

Suddenly, in March, it became known that the Russian Revolution was destroying not its children, according to historic pattern, but its parents, the Kronstadt sailors. A rising had taken place in that ice-locked base, and the Bolsheviks were mobilising great strength in order to repress it.

Trouble had broken out on March 2nd. Trotsky had appointed Raskolnikov as one of the heads of the political control of the Baltic fleet, with orders to destroy the powers of the ships' committees or Soviets, appoint officers whose orders were to be carried out implicitly and commissars who were to look after the officers. The powers of the commissars meant little to the lower deck. As far as they were concerned officers were back with much the same authority as they had had in the Tsar's day, and, in fact, they were nearly all the same men—former Tsarist officers or promoted Tsarist petty officers. At the same time there was much grumbling amongst the workers in Kronstadt, who thought that the strict discipline of the Civil War should be relaxed so that they might be able to enjoy the fruits of revolution and of peace.

The first sign of discontent had appeared at Kronstadt on February 28th, when the crews of the *Petropavlovsk* and *Sevastopol* met on board the former ship and passed a resolution calling for free elections, with freedom of speech and freedom of the Press (for Anarchists and Left Socialists only), freedom of assembly, the liberation of political prisoners who were members of Socialist parties, the creation of a committee to review the cases of those held in prisons and concentration camps and various other concessions which would mean the loosening of Communist control.

The Russians at Sea

But, as Dr. George Katkov points out in his study of the rising:[1]

The sailors did not for a moment think of breaking away from the Soviet Union and of establishing a border government similar to the counter-revolutionary governments of the White generals . . . They considered themselves to be a political pressure group and not conspirators.

After this, on March 1st, the only solidly Communist body in Kronstadt, 200 students attending the Party School, left hastily across the ice for Krasnaya Gorka. The Kronstadt rebels started to look for allies and thought that they had found them among the personnel of the nearest naval air station, at Oranienbaum, but within five hours a party of Kursanty—cadets from the Communist officers' schools— had arrived from Petrograd and extinguished the Oranienbaum mutiny.

Thus the Kronstadt rebels had to fall back on their own resources and their 140 guns, of which the biggest were the twenty-four twelve-inch mounted by the *Petropavlovsk* and *Sevastopol*. These ships, however, were lying alongside each other, frozen in the ice, so that each blocked part of the field of fire of the other.

It was an enormous handicap for the rebels that the ships were thus imprisoned in the ice. An attempt was made to seize an ice-breaker in Petrograd which might have been able to free the two battleships and some of the other vessels in Kronstadt harbour, but this failed, as did attempts by a party of 200 delegates to propagandise the cause of Kronstadt in Petrograd and nearby towns.

On March 6th the Petrograd Communists began to round up the relatives of all the men known to be in Kronstadt, and carried out leaflet raids from aircraft urging the rebels to surrender. This the leaders refused to do; they also refused to listen to those of their followers who urged upon them the necessity of striking first, before the authorities upon the mainland had time to gather their forces. They believed that they could not hope to succeed with an offensive across the ice against the much stronger Communist forces, but they did hope that within a month, and perhaps sooner, the ice would melt. Then the *Petropavlovsk* and *Sevastopol* could leave harbour and steam up to Petrograd, to be met, they believed, by joyous crowds of sympathetic workers.

On the other hand, for fear of the ice melting the Communists did not wish to risk delay by trying to starve the island and, after a

[1] Published in *St. Antony's Papers, No. 6. Soviet Affairs*, no. 2, p. 27, edited by David Footman, Chatto & Windus, London; Frederick A. Praeger, New York, 1959.

preliminary exchange of bombardments on March 7th, launched an infantry attack across the ice next day in a snowstorm. This failed.

The commander of the attack, Tukhachevsky, at the age of twenty-seven, was a general. Four years earlier, when the Revolution broke out, he had been a lieutenant of the Imperial Guard. As a leader of Red armies he had gained great victories against Kolchak in Siberia, against Wrangel in the south and had come within an ace of taking Warsaw in the summer of 1920. In 1937 he was arrested and shot, the most prominent of Red soldiers to fall a victim to Stalin's first great purge.

Tukhachevsky's second offensive against Kronstadt began on March 16th, with a bombardment of the rebel positions; at nightfall the infantry attacks opened over the ice. Patches of fog hung about so that the attacking groups, in great compact blocks, were out of sight within a few minutes of leaving the shore; later they passed in and out of the fog, sometimes lit by the beams of searchlights, sometimes unable to see more than a few yards ahead despite the diffused glow of the searchlight beams.

In the midst of the noise of artillery, automatic weapons and rifle fire, heavier roaring sounds were heard. While the main attack had come from the south side of the Gulf another force from the north side was also advancing against Kotlin island, and this force, losing its way in the fog and mist, came upon a minefield frozen into the ice. The great weight of the men detonated a few of the mines and the explosion of these set the rest off by countermining action and the night was full of the flashes and sounds of exploding mines, the crash of breaking ice and the shouts of the men who found themselves in the freezing water.

But the attack from the south reached the Petrograd Gate of Kronstadt at about five o'clock in the morning of March 17th, crossed the old moat and began to fight its way through the streets of the town, led by volunteer 'shock troops'.

Fighting went on throughout the day. At four o'clock that afternoon the rebels counter-attacked and very nearly drove the Bolsheviks from the town. Only the arrival of artillery over the ice answering a SOS in the nick of time saved the Reds. Attacking once again, they broke into the prison and liberated 300 diehard comrades who had refused to join in the insurrection. Next morning, at daylight, the rebels could see that their situation was fatal and they began to surrender. On board the *Petropavlovsk* and *Sevastopol* demolition charges were placed in position to scuttle the ships, but before they could be fired the triumphant Bolsheviks swept on board, seized the ships and cut the fuses. Those rebels who could fled across the ice to Finnish territory, and resistance continued in Fort Todleben alone. Finally, at midnight on March 18th–19th, this position capitulated.

Altogether, it is reported by Soviet sources that the garrison of Kronstadt lost some 700 killed and 2,500 wounded, while the storming Bolsheviks lost 600 killed and about 1,000 wounded. The losses of the garrison, however, in all probability, do not include those who were killed after they had surrendered.

Mr. Isaac Deutscher in *The Prophet Unarmed*,[1] the second of his two books on Trotsky, states that Lenin's reaction to the Kronstadt rising, after it had been put down, was to order the disbandment and scuttling of the entire fleet, on the grounds that it was troublesome, useless and consumed an unjustifiably large part of the country's resources in men and equipment. Trotsky, however, according to Mr. Deutscher, intervened and succeeded in persuading Lenin to change his mind. Taking the fleet under his own wing, Trotsky then began to pull it together and, at the same time, to secure technical assistance for it from German sources. This assistance does not appear to have materialised until five years later, but the first bridges appear to have been built at the time of the signing of the Russo-German Treaty of Rapallo in 1922.

When spring came in 1921 nearly all of the ships of the Russian navy still in existence were out of commission and badly in need of the refits which they had gone without for the past four or five years. Those of their crews who remained were divided by politics and united by a strong desire to go home.

Ashore the Civil War was over and so were Russia's wars against her neighbours, although it was not until Christmas Day 1922 that the Japanese withdrew from Vladivostock and not until May 1925 that they left northern Sakhalin. When this happened the *de facto* boundaries of the Soviet Union assumed, at last, the form which they were to have until 1939.

In 1922 the Moscow Government began to re-form the Red navy. Since 1919 very little had happened afloat; some light craft had been operational during 1920, while in November of that year the behaviour of the surviving Red submarines in the Black Sea had been described as 'threatening' by the British Government and Moscow had been accordingly warned that they should not interfere with the evacuation of Wrangel's forces from the Crimea.

The first definite step to be taken in the remaking of the Russian

[1] Oxford University Press, 1959.

navy was the decision that 3,000 Komsomols—Young Communists— were to report to the various naval schools for training as seamen. The choice of these young men, the most carefully indoctrinated of young Russians, was natural enough after the various shifts in the opinions of the lower-deck ratings through the years from 1917 to 1921—through Tsarism to democracy, to anarchism, to Bolshevism and to mutual self-destruction in the Kronstadt rising.

Altogether, during the four years 1923–7, 10,000 Komsomols were directed into the navy. They provided the vital cadres upon which the fleet of the future was to be built, although to begin with their first task was very often to empty their ships of the tons of filth which had accumulated on board over a period of five years or more in harbour. In addition, for the first time since 1917 the navy was reinforced by new tonnage as the furthest advanced of the ships building at the outbreak of the Revolution were finally completed.

Re-forming the fleet was very slow work. In 1922 the first exercises since the end of the war were held in the Gulf of Finland. By 1923 in the Baltic there were in commission one battleship, the eternal *Petropavlovsk*, now renamed *Marat*, five destroyers and six submarines. In the Black Sea at this time there were six destroyers and eighteen submarines, on the Volga and in the Caspian eleven destroyers and eight submarines, all brought from the Baltic via the inland water-ways, and in the White Sea a single submarine.

A German report of this time speaks of a naval air service of 250 planes, and as this was just at the beginning of the period of Soviet-German collaboration in the field of armaments, the figure was probably accurate. However, although the Germans worked closely with the Russian army and air force in secret violation of the Treaty of Versailles, there was much less of such collaboration in naval matters.

In February 1924 the Red navy had made only a very humble beginning to a come-back, but in that month the Russians showed that they were setting their sights high. The major naval powers, then the United Kingdom, the United States, Japan, France and Italy, had agreed to limit their capital-ship and aircraft-carrier strength by the Washington Treaty of 1922, while the strength of the German navy had been laid down by the Treaty of Versailles.

The remaining naval powers met in a conference at Rome to try to apply the principle of the reduction and limitations of naval armaments to themselves, and at this meeting the Russians demanded a capital ship tonnage of 490,000—nearly equal to that of Britain and the United States. In reply to the protests occasioned by this demand

The Russians at Sea

the Russians agreed to accept 280,000 tons, provided that Wrangel's ships at Bizerta were returned to them, that no foreign states were allowed to send warships into the Baltic or the Black Sea and that the Straits of Korea were demilitarised. At that time the Russians possessed only three capital ships of a total of 70,000 tons. The demand for a vast increase in permitted tonnage made disarmament discussions impossible and the conference broke up.

The refurbishing of old ships was continued, including that of the *Sevastopol*, now renamed *Pariskaia Kommuna*. In 1925 the most elaborate manoeuvres so far held took place in the Gulf of Finland and were marked by a series of fairly minor accidents—a torpedo boat was lost on a mine, there was a gunburst on board a cruiser, a couple of collisions and a submarine was damaged by bottoming too hard.

In the spring and summer of 1926 Russo-German arms talks had got so far as to permit the dispatch of a German naval mission to Russia led by Admiral Spindler, the official historian of the U-boat campaign of World War I. The Germans were asked to furnish plans of the most successful types of submarines as well as details of operational experience and the service of selected experts. They visited the show ships of the Baltic fleet, which turned out to be the *Marat*, whose captain was described by the Germans as 'a sound torpedo coxswain type', the destroyer *Engels* (ex *Desna*) and the submarine *Batrak* (ex *Vepr*).

Apart from submarines the principal Russian interest was in designs for motor torpedo boats and for aircraft launching catapults. There was a certain amount of discussion of possible Russo-German co-operation in the event of either country finding themselves at war with a Franco-Polish coalition in the Baltic and the Mediterranean. As Mr. Erickson points out in *The Soviet High Command*,[1] it was never in Germany's interest to build up a naval rival in the Baltic. Nevertheless the Russians obtained various sets of U-boat plans, the most important of which were those of the B-III type, one of the most successful designs for a conventional submarine ever produced. Two hundred of them were ordered in the First World War, and the design was then developed to form the Type VII, more than 600 of which formed the backbone of the U-boat fleet in the Second War. In the meantime a variant of the design was built in Russia—first known as the 'N' class, and nick-named, 'Nemka' ('German girl') and later as the 'S' class.

Later in 1928–9, when the existence became known of the German

[1] Published by Macmillan, London; St Martin's, New York, 1962.

design for the 'pocket-battleships' of the *Deutschland* class, the Russians asked to see them as well.

In 1929 Soviet warships for the first time visited foreign ports, going to both Germany and Italy. In January 1931, in preparation for the Disarmament Conference which met in the following year at Geneva, the Soviet Union published, for the first time, an official return of the strength of its fleet—three capital ships (*Marat, Pariskaia Kommuna* and *Oktiabrskaia Revolutia*, formerly *Gangut*), two cruisers, *Tchervonaia Ukraina* (ex *Admiral Nakhimov*) and *Profintern* (ex *Svietlana*), seventeen destroyers, sixteen submarines and a number of training ships, which included two of the old cruisers—*Avrora* and *Komintern* (ex *Pamiat Merkuria*).

The *Pariskaia Kommuna* had been sent to the Black Sea in 1930; on the way there she met a detachment of the British Atlantic fleet and salutes were exchanged between British and Russian warships for the first time since the Revolution.

The year 1933 saw Hitler in power and the failure of the Geneva Disarmament Conference. It also saw the beginning of talks between the Russians and French and Italian naval architects and shipbuilders on the possibility of laying down new ships for the Russian navy. These were to be the first major warships begun since 1916, other than submarines, which, by 1936, according to German sources, already reached a total of 116 boats, nearly all of post-war construction.

From 1935 dates the first of the big destroyers of the *Leningrad* class (2,900 tons), which showed many signs of French design. But the bigger ships which were now coming along were of Italian inspiration, built in Russia—except for one destroyer—to Italian plans and under Italian supervision, although machinery for some was manufactured in the United Kingdom—the manufacturers being supplied with blank plans of the ships, showing only the dimensions of the machinery spaces and a 'torpedo compartment'. The first of these was the 7,000-ton cruiser *Kirov*, which has been followed by over twenty heavy cruisers of the *Chapaev* and *Sverdlov* classes and similar designs which are in existence at the present day.

The fact that the Communist and Fascist régimes were working hand in hand on this project is, to this day, somewhat piquant, as is the fact that when the Italian-built Soviet destroyer *Tashkent* was launched at Livorno in 1938 she was blessed by a Catholic priest and flew the Italian flag.

This rebirth of an important Russian surface fleet under the personal auspices of Stalin was accompanied by the creation of the first Soviet admirals—though for the sake of the pure Communists they were known as 'flagmen'. One of the first of these flagmen was Kuznetzov, who was to be responsible for the Russian fleet for years after the end of World War II. Commander-in-chief in the Pacific at the time of the 1937–8 purges, he was the only fleet commander to survive. Another flagman of 1935 was Viktorov, who had been commander-in-chief in the Baltic and had been removed owing to an indiscretion of a political nature committed by his wife. After this he had been given a chance to rehabilitate himself in the Pacific which he had been able to take.

In 1937 the German Minister of Defence, General von Blomberg, announced that Russia would soon have the biggest submarine fleet in the world, about 150 boats, and it was about this time that priority was given to the building of some fifty submarines for service in the Far East. Relations between Russia and Japan became so bad that during the next year an undeclared war flickered up and down the frontier in Siberia between Soviet-held territory and that occupied by the Japanese.

In the meantime, during 1937 events in the Mediterranean showed strikingly the importance of seapower in an age which half expected its wars to be won by aircraft and tanks alone.

From the outbreak of the Spanish Civil War in 1936 the Germans and Italians, in violation of international law, sent troops, ships, weapons and supplies to aid the rebel forces under General Franco. The British and French Governments proclaimed and practised the doctrine of non-intervention, while the Russians aided as best they could the legitimate Republican and democratic Government.

This went on until the spring of 1937, when a Russian merchant ship, the *Komsomol*, carrying a large number of crated fighter aircraft, was sunk by a unit of the rebel navy. This showed the Russians clearly that, unless they were prepared to sail convoys which could fight their way through the Mediterranean from the Black Sea, it would be impossible to send further war materials to the Republicans on a large scale. From that time, although Russian, Spanish and foreign Communists alike did what they could to strengthen the Republicans and, of course, the Communists, in Spain, there could never be any question of material assistance to the legitimate Government from Russia on the same massive scale as that which was being received by Franco from Hitler and Mussolini.

Stalin drew his own conclusions and the expansion of the Soviet navy entered another phase, with plans for building capital ships of the greatest size and power, as well as very large cruisers to counter the German pocket-battleships of the *Deutschland* class.

The three capital ships ordered were improvements of the Italian *Vittorio Veneto* class of 35,000 nominal tons, actually a good deal larger, with nine sixteen-inch guns instead of nine fifteen-inch.

The large armoured cruisers would have been about 22,000 tons, each armed with two of the triple fourteen-inch turrets from the *Kinburn* class battle cruisers laid down in 1912.

At the same time as these designs were selected attempts were also made, without success, to persuade the Americans to make available their latest capital-ship designs. A similar attempt to obtain assistance in the construction of the biggest warships was made to Hitler during the period of Russo-German rapprochement during 1939–41. The Russians wished to buy the 10,000-ton cruisers *Prinz Eugen* and *Seydlitz*, as well as the eight twin sixteen-inch turrets intended for the two battleships of the improved *Bismarck* class. In the end all that they could obtain was the cruiser *Lützow*, a sister ship of the *Prinz Eugen* and *Seydlitz*, but without her main armament of eight-inch guns, which had been taken by the German army.

The hull of the *Krasnaya Ukraina*, one of the 35,000-ton ships, was captured half completed by the Germans at Nicolaiev in 1941. Machinery for one of the vessels of this class was ordered in Switzerland, and before it was ready for delivery war had started between Russia and Germany and the machinery remained in Switzerland. Fearing a German attempt to buy it and install it in the captured hull, the British Government made a pre-emptive purchase and it remains in packing-cases in Switzerland to this day.

At no stage during the planning of the Soviet fleet was any attention given to the building of aircraft carriers—presumably Stalin, like Mussolini, thought that this type of warship could be disregarded by a country which was planning to conduct its main naval operations in enclosed waters, whether of the Baltic, the Black Sea or the Mediterranean. In fact, as far as Mussolini was concerned, possession of carriers would have been the only thing that could possibly have saved the Italian surface fleet from its eventual end. This was tardily recognised, so that an attempt to provide carriers by converting two large liners was made—too late; but there has never been any definite news of a Russian carrier.

Bit by bit, as the Soviet navy developed during the 1930s from a collection of obsolete survivors of war, revolution and civil war to the beginnings of an important fleet, there developed also a doctrine for its use in time of war, everything, of course, justified by reference to whatever was the current Communist teaching.

This development was described in an important article in the

Journal of the Royal United Services Institution for August 1935 by Mr. Fedotov-White, who pointed out how teachings had varied as personalities and ideas changed within the Kremlin.

At the beginning of the Soviet régime Trotsky had said to the Eleventh Congress of the Russian Communist Party:

> How can one develop war practice on the basis of Marxian methods? This would be similar to the evolution on Marxian lines of a theory of architecture or a veterinary text-book.

But once Trotsky was out of the way, Soviet thinkers started to do just what he had advised them not to do. Thus A. P. Alexandrov, writing in the *Morskoi Sbornik*, ended up *A Critical Analysis of the Theory of the Command of the Seas* with the rousing conclusion: 'Down with the doctrine of the command of the seas!'

His reasoning was fairly clear. Any war in which she was engaged the Soviet Union would win. As she did not have a navy strong enough to enforce command of the seas, the war would be won without it; therefore it did not matter.

In 1930 Muklevitch, then Chief Commissar, a fat, sturdy, round-faced man who perished in the purges seven years later, outlined the very limited role planned for the navy at the time:

> In war the fleet would accompany the army during its advance and it would not be guided in its activities by lessons drawn from the study of the Battle of Jutland, because it would not seek to solve its problems by an open sea encounter with the enemy's fleet, but would carry on a 'small war' relying on minefields, submarines and naval aircraft, as well as on a superior knowledge of the theatre of war.

In other words, nothing more was judged possible than coastal operations in the Baltic and Black Sea. What would happen if the Red army, instead of advancing along the enemy coast, withdrew into the heart of Russia, as had, after all, happened in 1812 and in 1915, was not mentioned.

However, as Mr. Fedotov-White pointed out in his article, the development of Russia's industrial potential made a much more ambitious shipbuilding programme possible and more ambitious plans for future war as well.

This 're-thinking' of the role of the Soviet navy in war was carried out in a smoke screen of denunciation of 'bourgeois' theories of naval warfare, and it was interspersed with such glimpses of the obvious as the statement, in 1932, that 'the naval forces of the Red Army of Workers and Peasants would employ mixed tactics of surface, submarine and air'.

But Mr. Fedotov-White commented:

One is inclined to think that the Marxist-Leninist version of naval doctrine is merely a rationalisation in terms of Marxian dialectics of a solution already arrived at by the leaders of the young Soviet school without the assistance of that theory, and that as the Soviet navy is not the only one moving in that direction one hesitates very much to call it Soviet or Communist. One is rather inclined to consider it merely an intelligent, modern answer to the peculiar geographical as well as industrial conditions of the Soviet Union.

But as the Soviet navy was beginning to reach a material strength which might make it an important factor in the Second World War, the purges dealt it a very heavy blow, one from which it had not recovered by the time of the German attack in June 1941.

Amidst the great purge of the services which followed the arrest and execution of Tukhachevsky, just about all the senior officers of the Red navy disappeared. Very few survivors of these men have been heard of since, and it must be supposed that nearly all of them lost their lives, either before a firing squad or in a prison camp.

The immediate sequel in the navy was a mass promotion of junior officers to take the place of those who had been liquidated. Those making the new appointments to flag rank were obliged to dip deep down among the lists of officers who were of rank equivalent to that of lieutenant-commanders or commanders. In theory, of course, this was no bad thing. Many junior naval officers were appointed to command of destroyers and submarines within a year or so of leaving the naval school, and this probably did very little harm—young British and U.S. reserve officers of good quality showed themselves perfectly suitable for command after very few years at sea, but the question of the Russian senior officers, the flag officers, was a different one.

In the first place, promotion to flag rank came without the new admirals having had any experience at all and in the second place, even more important, was the shattering effect on morale of the Tukhachevsky purge. Senior—and junior—officers disappeared entirely in great numbers because of political charges brought against them. It is hard to believe that the Russian officers who survived the purges of 1937–8 really accepted the fact that their comrades and commanders whom they knew well had actually been engaged in a vast secret conspiracy to overthrow the régime. Everyone, however innocent, must have felt that he might be next to go. People with blameless service records disappeared, but the avoidance of mistakes might at least offer some prospect of avoiding the same fate, so that there was a very high premium on taking no risks.

As far as lack of experience in flag rank was concerned it is true that the Russo-German war at sea about to open was not one for squadron and fleet tactics, but there was nevertheless a need for qualities of experienced command and leadership, these things which can never be improvised save by genius.

In addition to this lack of experience among the officers there was also the same lack of experience in the crews from which they had suffered in the Russo-Japanese War and the First World War. They had almost no deep-sea experience, no long cruises and no feeling of being at home on the sea—the essential condition which Makarov had laid down forty years previously for the successful waging of naval war.

CHAPTER XVIII

SECOND WORLD WAR

1941–1945

EVER since the foundation of the Soviet State its leaders had warned their followers against the dangers of an unprovoked attack against the Soviet Union by one or more of the capitalist countries. Nevertheless, the German attack on June 22nd, 1941, found the Russians as completely unprepared as they had been at Port Arthur. And this was not for want of warning. Not only had Stalin been warned by Churchill, he had also been warned by his own naval intelligence authorities of what might happen.

The first worrying symptom which had been picked up was the fact that, at the end of May, the German naval mission supervising the completion at Leningrad of the cruiser *Tallin* (ex *Lützow*) was withdrawn. Then, on June 16th, the Germans stopped the sailing of their merchant ships to Russian ports and prohibited Russian ships from leaving German-controlled ports.

Two days earlier German minelayers and escort vessels had left the ports of the Reich and secretly taken up position among the lonely islands at the entrance to the Gulf of Finland.

When war between Russia and Germany did begin the German moves at sea were of an entirely novel kind, dictated by the fact that all the conventional German surface warships and nearly all the U-boats were occupied against the British navy. On the other hand, the Russians were believed to have in the Baltic two old battleships (*Marat* and *Oktiabrskaia Revolutia*), two modern cruisers (*Kirov* and *Maxim Gorki*), forty-one destroyers, old and new, nearly 100 submarines and over 100 motor torpedo boats. In addition, there were under construction for the Baltic fleet a very large cruiser, three *Chapaev* class cruisers, twelve destroyers and about fifty submarines.

Against these the Germans could only set their own motor torpedo boats, known to them as S-boats (*Schnellboote*) and to the Western allies as E-boats, various small auxiliaries and a number of former excursion steamers. These latter were about the same size as the ships used on the routes across the English Channel and the North Sea, and had been fitted as minelayers. With some 5,000 mines on board they began the first naval operation of the war—the sealing of the Gulf of

Finland. Farther back in the Baltic a second line of German mine defences was formed, running east from the Swedish island of Oland, and finally there was a kind of long-stop position amongst the Danish islands, with mines guarded by the ancient battleships *Schleswig-Holstein* and *Schlesien*.

Between the Swedish mainland and Oland the Swedes had, as a result of German pressure, been persuaded to lay a field of their own, but the German ships who should have known were not told of this and three of their biggest minelayers, *Tannenberg*, *Preussen* and *Hansestadt Danzig*, were lost in a single night—July 9th, 1941—in the Swedish field.

In fact, there was no need for the German minefields outside the Gulf of Finland. The Russian surface ships showed no desire to emerge from their home waters to make for Sweden and internment or to make a break for British waters through the western end of the Baltic. All that the Baltic minefields achieved was to sink a number of German merchant ships, in addition to the minelayers already mentioned.

During the first few weeks of the war, as the German and Finnish armies advanced on this front towards Leningrad, the first Russian concern was to defend the ports of Tallin (formerly Reval) and Hangö. When the defence of these places became hopeless the Russians tried to evacuate them by sea, as they were, by then, cut off from communication by land with the main body of the Russian armies.

The evacuation of Tallin under these circumstances led to what the Swiss historian Juerg Meister has called 'the mine battle of Reval . . . the most successful mining operation in naval history'.[1]

By August 28th Tallin was surrounded on land by the German army and at sea by German mines. The Russians had made very little resistance to the enemy minelaying operations, despite the fact that the cruiser *Kirov* and a dozen destroyers were lying in Tallin harbour. When the Germans reached the outskirts of the city the Russians loaded the survivors of three infantry divisions and a number of Estonian deportees in 170 ships, great and small. Although the *Kirov* was damaged and under tow by three destroyers, she gave the protection of her seven-inch guns, while the convoy was covered by clouds of smoke blown out to sea from the vast forest fires. In command of the operation was Vice-Admiral Drozhd, in the destroyer *Stoiki*. The columns of ships were preceded by minesweepers and

---

[1] In his book *Der Seekrieg in den Osteuropaischen Gewassern*, 1941/45, J. F. Lehmanns Verlag, Munich, 1958.

sperrbrechers—merchant ships specially fitted to go ahead of convoys and detonate any mines in the way.

Soon the explosions began as the *sperrbrechers* and minesweepers started to force a passage. German artillery ashore opened fire, and German aircraft attacked as well, but the fire of the *Kirov* prevented them from doing any great harm for the moment. When gaps had been blown in the minefield by the sweepers or by the sinking of ships, the rest of the convoy followed through the breaches thus formed in the defences. Many ships were, however, lost and at nightfall the rest anchored where they were and began their voyage again at daybreak. After an unsuccessful attack by Finnish M.T.B.s, next morning, August 29th, the main body of Russians sailed on; in all about fifty of the Russian ships were sunk during the voyage eastward, but, as Herr Meister writes: 'Thanks to their usual fearlessness in the face of loss, the Russians managed to get the majority of the convoy through.'

Altogether they had had to contend with over 4,000 mines, laid so close together that the distance between the individual mines varied only between 25 and 30 feet.

The *Kirov* was one of the survivors of this battle, but she was so badly damaged that she was out of action for months. At this time the *Marat*, which had resumed her former name *Petropavlovsk*, was sunk by dive bombers on September 22nd. She settled on the bottom for the second time in her career, but two of her turrets still remained in action. During the same raids the *Oktiabrskaia Revolutia* and *Maxim Gorki* were also damaged. The *Maxim Gorki* had earlier struck a mine and lost about 45 feet of her bow.

During the month of September all of the available German big ships were brought into the Baltic—the *Tirpitz*, the pocket-battleship *Admiral Scheer*, the light cruisers *Köln*, *Nürnberg*, *Emden* and *Leipzig*, with escorting destroyers. But, after venturing as far north as the Åland islands, this task force went away again, for there was nothing that it could attempt of importance commensurate with the risks that it ran.

Before the winter set in submarines on both sides were in action, with very little success. The Germans and Finns had only ten boats and the Finns very soon nearly lost one of theirs, the tiny *Saukko*, only 107 feet long, which attempted an attack on ships lying in the harbour of Someri, an island in the Gulf of Finland. As the boat came close to the harbour a torpedo began to run in its tube, the gas generated made unconscious all but two of her crew of thirteen, and she drifted out of control and ran aground, being rescued with great difficulty by the two members of her crew still conscious.

The Russian submarines had a very disappointing time; to this day nobody can really say exactly why.[1]

In the first place very few boats were ready for sea at the outbreak of war, and most of those were in a very early stage of training, so that they were generally unskilfully handled. In early attacks the boats' trim was often so faulty that, when they fired their torpedoes, they surfaced in full view of the enemy.

Although there were ninety-four Russian submarines ready at the outbreak of war in the Baltic, according to German sources, only about twenty-five seem to have been operational. Of the rest, nineteen were sent by canal to the White Sea, ten were scuttled in Libau before the place was evacuated, and five were sunk by the enemy, while thirteen were training boats and about a dozen were under repair or working up when war began. It is worth noting that not one single boat was on station before the outbreak of war. On the other hand, German and Finnish submarines soon found that the Russian anti-submarine technique was much better than they had expected, despite the fact that the Russians were without sonar or radar.

With the beginning of winter and the freezing of the Gulf of Finland conventional naval warfare came to an end—but the mining campaign went on, for the Germans dragged mines across the ice on sleds, cut holes in the ice and dropped the mines through them, ready for the spring.

But when the spring came the German attack on Leningrad slackened and a semi-siege took its place. The main weight of the German thrust was directed in a south-easterly direction, across the Ukraine, and the Italians hopefully collected a team of M.A.S., their version of E-boats and S-boats, which was carried half-way across Europe by road and prepared for operations in the Caspian Sea which were never to take place.

In the meantime there was a lull in the Baltic, except for the Russian flotilla on Lake Ladoga, thanks to whose work it was possible to bring into Leningrad the most necessary supplies, in quantities which were sufficient to enable the city to hold out, but not sufficient to prevent the citizens of Leningrad from dying by the thousand of privation.

For the rest, small parties of men, Russian, Finnish and German, carried out raids, commando-style, on each other's coastal and island positions, and small flotillas of landing craft, trawlers, gunboats, and

[1] In addition to *Der Seekrieg in den Osteuropaeischen Gewaessern* see also *L'Enigme des Sousmarins Sovietiques*, by Lieutenant de Vaisseau Claude Huan, Editions France Europe, Paris, 1959.

ice-breakers fought brief actions between themselves without any real effect on the situation.

When the German attack on Russia was planned no one on the German side had given any thought to the question of naval operations in Arctic waters, for the Germans expected that the whole campaign would be terminated so speedily and so successfully that there was no need to worry about the need for interrupting communications between Russia and the outside world via the North Cape. In fact, this area of sea was to become one of the most important in the whole war, as the Allied convoys came to play an increasingly important role in strengthening Russian resistance.

Nevertheless, in the terrific Arctic convoy battles of 1942–3 the Russians could only play a comparatively minor part, for in June 1941 their Northern fleet was without ships or experience. Apart from some forty submarines, it comprised only a dozen destroyers, with light craft and converted auxiliaries. The destroyers were mostly big modern boats of Italian design, and this was to be a handicap of considerable magnitude, for they were built with the Mediterranean in mind and not the Arctic, so that their open bridges in bad weather iced up so thoroughly that fire control gear, bridge telephones and the rest became unusable. The Russians were, however, not alone in this mistake, for the British suffered very nearly as badly.

But Russian inexperience in the handling of the destroyers and escort craft showed clearly—they usually seemed, to Allied observers, to be steaming at full speed, with the disappointing result that they ran out of fuel and had to return home far sooner than would otherwise have been necessary, thus laying an even heavier burden on the escorts provided by the Western Allies.

When it became clear that the Russian armies would not be overwhelmed before the spring of 1942, Hitler, who spent his entire war expecting an Allied landing in north Norway, began to build up his naval forces there. The newly completed *Tirpitz* was sent, with cruisers and destroyers, while the *Scharnhorst*, *Gneisenau* and *Prinz Eugen* were ordered to make their famous dash up the Channel from Brest to support them.

Only once—on December 16th, 1941—were Russian and German surface ships in action with each other, and then without result. For the rest, while the Russians were mostly engaged on escort duty, the Germans, after a number of tip-and-run bombardments of Russian coastal positions, settled down to interfere as much as they could with the Allied convoys on their way to and from Murmansk and Archangel.

An attempt to raid farther afield was made by the pocket-battleship *Admiral Scheer*, which, between August 16th and 30th, 1942, cruised for a fortnight in waters north of Siberia, along the edge of the ice, going as far east as the entrance of Vilkitzy Strait, looking for merchantmen using the famous north-east seaway linking the Atlantic with the Pacific (800 miles from the North Pole), one of the few areas of the world where, hitherto, no war had even been fought. This was called 'Operation Wonderland' and it all came to very little, because the *Scheer*'s float seaplane was written off in an accident and the captain of the pocket-battleship decided that, without adequate ice reconnaissance, it was too risky to continue the cruise.

He fired about 500 rounds against the Russian base at Port Dickson to destroy the big radio station, which was a key point for the control of seaborne traffic through the northern ice, sank two merchant ships and came home. One of the merchantmen was the icebreaker *Sibiryakov* which fought with great courage a hopeless fight, putting the *Scheer*'s men in mind of their ship's fight with the *Jervis Bay* in November 1940.

There was no other long-range operation by German surface craft in Siberian waters. Several were planned, but by now the Germans were running very short of big surface ships and did not wish to add risk of ice damage to the other hazards of war. Accordingly, the burden of the war at sea was borne by submarines and anti-submarine vessels, by minelayers and minesweepers.

In the summer of 1944 the Russian forces in the White Sea were strengthened by the transfer to the Soviet Union of a British battleship, *Royal Sovereign*, an American cruiser, the *Milwaukee*, nine of the former American Lease-Lend destroyers and four British submarines. The battleship and the cruiser, which received the names of *Archangelsk* and *Murmansk*, were objects of prestige rather than usefulness, loaned to Russia because the British and American fleets had been considerably strengthened in the Mediterranean when most of the Italian navy had come over to the Allied cause. On the other hand, the destroyers, though ancient, and the submarines were of practical value. All these ships, except one of the destroyers and one of the submarines, which were lost, were returned to their original owners after the war, when the Russians received a proportion of the former Italian ships.

A little earlier the Russian Northern fleet received reinforcements from another source—the Russian Pacific fleet, which dispatched five submarines to the Arctic Ocean via the Panama Canal. One was torpedoed and sunk in error by a Japanese submarine, which took it for an American. (Russia did not declare war on Japan until August 1945.) In addition, three destroyers and various auxiliaries were sent from Vladivostock to Murmansk by the North-East passage.

In the Black Sea, as in the Baltic, the Russian fleet at the outbreak of war was surprised by a well-planned minelaying campaign. In the Baltic there had been enough ships available to lay the mines which sealed up the Russian ports, but there were no German warships in the Black Sea, and only a few Rumanians, so that the mines had to be dropped by the air. In this way, on June 22nd, the first day of the Russo-German war, seventeen submarines were caught at Sevastopol, trapped until the exit from the harbour could be swept.

At the beginning of the war the Russian Black Sea fleet numbered fifty-one submarines in various states of operational readiness, plus the obsolete battleship *Pariskaia Kommuna*, which resumed her old name of *Sevastopol*, six cruisers (four of them obsolete) and twenty-seven destroyers and torpedo boats.

On the other hand, the only Axis warships in the Black Sea were four Rumanian destroyers and one submarine, which proved to be too big and too clumsy for operational purposes in confined waters. The Bulgarians were never officially at war until the very end of the Balkan campaign, although their bases were at the disposal of the Germans.

The Germans rose to this situation with energy and improvisation of the highest order. No less than 428 vessels, including submarines, were brought by road, rail and river from the North Sea and the Baltic to Constanza; to these were added nearly 100 more that in peacetime plied upon the Danube. Ships from the North Sea got as far as Dresden on the Elbe and then were placed on giant trailers and towed along the *Autobahn* to Ingolstadt on the Danube, where they were once more put afloat. The U-boats, six of them, presented the toughest problem, as they drew too much water for the shallower parts of the rivers and were also too tall to pass under the bridges over the *Autobahn*. Accordingly, they were stripped, so that their weight was reduced from 350 to 200 tons, and placed on their sides between six special pontoons which carried them through the shallow waters to Constanza.

The talent shown in the organisation of supplies for the Axis naval forces in the Black Sea was the more remarkable in that when the Operation Barbarossa—the invasion of Russia—had been planned little attention had been paid to the possibilities of war in the Black Sea, probably because it was believed that the German army would be able to win the war by itself within a few weeks by its own resources. It will be recalled that a similar miscalculation was made in respect of the Arctic Ocean.

Because of this lack of German naval preparedness the Russians were first off the mark, once they had dug themselves out of mine-fields laid by the enemy. On June 26th, at first light, the big destroyers *Moskva* and *Kharkov* appeared out of the fog off Constanza and began to shell the town. They were answered by the eleven-inch guns of the Tirpitz battery, brought to Rumania from the North Sea coast of Germany via Holland. The Russians zigzagged to dodge these shells, any single one of which could have sunk them, and in doing this the *Moskva* caught a mine in her sweep. Instead of cutting the mine's mooring cable the sweep drew it into the ship's side, where it exploded, breaking the ship in half. Hours later sixty-six survivors were picked up by the Rumanians, the *Kharkov* having disappeared back into the fog.

The first check to the eastward advance of the combined German, Italian, Rumanian and Hungarian armies on the Black Sea flank of the Axis advance was provided by the Tobruk-like defence of Odessa, which, surrounded to landward, held out from mid-August until mid-October. During the siege it was supplied by a continuous procession of small craft—like Tobruk—which finally brought away the garrison to Sevastopol, where it formed the nucleus of another, and even greater siege of the Tobruk pattern, which lasted 209 days, from October 29th, 1941, until July 1st, 1942, when the city surrendered.

Russian surface ships and submarines kept the garrison supplied all through these days until, with complete command of the air, the Germans began their final attack on the fortress. The *Sevastopol* and the cruisers gave supporting fire to the garrison on several occasions, but the day-to-day, or rather night-to-night, work of supplying the place was done by the small ships, of which the most famous was the destroyer *Tashkent*, who made more than forty trips between Sevastopol and Novorossisk, in the course of which she was attacked by aircraft ninety-six times, dodging 400 bombs and ten torpedoes before she was finally sunk on July 2nd at Novorossisk by a dive bomber on the day after the siege of Sevastopol had ended.

Altogether, during the siege, the Russian losses totalled 97,000. The Luftwaffe dropped nearly 70,000 bombs, between June 12th and 23rd, while the artillery fired 45,000 tons of ammunition—1,300,000 rounds. In all German bomb disposal units found it necessary to deal with 137,000 land mines.

The whole operation established once again that in modern warfare, in the face of a resolute enemy, ports can be taken only from the land.

While Sevastopol was thus holding out the armies of Germany and her allies had flooded around the north shore of the Sea of Azov, come to the Volga and seemed to be about to reach the Caspian Sea. It was for this purpose that the light coastal forces were brought overland to the theatre of war; additional reinforcements were provided by a small contingent of the Croatian navy. All along the coasts of the Black Sea and the Sea of Azov a lively exchange of commando raids was carried on by both sides.

The German advance which deprived the Russians of Sevastopol overran Novorossisk as well, so that soon the Black Sea fleet was left with only the ports of Tuapse, Poti and Batum, none of them properly equipped.

Meanwhile the Luftwaffe, freed of its responsibilities at Sevastopol, was able to take further part in the struggle for the command of the Black Sea, which by this time may fairly be said to be divided into German and Russian sectors. The fact that the Germans were able to control the western part of the Black Sea, with no warships more important than half a dozen very small submarines of 280 tons, is an indication of the puzzle presented so often by the Russian navy through the ages. They had an overwhelmingly stronger force, they had brave seamen, some good ships and little idea of how to use them. The fault, however, was by no means exclusively that of the Russian navy—for one reason or another support from the Russian air force was almost never forthcoming.

At first, after the fall of Sevastopol and Novorossisk, it looked as though the Germans would be able to make a clean sweep of the Black Sea coast as far as the Turkish frontiers and deprive the Russian fleet of its last bases, but their advance broke down and never got beyond Novorossisk—which port the Germans were unable to use, as it remained, throughout the year during which they occupied the place, under fire from the Russian guns on Cape Doob.

After Stalingrad the Russian counter-attack for the recapture of Novorossisk developed into one of those combined operations which, we have seen, had been long before laid down as the type of battle which it would be the duty of the Red navy to fight. The army attacked on the main front, small craft landed commandos to form bridgeheads behind it, and the air force, which by now had come within reasonable distance of achieving command of the air over the land, supported the operation on a large scale.

The final attack was made on the night of September 9th–10th,

1943. Russian M.T.B.s broke into Novorossisk harbour, firing torpedoes at everything they could see, and were followed by fifty landing craft carrying some 2,000 men, who landed on the waterfront of the town. All attempts to drive them off failed and, as the Russian pressure from the bridgehead, which the navy was able to keep supplied, and the army on land increased, the Germans were obliged to withdraw on September 16th—not merely from Novorossisk itself but also from the Kuban as a whole.

These operations were carried out without the support of the capital ships or the cruisers—*Sevastopol* had been damaged by air attack in September 1942 at Poti and the crew of this ship, as well as other spare naval personnel, were formed into units to fight ashore.

Despite the rapid growth of Russian airpower, the Luftwaffe could still do damage, as was shown on the night of October 5th–6th, 1943, when three Russian destroyers, *Kharkov*, *Boiki* and *Sobrasitelni*, bombarded German positions on the Crimea at Theodosia, Yalta and elsewhere. On their way home they encountered a patrol of German E-boats and the action which followed so delayed them that they were still within range of the enemy dive bombers at first light. In the course of three attacks the Germans succeeded in sinking the *Kharkov* and *Boiki*, while the *Sobrasitelni* sank while under tow, following another action with the E-boats.

This untoward day's work made the Russians even more unwilling to risk their major warships, particularly as no air cover was forthcoming, but they clearly continued to regard smaller craft as entirely expendable, and with them they began a series of raids on the coast of the Crimea, looking for a weak point where they could set foot. This they succeeded in doing, but the German light coastal forces were able to prevent the arrival of reinforcements by sea and eventually both of the bridgeheads which had been formed were wiped out. It would appear that the energetic use of the bigger Russian surface ships would almost certainly have avoided this reverse.

For four months after the liquidation of the last of the Russian bridgeheads on December 11th, 1943, there was a lull in the Crimean fighting. Then, on April 13th, 1944, the Russian army broke into the peninsula from landward and the struggle was soon over. Sevastopol surrendered just a month later, the Germans being evacuated by sea on May 12th. The German convoys were undisturbed by the Russian fleet, but harried by the Russian air force. Bombs and mines were the usual weapons used from the air, but there was at least one experimental attack by means of a torpedo parachuted from a height of 10,000 feet.

But if the Russians were unable to carry out properly conventional operations of sea warfare, they were once more able to spring surprises in the field of amphibious operations, thanks, in part, to air superiority.

With a force of 600 small craft the Russians landed, on August 22nd, at the mouth of the Dniester, behind the German lines, and then repeated the stroke at the mouth of the Danube, two days later. The Russian attack on Rumania from land and sea was followed immediately by that country changing sides in the war. This change took place with such verve and enthusiastic recklessness that, on mixed German and Rumanian anti-aircraft gun sites, the Rumanian gunners began firing on their erstwhile allies over open sights at zero elevation. Bulgaria, which had hitherto not been at war with the Soviet Union, had war declared on her by the Soviet Union a couple of hours after she had, herself, declared war on Germany. The Russo-Bulgarian war lasted for one day, after which the Bulgarians capitulated and also changed sides. These political happenings, caused and reinforced by the unbroken and massive triumphs of the Red army, destroyed the German position in the Balkans and there was nothing for it but a rapid retreat up the Danube.

About 200 German river craft of all sorts assembled on August 25th at Braila, under command of Engineer Rear-Admiral Zieb, and started for home, forming a line 25 kilometres long. They were unable to find pilots or charts, save for a tourist map of the river bought in a stationers' shop. Many of the Germans were drunk owing to the great quantity of liquor available, and some were for deserting or making their way to safety on foot. Finally the armada got under way, with a Greek pilot who gave orders in Rumanian to a woman who was able to translate them into German—sometimes a lengthy and confusing process, especially at Cernavoda, where a vigorous artillery action developed which ended in the destruction of the town and the successful passage of the German force. However, the huge railway bridge here, on the line from Bucharest to Constanza, was left intact, in case there were still German forces in the area who would need it in order to reach safety.

By now Zieb's force had been joined by many stragglers and numbered about 8,000 men and women—about half of them civilian refugees—very short of fuel, food, water, doctors and medical supplies. Guns which had been knocked out at Cernavoda were replaced by guns taken from the cargo of some of the lighters, steam was raised by burning willow trees in the boilers and casualties were replaced by men from a disciplinary battalion.

A Rumanian heavy battery of 5.9-inch guns in concrete emplacements was the next obstacle. Plans were made for it to be attacked from upstream and downstream by the ships and taken in the rear by a landing party; the sight of these preparations, plus the announcement that 200 Stukas were on their way to attack the Rumanian position—bluff, of course, as there were probably not 200 Stukas serviceable in the whole Luftwaffe at the time—led to the Rumanians' agreeing to hold fire while the Germans steamed slowly past, very slowly, because the willow trees proved poor fuel.

Women in the German party were set to work making bandages. The cargo of some of the barges revealed itself as being 2,000 tons of plums and almonds, so that there was, at last, something to eat and, for drinking water, there was the Danube. The Germans made their way peacefully to Ruschuk in Bulgaria, where the authorities provided coal, distilled water and bread—the latter by commandeering all the bakeries in the town and putting them to work. At Svistova, a little farther up the Danube, 700 wounded were landed and 300 women and children. A number of men of the disciplinary battalion tried to stow away with the wounded, but were detected.

Zieb addressed their unit and told its members that, if they behaved in the future, their records would be destroyed, which meant, of course, a pardon for their evildoings. The answer to this seems to have been a very high standard of conduct for the rest of the voyage. More bombardments and counter-bombardments between ships and shore followed, but still the Germans crawled slowly up the great river with, by now, the Russian forces in hot pursuit.

On the evening of August 31st, at Calafat, the strongest Rumanian resistance encountered so far was presented. Zieb's flagship, in peacetime a river and coastal cargo vessel, was badly hit. Her bridge was wrecked, aft she was making water, while forward she was on fire, with the women on board forming a human chain, passing water buckets from hand to hand in an effort to quench the flames, the pumps having been put out of action. Zieb and the women boarded a motor lighter and the fighting went on all night long, with the Germans slowly forcing their way against the stream at a top speed of two knots. Altogether 172 ships got through, while a score or more were sunk, despite the success of the Germans in blowing up one of the Rumanian positions.

At Prahovo, a small fishing village where the armada stopped to draw breath, 1,600 German wounded were landed in Yugoslavia on the morning of September 1st. The place became temporarily a German base, though under spasmodic fire from the enemy on the other side of the river, and Zieb flew off to Belgrade, still in German hands, to get orders for the next lap of his journey. Here the German commander-in-chief, Field-Marshal von Weichs, told him that the Russians had seized the Iron Gate between Prahovo and Belgrade, but that a counter-attack was to be made in order to regain the position and enable Zieb's armada to continue on its way.

But these attacks failed after September 7th, and Zieb was obliged finally to scuttle as much of his fleet as he could, only twelve units being taken by the Russians. Some civilians, mostly women and children, escaped by train, though one of these was wrecked by the partisans, and the rest of the survivors set off on a five-week march through the mountains to Belgrade, constantly under attack by Russian aircraft and Yugoslav partisans.

Zieb's operation had been one of the most remarkable in modern warfare, reminiscent of the fighting which took place on inland waters during the American Civil War.

During 1942 and 1943 the Gulf of Finland was a dead sea. Only the mines challenged the German and Finnish command of the waters, and what was left of the Russian Baltic fleet did not stir from besieged Leningrad and Kronstadt.

But, at the beginning of 1944, the Russian break-out began, first of all from the bridgehead around Oranienbaum on the south shore of the Gulf opposite Kronstadt, from which port the operations were supported by the guns of the *Oktiabrskaia Revolutia, Petropavlovsk* and *Tallin.*

The Russian break-out from Oranienbaum, successful on January 17th, coincided with a final and successful attempt to link Leningrad completely once more with the main body of the Russian armies, so that the siege was at an end. On January 31st the victorious Russian armies crossed the River Narva on their way westward. The Germans could only answer this threat with more minelaying at sea and a stubborn defence on land.

To check the minelayers and to give cover for their own mine-sweeping, the Soviet air force kept up a continuous harrying of the German ships, and the Russian M.T.B.s made their mark with a series of skilful attacks which won the admiration of the Germans. To be sure of their torpedoes getting home, the Russians would bring their boats, with great dash, to within a few yards of the ship which they had selected as their target before firing. The boats were, of course, unarmoured, and the fact that they were petrol-engined meant that thousands of gallons of aviation spirit were at the mercy of German shells and tracer bullets.

Following the advance to the Narva, on the southern shore of the Gulf, the Russians began a similar advance against the Finnish forces on the north shore. One of the objectives of this twin advance was to force a way out of the Gulf of Finland into the Baltic for the couple of dozen Russian submarines which were still serviceable. In the meantime the Russian minesweepers began to cut a way through the minefields, the greatest of which had the code name of *See Igel* (Sea Urchin) and ran in a crescent between Narva Bay on the Russian shore of the Gulf and the Finnish shore, via Hogland.

The form of naval fighting which had, by now, developed, was very like that which had been adumbrated by the Soviet writer Muklevitch.[1]

Dive bombers and fighters supported the M.T.B.s and mine-sweepers. Minelayers blocked the possibility of a German counter-attack, artillery ashore protected the small craft to the best of their ability and, bit by bit, the Russian ships on the flanks of the two armies were able to give offshore support as they inched their way along the coast, while commando-type operations were carried on by both sides amongst the islands. There were great numbers of ships on both sides, tiny craft mostly, apart from the M.T.B.s and extemporised coasting vessels.

Thus, when the Russian break-out from the Gulf of Viipurii began, in the first days of July, there were no less than 100 vessels used to carry out landings behind the German-Finnish lines and on the islands in the enemy rear.

To check these operations German and Finnish submarines did what they could, but the short white nights made operations very difficult, for none of these boats appear to have been fitted with schnorchels, and were accordingly obliged to surface to charge their batteries.

On the north shore of the Gulf, the Russians continued their advance along the coast, until the Finns asked for an armistice at the beginning of September. On the south shore, however, the main weight of the Soviet advance no longer followed the coast, but headed south-west, cutting off the corner of Estonia and heading directly for the Baltic at Riga and Libau.

Operations then followed for the recapture of the islands of Dagö and Ösel, which was the 1917 Battle of Moon Sound in reverse, and the Baltic was finally reached on August 18th.

With Finland out of the war, the rest of the fighting in the Baltic was the story of the German attempts to evacuate their troops, and

[1] See page 206.

later their civilians as well, by sea from territories which there was no hope of their being able to hold in the face of the overwhelming strength of the Red army.

For centuries men have fought for the vital crossing-places of the sea. From the British point of view there were the Western Approaches, the Straits of Gibraltar, the Suez Canal, the Cape of Good Hope and Singapore. The Americans had Panama and its approaches, the Germans had the Kiel Canal, the French had the lines of communication between North Africa and France itself and so on, but very few, before 1939, stopped to think that one of the most important geographical key points of the next world war would be the North Cape and the seas and lands about it.

Nevertheless, in 1939 the Germans planned to seize Norway, and did so in 1940, while the Allies, having mined Norwegian waters, spent five years trying to get control of them. Hitler and Churchill both repeatedly drew the attention of their subordinates to the fact that north Norway, north Finland and north Russia was an area in which the war could be lost or won. Ashore and in the air the struggles of 1941–4 for this area ended in stalemate, except for the original German attack of the spring of 1940, and it is possible to argue that the fate of Narvik in May–June 1940 was decided by the German panzer troops in north-west France rather than by the Allies and Germany fighting at the top of the world. Already in 1939–40 the Russians and the Finns had failed to come to a decision in their northern war—it had been the ability of the Russians to get through the Mannerheim line 700 or so miles to the south which had brought about the Finnish surrender.

Then, in the years between 1941 and 1943 the combined German and Finnish forces had never been able to break through the Russian positions in Karelia and Lapland. Finally, even during the victorious Russian campaigns of 1944 no break-through in north Finland took place, and it was the Russian advance in the southern part of the country that led the Finnish Government to ask for terms, as it had done in 1940.

During the stalemate on land the fight for control of this area was carried on by sea and air. Mostly the comparatively meagre forces of the Luftwaffe held command of the air, except for the few occasions upon which the British were able to obtain the local air superiority needed to escort a convoy or to knock out, and, finally, sink the *Tirpitz*.

The main burden of keeping the ports of north Russia open fell upon the British and Americans, but there were also a number of Russian destroyers, minesweepers and submarines taking part. The Russian submarines attracted most attention to themselves by the inaccurate claim of *K 21* to have torpedoed the *Tirpitz* during her foray against luckless convoy PQ 17. Although the German battleship was, in fact, not hit, it became a Russian article of faith for years after the end of World War II that she had been knocked out and thus rendered an easy target for the British midget submarines and aircraft of the Fleet Air Arm and of R.A.F. Bomber Command which did disable her and finally sink her.

This mistaken claim—wherein the greatest element of mistake lay in reiterating it years after it was known that the *Tirpitz* had never been hit at all—was accompanied by a number of other claims which also proved to be inaccurate but which continued to be publicly maintained long after the true facts had been made available by the capture of the German naval records; for example, the claim that Russian submarines sank 1,500,000 tons of shipping in all theatres of war although the actual figure was less than 300,000 tons.

Similar exaggerations coloured reports of the performance of the Russian M.T.B.s in the Arctic, but the fact remains that the Russian submarines, the M.T.B.s and naval aircraft did do damage to the enemy, and were always able to threaten a sortie. This compelled the Germans to use heavier escort forces than would otherwise have been the case, thus diverting German surface craft from the attacks on the Allied Arctic convoys which, between them, brought 3,500,000 tons of war material, just about half of all that was delivered by the United States and Britain to Russia, between 1941 and 1945, the rest arriving via the Pacific or the Persian Gulf.

Throughout the war flotillas of small craft fought on the inland waters of eastern and central Europe; the Russian genius for improvisation showed itself to the full and, given air cover, the small ships on the rivers and lakes were able to accomplish a great deal. Across Lake Ladoga the Russians were able to revictual Leningrad by a railway over the ice during the winter, but when the ice melted a fleet of paddle steamers, barges, lighters, tugs, customs launches and floating cranes played their part in moving 800,000 troops and 1,000,000 tons of stores into the beleaguered city. Command of the lake was contested by German, Italian and Finnish light craft without success, although the Finns alone had on these waters 150 vessels of one sort or another.

The capital ship of this operation, as far as the Russians were concerned, was a thirty-five-year-old destroyer, the *Konstruktor* (ex *Sibirski-Strelok*), while the backbone of the Axis forces were a number of Siebel ferries, originally built for the invasion of Britain and brought to the waters of Ladoga by train. Throughout the fighting on the inland waterways the Russians used their vessels for commando raids and the landing of agents.

On Lake Ilmen, Herr Juerg Meister calculates, the operations of a scratch Russian flotilla, manned by 500 men, kept 5,000 Germans tied down by continually raiding the lake shores behind the enemy lines.

The Russian Caspian fleet, made up mostly of obsolete vessels used for training, took part in the Anglo-Russian occupation of Iran in August 1941, and afterwards part of it travelled by the Volga to Moscow and fought on the River Moskva in defence of the capital. Another example of the extreme mobility, in terms of distance, of these forces is given by some of the craft from Lake Ladoga, which made their way through the vast network of inland waterways that Russia possesses to the Sea of Azov, the Black Sea and, finally, the Danube, where in the closing stages of the war armoured motor boats of the Russian Danube flotilla, with marines on board, pressing ahead of the Red army, seized the one intact bridge over the river at Vienna and cut the cables of the demolition charges. A little earlier naval engagements had taken place on Lake Balaton, in the heart of Hungary, though here the Russian units were merely rowing boats, armed with bazookas and tommy guns. In addition, in the last days of war in Europe, Russian warships—small craft but indubitably warships—were fighting on the lakes and rivers around Berlin.

The war in Europe ended on May 8th. Three months later, to the day, in accordance with her promise to the Western Allies, Russia declared war on Japan—a war which lasted only a week, during which time the Russian Pacific fleet carried out successfully amphibious operations against the Japanese-held Kuriles.

CHAPTER XIX

THE PAST TWENTY YEARS

1945-1965

At the end of World War II the Russian navy was once more at a very low ebb. It had been a disappointing war for a fleet which was only just beginning to be reborn after the Revolution and the Civil War. From 1941 to 1945 of the components of the Red navy, the Baltic fleet had been almost entirely bottled up in the Gulf of Finland, the Pacific fleet had had only seven days' fighting against an already beaten foe, the Black Sea fleet, though greatly superior numerically to the enemy, had never been able to exercise command of the sea; thus the ships of the fleet in the White Sea which had co-operated with the Western Allies in covering the Arctic convoys were the only Russian surface ships that had been able to contribute markedly to the Allied war effort at sea.

Examples given earlier are indications of the extent to which in seamanship and shiphandling the Russians, during World War II, were short of the requirements of modern naval warfare on the single ship level. At the level of the squadron or fleet there was a corresponding inability to combine ships in team work against enemy sea forces.

On the other hand, on occasion commando operations were handled in a most distinguished manner, and whatever was going on, there never seems to have been any fear of casualties or of losing ships. Co-operation between ships and land based aircraft was generally poor, but so it was in most other navies.

The foregoing sets problems which are still unresolved to this day.

Clearly the Russians were very often lacking in the training, experience and doctrine which were essential to a reasonable conduct of operations. Why this was so is hard to tell; probably it was because after the Revolution the whole navy had been restarted almost from scratch, a background of seamanship and wartime experience was almost entirely lacking and no one had been encouraged to experiment or criticise, for criticism and initiative could, during the Stalin age, lead straight to Siberia or to death. The 1937 purge had gone right through the navy, but when war came in 1941 officers who had survived but who had been banished to labour camps and the like were hastily recalled and, naturally, were not in a high state of morale or training.

After 1945 attempts were made to dissipate discouragement by publishing exaggerated accounts of what the navy had accomplished, despite the fact that once the war was over German records were in Allied hands and it was possible to see what, in fact, had happened. But something had to be said to re-create confidence in the fleet which, in the meantime, had almost ceased to exist as far as modern surface ships were concerned. Construction of new tonnage, apart from submarines, had almost come to a stop, for the urgent demands of the army and the air force had made it impossible to spare much for naval shipbuilding. As a result, in 1945 the total effective strength of the Russian navy amounted to two or three cruisers of pre-war design, between twenty and thirty destroyers of the same vintage and about 100 submarines.

It is remarkable enough that within ten to twelve years, despite these discouraging circumstances, the Russians were able to build themselves a navy bigger than any in the world except that of the United States. What is even more extraordinary is that this huge effort was made at a time when the Soviet Union was repairing the damage of an invasion which had destroyed literally 50 per cent of the country's resources, maintaining the most powerful army in the world, re-equipping a great air force and developing nuclear weapons and space vehicles. The building of the new Russian navy required an expenditure of men, materials and technical resources which no other country in the world, except the United States, could possibly have provided. As a preliminary to the task the title 'Red fleet', which had been borne since January 1918, was formally abolished in March 1947.

The rebirth of the Russian navy had modest beginnings; work was resumed on the cruisers and destroyers begun before the war and whose construction had been suspended shortly after the German invasion. Later on the first of the postwar ships were laid down. These differed very little from those already begun between 1934 and 1941, and the Russians received their first new ideas of naval architecture from the German warships captured at the end of the war. Far and away the most important of these were the U-boats. German submarines at this time were better than any other in the world, and this meant that in postwar submarine design the Russians started off level with other powers which also had access to the German designs.

The Russians, however, were still much behind in operational experience, and in constructional know-how. For this they tried to compensate by the use of Germans, experts and seamen alike, whose status in Russian hands varied between that of honoured, if enforced, guests to that of the more unfortunate types of political prisoners.

The efforts of the Russians to build a first-class navy did not, in the early years, attract much attention in the outside world. It seemed so unlikely. The war was won, the two navies of most immediate menace to Russia, the German and the Japanese, were destroyed. Moreover, new weapons, and above all the A-bomb, might be claimed to have made navies obsolete. This idea might be thought especially likely to appeal to a country which had never had a vital need for a navy, nor great success in the conduct of modern naval warfare. For that matter it was difficult for some in the West to see what purpose a fleet armed only with conventional weapons could fulfil in the atomic age, for it seemed that any war would be settled in a few days or hours by an exchange of missiles, long before seapower could play a part.

At this time the firing of atomic weapons from surface ships had barely been thought of and it was clear that the new Russian navy was designed for conventional wars. It soon also became clear that it was a great navy, not designed simply for 'brush fire' wars but also for war on a world-wide scale, waged by the four traditional Russian fleets—in the Baltic, the Arctic, the Black Sea and the Pacific, with, for the time being at least, a detachment of submarines in the Mediterranean based on Albania.

Important clues as to these developments were provided during the early 'fifties, when it became known in what types of ships the new Russian navy was specialising. The day of the battleship was already over, but, somewhat surprisingly, there was no attempt to build any aircraft carriers, although these had become the capital ship of the great navies during the Pacific war. Instead, the Russians were copying the German policy of 1939–45 and putting all the emphasis on the development of their submarine fleet, reinforced only by escort vessels, light torpedo and mine craft, with a few large surface vessels to act as raiders.

Applying a parallel between Hitler's planned navy of 1939 and Stalin's of 1947, the part of the German heavy ships, *Bismarck*, *Tirpitz* and the rest, was to be taken in the Russian navy by the big cruisers of the *Sverdlov* class, some twenty-four of which were originally ordered. The first of these, the *Sverdlov* herself, was seen in public for the first time at the Coronation review at Spithead in 1953 and created an enormous amount of interest. In the first place, she was the first large modern Russian warship to have appeared in foreign waters for over forty years. Secondly, she was big for her armament—15,000 tons and carrying twelve six-inch guns. Finally, she handled beautifully and was a fine-looking vessel, showing clear traces of the Italian influence in her design. But it was really surprising that she should have been built at all. The fate of the German surface ships in World War II had shown that the possibility of detecting and destroying them on the high seas had developed so much that by the end of 1942 they had lost nearly all chance of doing serious damage, although their mere existence in remote northern harbours was to pin down strong British forces for which there was plenty of work elsewhere.

Under these circumstances it was astonishing to see that the Russians had invested heavily in these ships, at once so powerful by pre-1939 standards, so handsome and of such very limited use. How this happened is by no means clear, but it would seem most likely that Admiral Kutznetzov, who was in control of the rebuilding of the Russian fleet after 1945, was so anxious to get modern ships of some size at the earliest possible moment that he settled for the *Sverdlovs* because they were the best type immediately available, and Kutznetzov, like Makarov fifty years before him, was above all anxious to get his crews to feel 'at home at sea'.

However, the vogue for these big cruisers did not long survive the arrival of Khrushchev in power and the retirement, owing to ill health, of Kutznetzov. In 1956 Khrushchev stigmatised these ships as being only suitable for taking statesmen about the world on good-will missions. It is ironical that one of these goodwill visits, that of Khrushchev himself and Marshal Bulganin to the United Kingdom on board the *Ordzhonikidze*, a sister ship of the *Sverdlov*, in 1956, was the occasion of such a notable display of Anglo-Russian ill-will.

Khrushchev, at about this time, also began to express doubt on the value of the aircraft carrier, but he never spoke slightingly of the submarine and the Russian submarine-building programme went ahead at a rate unparalleled by any country in peacetime, the annual total of boats coming into service exceeding for a time eighty units. In this way an increase in strength from 100 to 450 was reached within a few years. This total has been more or less stationary for the last few years, as new boats coming into service have replaced old ones built before the war. These latter were mostly designed for service in coastal waters, while their replacements are capable of operating throughout the world. Some of the latest submarines are certainly nuclear and some are equipped to fire guided missiles; the Russian Press has made much of these weapons, but publicity may have out-run, for the time being at least, the event which it is desired to publicise, for so far there is no indication that the Russians have a weapon equivalent to Polaris.

However, the number of Russian guided-missile submarines in service is, in any case, only a small proportion of the total of that country's submarine fleet, which is overwhelmingly made up of types designed to carry out the same sort of war against merchant shipping as the Germans waged in two world wars. Incidentally, its total strength is just about that of the German U-boat force at its most powerful during World War II.

Together with the submarine-building programme the Russians have continued to build escort vessels and other small surface craft, nearly 2,500 of them. The biggest of these ships are the *Kynda* class, while smaller types of escort vessels vary in size from 3,500 tons to 800 tons. There are in all some 440 of these escort vessels, whose armaments run through the whole spectrum of naval weapons: guided missiles, both surface to air and surface to surface, anti-submarines and anti-surface ship torpedoes, dual-purpose guns for use against surface ships and aircraft, automatic anti-aircraft guns and other anti-submarine weapons.

In addition there are about 1,000 motor launches and motor torpedo boats, the lineal descendants of the shallow-draft rowing boats and barges which were the flotilla craft of the Baltic wars of 200 years ago, and an important force of small ships, again numbering about 1,000, for mine warfare. These are another example of the continuity of Russian naval practice, since these ships, in their turn, descend from the very earliest Russian experiments during the Crimean War to hold off the Allied fleets with sea mines, and there is little doubt that, at the outbreak of any sea war, one of the first pre-occupations of the Russians would be to saturate their home waters with mines and, at the same time, use mines in an attempt to block the principal harbours of their enemies.

The foregoing ships are all, in their various ways, ordinary war-ships, recognisable as such; in addition, in recent years the Russians have made use, for naval purposes, of a considerable number of small merchant vessels, mostly of the general type and build of trawlers. These ships have been most in the public eye when they have turned up in the neighbourhood of NATO naval exercises to see, or more likely to listen, to what is going on, thus hoping to get information as to the workings of NATO communications, radar, etc. Quite apart from this, these semi-official trawlers provide valuable sea time for Russian officers and ratings.

Concurrently with the expansion of the navy there has been a very great increase in the number of genuine trading vessels—the total size of the Russian merchant fleet having increased in size from 1,300,000 tons in 1939 to 7,000,000 tons in December 1964. These ships again provide valuable training for officers and men who may one day be needed for the navy. This same need for training is the reason why almost all Russian warships not undergoing important repairs are kept permanently manned and in seagoing condition, whereas in the Western fleets a high proportion of ships are moth-balled or otherwise laid up in reserve. So thoroughly do the Russians apply the principle of keeping ships continuously ready that, instead of ships returning to their home ports to give leave periodically, usually to half the ship's company at a time as is the British practice, the Russians operate a system under which one-twelfth of the ship's company are allowed a month's leave at a time, so that the ships are always ready for sea.

In this way a huge navy was built up, a process which began at a time when all the principal navies in the world had been greatly reduced in size or ceased to exist altogether. While the Russians planned their defence policy for the future in the years 1945–7 they bent every effort towards producing their own nuclear weapons, but they were also obliged to plan a strategy in which their own conventional strength was to hold in check the atomic strength of the Americans. This was made easier by the massive cuts in the conventional forces of the West.

Thus there grew up a great disparity of power in 1947–9; powerful Russian and satellite forces were on the edge of Soviet-held territory, within a few hours' motoring of the Atlantic coast of Europe, while the western European powers tried feverishly to organise the military vacuum which was all that stood between them and another occupation, probably much more drastic and much more long drawn out than that from which they had just been delivered.

The formation of NATO and the provision of American aid created a balance between nuclear and conventional weapons which the first Soviet A-bomb did not fundamentally alter. It had been in order to increase this conventional strength that the Russians had once again begun to build a navy, with the principal emphasis placed on cruisers and submarines, for use against Allied sea communications. Whatever sort of war might be fought after the formation of NATO, it was clear that its course would depend on the aid provided by the United States. If there were to be a conventional war, it would be vital for the Russians to cut the sea communications across the Atlantic. If that could be done Russian success would be certain in a conventional war, and in the early days of NATO it might even have put a very different complexion on a war in which the Americans tried to use their nuclear supremacy, for there is a good deal of reason to believe that in those early days of NATO, fifteen years ago, American atomic weapons would not have been numerous enough or powerful enough to have defeated the Russians by themselves.

In the 1950s came the production of H-bombs by both sides. This brought about a new situation, but one in which the Russian navy was still of great importance, for it was soon clear that an exchange of H-bombs would be so totally destructive to both sides that the idea soon spread that they would be used only in the very last resort, and perhaps not at all. Therefore, if there was to be a great West and East war, without the use of nuclear weapons, the Russian navy would still have to play its vital role of trying to prevent the United States bringing help to Europe.

While a different kind of stalemate had grown up in Europe, a series of nibbles had gone on against the Western powers in Asia, Africa and America, either directly through local Communist forces or through nationalist leaders who saw Russian help as a means of paying off old scores they believed they had against Britain, the United States or France.

In this process the Russian navy also had its part; Russian warships of modern design provided, and provide, a powerful element in the forces of China, Cuba, Indonesia and Egypt, as well as those of satellite powers.

Submarines in Chinese, Indonesian or Egyptian hands might make an important difference in some future 'confrontation' with a Western power which was supporting its position with amphibious forces—aircraft carriers, assault craft and the rest. The risk represented by these submarines might mean that no amphibious operations could be attempted without full anti-submarine protection, and at the present time there are very few prepared to be quite sure that even the most recent and best-protected aircraft carrier would prove invulnerable to submarine attack. Of course, no warship, in fact, has ever been invulnerable, but from time to time there has been a disposition to believe that such a ship has been produced, and this belief has generally preceded a disaster.

In addition to the twenty-eight submarines provided for China, the nine for Egypt and six for Indonesia, Russia has also supplied surface vessels which might have an important influence on a 'localised' war. These include a few modern destroyers and considerable numbers of motor torpedo boats and motor gunboats—about fifty in the Vietminh navy, thirty-six in the Egyptian navy, twenty-eight in the Cuban navy and over seventy in the Indonesian navy (though not all of these are of Russian origin). These vessels would make blockades very dangerous to the blockaders. Many of them are armed with heavy ship-to-ship or ship-to-shore rockets, which, although only carrying warheads containing conventional explosives, could do serious damage against an extensive target. Although it is generally held that delivering high explosives by rockets is a very wasteful process because of the impossibility of accurate aim, there is plenty of harm that could be done under certain circumstances. For example, fast Egyptian rocket-launching craft could cause great damage to Tel Aviv or Haifa, coastal towns which hold the principal concentrations of Israel's economy.

A third way in which Russian naval aid might be covertly supplied to 'emerging' powers in dispute with Western nations would be by the provision of personnel and material for mine warfare. This was done during the Korean War, when on at least one occasion the United Nations command of the sea was brought to nought by a skilful and thorough minelaying campaign. This involved about 1,000 mines and was carried out by the North Korean sampans using Russian mines, presumably with the help of Russian experts.

A similar effort against commando operations such as those carried out in Malaysian waters in 1963–5 would tax very heavily the work of any task force, for it would make necessary a full-scale mine-warfare campaign to protect, not only the commando operations but also the nearest big ports from which the commando operations were supplied.

The triple threat of Russian submarine and mine warfare—its ability to fire nuclear weapons, to carry out a full-scale war against merchant shipping and also to intervene in little 'local' wars, together with Khrushchev's laughing reference to surface warships as nothing but the coffins of their crews—tends to obscure the fact that the Russian navy has some 2,000 of these 'coffins', warships ranging in size from 15,000 tons downwards. Upon these ships may well depend the command of both the Black Sea and the Baltic. This command could permit the exit of submarines into the Mediterranean and the Atlantic, and would also permit these seas to be used for the transport of Russian armies driving west or south towards Istanbul and Copenhagen.

Ability to use sea transport in the case of such attacks would be of the greatest value, because, even without nuclear attacks on road and rail communications, enough conventional damage might be done by air attack to hamstring an invading army which was obliged to move by road and rail alone. It will be seen that to release the navy from the inland seas the Russian army and air force would have to launch two great offensives which might, in their turn, depend for success upon the navy's command of the sea, the whole scheme involving triphibious operations on the grandest scale.

All this presupposes, of course, a war which is not ended in a few days by a nuclear war but a war which could last for years, and it is for such a war that the Russian navy has prepared and is preparing.

In the event of such a long-drawn-out war it would be the task of the Russian submarines to break the Atlantic alliance in two. The threat of this attempt was perhaps best summed up in November 1962 by Vice-Admiral R. M. Smeeton, Royal Navy, who was at the time deputy to Saclant (Supreme Allied Commander Atlantic). Addressing a meeting of NATO parliamentarians he said:

> You all know that the Soviets have today the largest submarine force the world has ever known. We must assume that this force possesses every deadly weapon that we possess. We must assume that this force has a simple mission . . . it is to divide and destroy the physical structure of N.A.T.O., not by frontal attacks on our defended periphery but by the infiltration of submarines into our geographical core and from there striking out at the soft and exposed area behind our fighting front. The mission of the Soviet submarine force is obvious, the danger to our alliance is ever present. Actually, the danger may be greater than we realise, for since World War II the Soviet have built a new powerful navy and a large modern merchant fleet. They have the largest trawler fleet in the world. They have ventured upon the high seas, something unusual in Russian history. The Communists are moving into the arena of sea power. They are no longer entirely 'land animals'.
>
> We should first examine in a general way what measures we should take to cope with the Soviet submarine threat. It is obvious I think that N.A.T.O. should try to stop any Soviet submarines from getting into the Atlantic by closing the Baltic and Turkish straits and by establishing a control in the North Atlantic. Those submarines that are out in the ocean areas to begin with should be harried and destroyed. In an all-out war we would hope to prevent them from ever returning home and resupplying by destroying their facilities in the Northern sea area.
>
> To carry out this latter task it would be necessary to use nuclear weapons. The reason is quite simply the size of the job to be done and how many tools we have to do it with.
>
> We simply do not have enough forces. Let me make this clear. Contingency operations of a limited nature, surveillance of the seas, harassment to make our purpose and resolve clear to an enemy, these we can do without using nuclear weapons. We can take steps to make sure the enemy is fully aware of where his course of action is leading him without

using nuclears. But we cannot go to war that way. To conduct a non-nuclear war at sea, with hope of success, Saclant would need several times the present allocated number of anti-submarine vessels, escorts and maritime patrol aircraft. Several times the number presently earmarked for Saclant. Even to fight an all-out war in the Atlantic, Saclant needs more modern anti-submarine warfare vessels, more escorts and more maritime patrol aircraft. Saclant's force requirements were set at the very minimum and they have not been met. The Soviet have a more modern navy than we do.

From the foregoing it will be seen that, at the present time, there is no prospect held out of being able to avoid the use of nuclear weapons if the Russians were to launch a conventional submarine war. It is the general consensus of opinion in the West that once nuclear weapons have been used by one side or the other the conflict will very rapidly escalate into a full-scale nuclear struggle, with ruin for both sides within a few days or hours. It is interesting, therefore, to observe that this is not what the Russians think—or at least it is not what the Russians say that they think.

Since the year 1926 only one comprehensive book on the present and future practice of the art of war has been published in the Soviet Union. This is *Military Strategy*, edited by Marshal V. D. Sokolovsky, Chief of the General Staff from 1953 to 1960, which appeared in Moscow in September 1962 and in the following year was published in translation.[1]

This book, under Marshal Sokolovsky's editorship, was prepared by a group of army officers, comprising nine colonels, four major-generals and one professor colonel-general;[2] it devotes comparatively few of its 395 pages to naval matters, but what it does have to say about them is full of interest, for it shows clearly how the Soviet Union envisages the kind of war which NATO would have to fight at sea.

It begins with one of those glimpses of the obvious which, at least at first, seem striking only by their *naïveté*:

The world oceans will be the navy's theatre of military operations.

On reflection, however, this would seem to mean that in a future war the Russian navy would not find itself confined to the Baltic, the Black Sea and to coastal waters in the Far North and the Far East, but would be out on the high seas.

[1] Published in New York by Frederick A. Praeger, Inc., and in London by the Pall Mall Press Ltd.
[2] It is worth noting that apparently there was not, in 1961–2, a single Soviet naval officer who was considered suitable as a contributor to this book.

The main aims of operations in naval theatres will be to defeat the enemy fleet and disrupt his naval and sea communications. In addition, there may be the tasks of delivering nuclear-missile strikes against coastal objectives, supporting the ground troops, carrying freight and protecting our own naval communications lines . . .
The most important task from the very outset of the war will be to destroy enemy carrier based units.

It is pointed out that these units will be used to make surprise nuclear attacks against important objectives in 'the socialist countries'. 'An effective means of combating carriers,' the book goes on, 'are rocket-carrying nuclear submarines.'

In the aggressive plans of the Anglo-American bloc, great significance is attached to the use of nuclear submarines for nuclear [i.e. Polaris-type —D.W.] attacks deep within the territory of the socialist countries . . .
Submarines have become the main striking force at sea, not only in the Soviet navy, but in the navies of the Anglo-American bloc.
Among the main tasks of the navy in a future war will be the disruption of enemy ocean-going and coastal shipping and the disruption of his communications. We must consider that up to three-fourths of all the probable enemy's equipment and personnel lie across the ocean. According to the calculations of certain military theoreticians, 80–100 large transports would arrive daily at European ports in the event of war, and 1,500–2,000 ships . . . would be *en route* simultaneously.

These ships would be targets for nuclear and conventional submarines, whether armed with Polaris-type rockets or with conventional torpedoes, and at the same time nuclear attacks would be made by Soviet forces on sea bases and ports, shipbuilding and ship-repairing centres and the Anglo-American convoys. Mine warfare would also be used to hamper the movements of NATO shipping.

All this would require the use of scores of nuclear missiles—but apparently the Russians believe that an exchange on this scale would not result in the immediate destruction of either side.

The willingness suggested by Sokolovsky's team of writers to smother even comparatively minor naval targets with nuclear weapons tends to confirm the belief that the Russians have a very large number of medium-range missiles, suitable for use against targets in Europe and European waters, while long-range weapons for direct attack on American targets are in short supply.

In addition, there may be the Russian calculation that Soviet medium-range missiles on European targets will not be answered by American long-range ones on Russian targets so long as the United States itself is not subject to nuclear attack.

Here, then, we have the redoubtable Russian navy, certainly equipped with a rich armoury of nuclear and conventional weapons and prepared to use whatever it has got if war starts. The outlines of the beginning of such a war at sea are clear from a comparison between the expressed official views, both NATO and Soviet. To begin with there is agreement on both sides that the first targets for the Russian submarines would be NATO convoys and NATO aircraft carriers.

Because of a shortage of conventional anti-submarine forces the NATO reaction to such attacks would be nuclear counter-attacks, in the first place on submarine bases.

Thus at present form an all-out submarine campaign, even without the use of nuclear weapons by the Russians, could bring a nuclear reply by the West, because there are not sufficient anti-submarine craft available successfully to resist a conventional Russian attack.

The West, at the present time, is much preoccupied with the need for increased conventional forces, and in this connection anti-submarine forces have a high priority for attention, for they would give us the possibility of confronting enemy submarines without being forced to use nuclear weapons.

Whether or not more anti-submarine ships and aircraft have been provided, there remains the need for continued scientific anti-submarine research. Enormous efforts are being made to solve the problems of the detection and destruction of submerged submarines, but there has been no break-through yet, although we have been working on the problem for fifty years. During that time some scientists, and even more science writers, proud of the fantastic achievements of the members of their mystery, have regularly announced the arrival of the answer to the submarine; each new experiment is hailed with cries of triumph and then with a great silence, as it transpires that the new arrival is not the answer which is sought.

This is a state of mind which has been particularly important during the recent arguments for or against Polaris, since, if an effective anti-submarine weapons system were devised, the case for the Polaris would be at least much weakened.

Of course, it is impossible to say that such a system will not be found, but at best a considerable number of years will elapse before it has been discovered, developed and put into service, and during that period all the navies of the world will have to fight the submarine with the methods which exist at the present time, refined thanks to constant research.

This research must be not only scientific but historical as well. The importance of this latter has been far from well recognised—so far that, between the wars, the British navy abandoned it altogether to save a few hundred pounds a year, despite the fact that, from a careful study of the submarine and convoy operations of the past, it would have been possible to avoid the disasters of the battle of the Atlantic.

But even more important than more weapons and more research for the West is the maintenance of the North Atlantic alliance in good repair. If anything ever happens to cause the Russians to doubt that the Americans will intervene in a naval war with everything they have got, then the West will be faced with a submarine menace even greater than those of 1917 or 1943.

Even a strong NATO will not cancel out the threats of minor naval operations which could be of the greatest importance in the Far East, the Middle East or in Latin American waters.

Whether British or American naval forces are ever challenged in those places by forces of Russian origin will depend upon the adequacy of those forces, and policy-making decisions in Moscow and in Peking. At the time of writing the Russian attitude seems much more propitious than for a long time past. But whatever happens, short of total disarmament by all the world, the Soviet navy will continue to play a paramount role in the planning and implementation of Soviet policy and in the calculations of the Soviet Union's potential adversaries.

As for China, the fact that that threat seems remote in terms of time and of technical development and half-hidden behind a threat much more immediate does not alter the fact that it is there, just the same.

ACKNOWLEDGMENTS

Any study of the Russian navy of the sailing ship era must be based upon two sturdy pillars, books written about forty years apart by Dr. R. C. Anderson—*Naval Wars in the Baltic*, published in 1910, and *Naval Wars in the Levant*, published by the Liverpool University Press in 1952. It is therefore fitting that in the first place I should thank Dr. Anderson and the Liverpool University Press for their kindness and generosity in letting me borrow from the two books.

I am also much indebted to Mr. Richard Hough and Messrs. Hamish Hamilton for permission to use parts of *The Fleet That Had to Die* and *The 'Potemkin' Mutiny*, Messrs. Sampson Low, Marston & Co. for use of *Ironclads in Action* by H. W. Wilson, Messrs. William Clowes and Sons, Ltd. for material taken from *Brassey's Naval Annual* for various years and Messrs. Faber and Faber Ltd. for permission to quote from *The Real War* by Capt. B. H. Liddell Hart.

The Oxford University Press gave permission to use material from *The Prophet Unarmed* by Mr. Isaac Deutscher, *History To-day* to adapt an article which I wrote entitled *The Russian Armada*, as well as to copy their map, and the Journal of the Royal United Service Institution to quote from an article by Mr. D. Fedotoff-White, and Mr. Fedotoff-White's publishers, Princeton University Press, allowed me to use his book *The Growth of the Red Army*, Messrs. Macmillan also permitted me to quote from *The Soviet High Command* by John Erickson.

Editions Payot, Paris have kindly given permission to quote or adapt from *Histoire de la Marine Russe*, by Monasterev and Tereschenko, *La Guerre Navale Russo-Japonaise* by Tereschenko, *La Marine Russe dans la Guerre et dans la Revolution* by Graf, and *Dans la Mer Noire*. Editions France-Empire have similarly given permission to use *L'Enigme des Sous-Marins Sovietiques* by Lieutenant de Vaisseau Claude Houar.

J. F. Lehmanns Verlag, Munich, have given permission to reproduce information contained in Herr Juerg Meister's *Der Seekrieg in den osteuropäischen Gewässern*.

Her Majesty's Stationery Office have permitted quotation from British Documents on the Origins of the Great War. The Navy Records Society have similarly permitted use of *A Memoir of James Trevenen* and *History of the Russian Navy under Peter the Great*.

The Pall Mall Press Ltd. similarly agreed to my use of *Military*

Strategy, by Marshal Sokolovsky and Messrs. Chatto and Windus allowed me to borrow from St. Antony's Papers: Number 6, material contained in an article by Dr. George Katkov entitled *The Kronstadt Rising*. Gerald Duckworth & Co. Ltd. allowed me to quote from Admiral Ballard's *Influence of the Sea on the History of Japan*.

Mrs. de Vries has given permission for me to quote from *The Imperial Russian Navy* by her father, F. T. Jane.

Finally, there are those three last—and first—resorts of those seeking information on naval topics: the Naval Library, Ministry of Defence, the Library of the Imperial War Museum and the Library of the National Maritime Museum, all in London.

To all the foregoing, I owe my deepest thanks.

In addition to the books mentioned above, the following are of special interest:

Bekker, Cajus. *Ostsee: Deutsches Schicksal 1944/45*. Oldenburg: Stalling, 1959.

Breyer, Siegfried. *Die Seerüstung der Sowjetunion*. Munich: Lehmann, 1964.

Clarke, Colonel Sir George Sydenham. *Russia's Sea-Power, Past and Present*. London: John Murray, 1898.

Falk, Edwin A. *Togo and the Rise of Japanese Sea Power*. London and New York: Longmans, Green, 1936.

Graf, H. (Garold Karlovich). *The Russian Navy in War and Revolution from 1914 up to 1918*. Munich: Oldenbourg, 1923.

Harbron, John D. *Communist Ships and Shipping*. London: Adlard Coles, 1962.

Jensen, Gustav. *Japans Seemacht*. Berlin: Siegismund, 1938.

Mitchell, Mairin. *The Maritime History of Russia, 848–1948*. London: Sidgwick and Jackson; New York: Macmillan, 1949.

Ogasawara, Vice-Admiral Viscount Nagayo. *Life of Admiral Togo*. Tokyo: Seito Shorin Press, 1934.

Saunders, M. G. (ed.). *The Soviet Navy*. London: Weidenfeld & Nicolson; New York: Praeger, 1958.

Wilson, Herbert Wrigley. *Battleships in Action*. 2 vols. London: Sampson Low, Marston; Boston: Little, Brown, 1926.

————. *Ironclads in Action*. 2 vols. London: Sampson Low, Marston; Boston: Little, Brown, 1896.

INDEX

INDEX

Abdul Hamid the Damned, 173
Aberdeen, Earl of, 90
Åbo, 23, 25
Adana, 97
Admiral Kornilov, 118
Admiral Makarov, 169, 173, 186
Admiral Nakhimov (later *Tchervonaia Ukraina*), 152, 203
Admiral Scheer, 211, 214
Admiral Seniavin, 152
Admiral Ushakov, 152
Adolf Frederick of Holstein-Gottorp, 39
Adrianople (Edirne), 96
Adrianopol, 100
Adriatic Sea, 81, 86, 90
Adzuma, 148
Aegean Sea, 53, 55, 85, 96
Aegina, Gulf of, 49
A G 15, 185
Agar, Lt. A. W. S., 194
Akagi, 147
Akatsuki, 123
Akebono, 128
Akerman, 32, 62
Akiyama, Cmdr., 148
Aland Islands, 23, 25, 38, 77, 78, 104, 189, 211
Alaska, 105, 109
Albania, 62, 81, 228
Albatros, 169
Alexander I, Tsar, 15, 75, 76, 79, 84, 85
Alexander II, Tsar, 107
Alexander Nevsky, 94
Alexandria, 93
Alexandrov, A., 206
Alexiev, Ad., 122, 129, 132, 139
Algiers, 46
Ali Pasha, Governor of Egypt, 55
Ali Pasha of Janira, 86
Alma, 195
Almaz, 152, 175
Almirante Villar see *Kapitan 2 R Kingsbergen*
American Civil War, 11, 109, 121
American War of Independence, 14, 43, 82
Amiens, Treaty of, 76, 83
Amur, River, 97, 107
Amur, 141, 167
Anapa, 86
Anatolia, 15, 49, 61, 97, 99, 102, 175, 176, 178
Ancona, 82, 83
Anderson, Dr. R. C., 30, 60, 61, 65, 68, 88
Andrei Pervosvanni, 162, 181, 182, 194

Angola, 141
Angra Pequena, 141
Anholt, 76
Anne I, Queen of England, 42
Anne, Tsarina, 34, 167
Anzio, 73
Apraxin, Ad. Count Feodor, 22, 23, 24, 25, 27, 28
Apulia, 81
Arabat, Tongue of, 35
Archangel, 43, 66, 78, 80, 106, 172, 188, 213, 214
Archangelsk see *Royal Sovereign*, 214
Arcona, Cape, 167
Arctic, 106, 127, 175, 213, 216, 228
Arondel, 26
Asahi, 147
Asama, 130, 148
Asashio, 123
Asia, 93, 94, 95
Askold, 128, 130, 137, 179
Aspö, 38
Assar-i-Chevket, 114, 115, 116
Athos, Battle of, 87–88
Atlantic, 11, 14, 19, 108, 191, 231, 233, 234, 235, 238
Augsburg, 165, 170
August 10th, Battle of, 135
Augustus III of Poland, 37
Austerlitz, Battle of, 84
Austrian Succession, War of, 37, 39
Avni-Illah see *Rafail*
Avrora (1), 105
Avrora (2), 16, 140, 151, 163, 181, 186, 203
Azard, 194
Azov, 32, 33, 34, 36, 55, 56
Azov, 94, 95, 100
Azov, Sea of, 32, 35, 36, 109, 217, 225

Babushkin, Seaman, 144
Bacchante, 90
Bakhirev, Ad., 186
Baku, 34
Balaton, Lake, 225
Balkans, 96, 219
  First Balkan War, 174
  Second Balkan War, 174
Ballard, Ad., 136
Balle, Cmdr., 69
Bari, 81
Barsh, Cde., 48
Bartrak see *Vepr*

243

Index

Bathurst, Capt., 95
Batum, 99, 113, 114, 115, 217
Bayan (1), 130, 139, 141, 142, 144
Bayan (2), 163, 169, 185, 186
Bayern, 185
Bedovy, 153
Beirut, 55
Belgrade, 221
Belli, Capt., 82, 84
Bender, 62
Bentham, Col. Samuel, 59
Beresford, Lord Charles, 140
Berlin, 40, 186, 225
Berlin, Treaty of, 117, 125
Berutch Spit, 36
Bespokoini, 192, 196
Bessarabia, 62
Bezobrasov, Ad, 132
Bismarck, 138, 205, 228
Bizerta, 196, 202
Blomberg, Gen. von, 204
Bodry, 153
Bogatyr, 137, 163, 167, 169
Boiki, 218
Bomarsund, 104, 105
Boretz za Svobodu see *Kniaz Potemkin Tavricheski*
Bornholm, 26, 167
Borodino (1), 150, 151
Borodino (2), 160, 162
Bosphorus, 86, 95, 96, 97, 99, 112, 125, 176, 178
Bothina, 25
Boyarin, 126
Braila, 62, 112, 219
Brassey, Lord, 108
Braunschweig, 166
Bredal, Ad., 34, 35, 36
Bremen, 26
Bremen, 170
Breslau, 16, 174, 176, 178
Brest, 82, 213
Brest Litovsk, 187, 189
Briansk, 32, 34
Bridge, Vice-Ad. Cyprian A., 23, 29
Brindisi, 81
Bruix, Vice-Ad., 82
Bruster Ort, 40, 167
Bucharest, 219
Bucharest, Treaty of, 174
Bug, River, 57, 62, 63
Buiny, 150, 153
Bukhvostov, Capt., 149
Bulganin, Marshal, 13, 229
Burevestnik, 196
Busk, Hans, 108

Byron, Lord, 91, 92
Bywater, H. C., 108

C 26, C 27, C 32, C 35, 172
Cadiz, 79, 84
Calafat, 220
Calmar, 27
Canada, 171
Caspian fleet, 225
Caspian Sea, 33, 34, 201, 212, 217
Cassandra, 193
Catherine I, Tsarina, 37
Catherine II (the Great), 14, 41, 42, 44, 45, 55, 64, 69, 71, 72
Cattaro, 84, 85, 90
Caucasus, 96, 97, 101, 105, 106, 111, 112, 114, 115, 175, 176, 178
Centaur, 77
Cephalonia, 81
Cerigo, 81
Cernavoda, 219
Channel Islands, 73
Chapaev, 203, 209
Charles XII of Sweden, 20, 22, 25, 26, 27, 32, 33, 102
Charles XIII, 64, 68, 70, 78
Chatham, 74
Chefoo, 137
Chemulpo (Inchon), 123, 124, 142, 179
Cherbourg, 43
Cherigo, 196
Chihaya, 150
Chile, 92, 126
China Seas, 153
Chios, 49
Chitose, 130, 137
Chotin, 55
Christian VI of Denmark, 39
Christian VII of Denmark, 79
Churchill, Sir W., 160, 209, 223
Clapier de Colongue, Capt., 139
Clowes, Sir W. Laird, 93
Cochrane, Thomas, Earl of Dundonald, 91, 92, 93
Codrington, Sir E., 93, 94, 95
Coles, Capt., 109
Collingwood, Ad., 86, 88
Constantin, 194
Constantine, Fort, 183
Constantine, King of Greece, 179
Constantine, Grand Duke, 107, 108
Constantinople, 32, 34, 36, 46, 48, 52, 58, 63, 82, 86, 88, 92, 95, 96, 97, 99, 111, 112, 117, 175, 176, 177, 178, 193
Constantinople, Treaty of, 55
Constanza, 158, 159, 215, 216, 219

244

Copenhagen, 14, 26, 27, 39, 40, 43, 57, 66, 67, 68, 75, 76, 233
Copenhagen, Battle of, 65, 75
Corfu, 81, 84, 85, 90
Corunna, 76, 78
Courland, Duchy of, 28, 30
Crabbe, Cmdr., 13
Crete, 92, 111
Crimea, 34, 35, 36, 55, 62, 101, 102, 105, 106, 189, 195, 196, 200, 218, 230
Crimean War, 12, 15, 98–106, 107, 108, 109, 110, 111, 117, 167, 177
Croatia, 217
Cronin, Lt., 67
Cronin, Mrs., 67
Cuba, 128, 232
Curzola, 84, 85
Cyril, Grand Duke, 131

Dago, 186, 222
Dalecarlia, 39
Dalmatian Coast, 84, 85, 86, 90, 91
Damietta, 55
Danzig, 37, 39
Danzig, Gulf of, 40
Dartmouth, 93, 94
Deane, 22
Den Helder, 73
Denikin, Gen., 195
Derbent, 34
Derski, 192, 196
Deschenes, Admiral P., 103
Desna, River, 32
Desna (later *Engels*), 202
De Tott, 53
Deutschland, 203
Devastation, 104, 105
Dewa, Vice-Ad., 150
Diana, 130, 133, 137, 163, 173
Djigit, 113
Dmitri Donskoi, 153
Dnieper, River, 32, 35, 36, 37
Dniester, River, 63, 219
Dogger Bank, 140, 143
Don, River, 21, 32, 34
Doob, Cape, 217
Dreadnought, 162
Dresden, 215
Drozhd, Vice-Ad., 210
Dubasov, Lt., 112
Duckworth, Vice-Ad., 86
Dugdale, Capt., 51
Duncan, Admiral, 72
Dvienadsat Apostolov, 158
Dvina (1), 105
Dvina (2). See *Pamiat Azova*

Dybenko, P.E., 171

E 1, 167, 170
E 8, 167, 170
E 9, 167, 169
E 13, 167
E 18, 167, 172
E 19, 167, 170
Eberhardt, Vice-Ad. A., 175, 176, 178
Ehrenskiold, Ad., 23, 24
Eisenstein, 156, 157
Ekaterinburg, 131
Elbing (Elblag), 22
Elizabeth, Empress, 39, 41, 73
Elliott Islands, 130
Elphinston, Rear-Ad. John, 43, 44, 45, 46, 47, 48, 49, 50, 52, 53, 54, 55, 57
Emden (1), 118, 179
Emden (2), 211
Engels see *Desna*
Enkvist, Capt., 151
Enos, 53
Entente Cordiale, 118, 121
Enver Pasha, 174
Epirus, 86
Erickson, J., 202
Ermak, 127
Essen, Adm., 129, 133, 142, 163, 168
Euboea, 49
Europa, 51
Eurus, 30
Evstafi (1), 50
Evstafi (2), 176
Ezekiel, 94

Fedotov-White, D., 188, 206, 207
Félicité, 43
Ferdinand VII of Spain, 79
Finland, Gulf of, 17, 23, 38, 68, 70, 71, 165, 168, 171, 172, 173, 187, 193, 201, 209, 210, 211, 222, 221, 222, 226
Fisher, Ad. Lord, 40, 167
Fitzroy, Lt. G. W. H., 94
Fiume, 90
Flanders, 185
Foggia, 82
Folkershamn, Rear-Ad., 140, 145, 149
Forester, C. S., 77
Fortescue, Sir John, 83
Fox, Charles James, 63
Franco, General, 17, 204
Franco-Prussian War, 15, 109, 110
Frankfurt on the Oder, 40
Frederick the Great of Prussia, 39, 40, 41
Frederick of Sweden, 39
Frederikshamn, 69, 70

French Revolution, 14, 63, 72, 73, 83
Friedrich Carl, 167
Fuji, 147, 149, 151

Gadd, Capt., 182
Gagara, 196
Gagern, Comdr., 51
Galatz, 62, 112
Galicia, 166, 176
Gallipoli, 53, 86, 102, 176
Gangut, Battle of, 23, 25, 32
Gangut (1), 94, 95
Gangut (2) (later *Oktiabrskaia Revolutia*), 160,
    161, 202, 203, 209, 211, 221
Garnier, M., 104
Gavryil, 195
General Admiral, 109
General Admiral Apraxin, 152, 153
General Alexiev see *Imperator Alexander III*
General Kornilov, 196
Genitchesk, 35, 36
Genoa, 95
George I of England, 25, 26
George III of England, 76
Georgi Pobiedonosetz, 158, 196
Gibraltar, Straits of, 223
Giliak, 141
Giliarovsky, Cmdr., 157
Gineysse, M., 104
Gnievni, 190, 196
Goeben, 16, 174, 175, 176, 177, 178, 191, 193
Golden Hill, 128
Golovin, Adm., 38
Good Hope, Cape of, 140, 223
Gorschkov, Adm., 11
Gothenberg, 66, 76
Gotland, 77, 168, 169, 171
Grajdanin see *Tsarevitch*
Gravelines, 52
Great Fish Bay, 141
Great Northern War, 14, 20, 25, 28, 31, 32
Greig, Commodore S., 51, 64, 65
Greig, Cmdr., 88
Grenfell, H. G., 164
Grom, 186
Gromoboi, 137, 163
Grosse Haff, 40
Grosser Kurfürst, 185
Guernsey, 74
Guichen, 43

Habenicht, Gp. Capt., 165
Hadji Bey, 61, 62
Haifa, 55, 233
Hamburg-Amerika Line, 141, 143
Hamilton, Lt., 165, 166

Hangö Head, 23, 24, 38, 67, 189, 210
Hannibal, 51
Hannibal, Gen., 130
Hanover, 76
Hansestadt Danzig, 210
Hassan Pasha, 46, 50, 54, 60, 61
Hatsuse, 132
Havana, Siege of, 43
Hecla, 104
Heinrich, Gross Ad. Prinz, of Prussia, 163
Heligoland, 76
Hellville, 142
Helsingfors, 23, 38, 69, 103, 104, 181, 182,
    183, 187, 188, 189, 193
Heyden, Ad., 93, 94, 95, 97
Hill, 203-metre, 141
Hindenburg, F. M. von, 22
Hitachi Maru, 138
Hitler, Adolf, 22, 203, 204, 213, 223, 238
Hobart-Hampden, Hon. A. C. (Hobart
    Pasha), 111
Hogland, Bay of, 64, 65, 173, 222
Hokkaido, 137, 138
Holstein, Duchy of, 20
Hondo, 138
Hood, 138
Horton, Capt., 169
Hoste, Capt. W., 90
Hough, Richard, 154, 157
Howard of Effingham, Lord, 45
Howe, Ad. Lord, 43
Huan, Lt. Claude, 212
Huascar, 115
Humber, River, 144
Hyde Parker, Ad., 75
Hydra, Island, 48

Ibrahim Pasha, 93, 97
Idjilalich, 113
Idzumo, 146, 148, 149, 151
Ikazuchi, 123
Illyin, Cmdr., 51
Ilmen, Lake, 225
Imperator Alexander III (later *Volya*, later
    General Alexiev), 149, 150, 183, 189,
    190, 191, 192, 195, 196
Imperator Nikolas I, 152
Imperator Pavel I (later *Respublika*), 162,
    181, 182, 183
Imperatritza Ekaterina II (later *Svobodnaya
    Rossia*), 177, 183, 189, 190, 192
Imperatritza Maria (1), 177
Imperatritza Maria (2), 177, 178, 193
Implacable, 77
Inazuma, 123
Indian Ocean, 118, 125, 144

246

Index

Infante, 43
Ingolstadt, 215
Ingria, 28
Intikbah, 115
Ioann Zlatoust, 176
Ionian Islands, 81, 83, 84, 86
Iran, 225
Irben Strait, 170
Ischia, 82
Ismail, 62
Ismail, 160
Israel, 233
Istanbul, see Constantinople, 233
Istomin, Cmdr., 94, 103

Jacobs, Robert, 52
Jane, Fred, 19, 27, 42, 68, 108, 116
Japan, Sea of, 133, 134, 137, 138, 143, 145, 147
Jarki, 192, 196
Jassy, 36
Jassy, Treaty of, 63
Jemtchug, 151, 179
Jena, 76, 86
Jenkins' Ear, War of, 37
Jersey, 74
Jervis Bay, 214
Jivoi, 192
Jutland, Battle of, 138, 154, 161, 171, 206

K 21, 224
Kagul see *Otchakov*
Kaliakria, Cape, 63
Kamchatka, 105
Kamimura, Ad., 133, 134, 137, 148, 151
Kamranh Bay, 144
Kapitan 2R Isilmetiev, 188
Kapitan 2R Kingsbergen (later *Almirarnte Villar*, *Wambola*, *Spartak*, and *Mikula Maklay*), 196
Kapitan Saken, 196
Karelia, 223
Karin, Vice-Ad., 168, 172
Karlskrona, 25, 66, 77, 68
Kasagi, 130, 150
Kassar Bay, 186
Kasuga, 132, 147, 149
Kasumi, 123
Kathen, Gen. von, 185
Katkov, Mr. G., 198
Kattegat, 67, 79
Kazarski, Cmdr., 96
Kerensky, A., 184, 185, 186
Kertch, Straits of, 56, 62
Kertch, 192
Khabri, 186

Kharkov, 216, 218
Kherson, 58
Khruschchev, Nikita, 13, 229, 238
Kiel Canal, 119, 223
Kilia, 114
Kinburn, 35, 36, 56, 57, 58, 62, 105
Kinburn, 160, 205
Kioge Bay, 40
Kirov, 203, 209, 210, 211
Klado, Capt., 143
Kniaz Potemkin Tavricheski (later *Panteleimon* later *Boretz za Svobodu*), 16, 156, 157, 158, 159, 174, 176, 183
Kniaz Suvarov, 141, 162
Kolberg, 40, 41
Kolchak, Ad., 129, 163, 171, 172, 178, 183, 189, 199
Köln, 211
Komintern see *Pamiat Merkuria*
Konia, 97
König, 186
Königsberg, 40
Konstruktor see *Sibirski-Strelok*
Korietz, 124
Kornilov, Admiral, 94, 102, 103, 184
Koryu Maru, 130
Koslanianov, Ad., 68
Kotlin Island, 21, 199
Krab, 161
Krasnaya Gorka, 195, 198
Krasnaya Ukraina, 205
Kreiger, Vice-Ad., 158
Kretchet, 182, 188
Krithia, 176
Kronprinz, 186
Krupp, 133
Kruse, Ad., 70
Kuchuk Kanardji, Treaty of, 56
Kuivaast Roads, 186
Kunersdorf, 40
Kuriles, 225
Kurino, Minister, 122
Kurische Haff, 40
Kutalia, 97
Kuznetzov, Ad., 204, 229
Kymmere, River, 39
Kynda, 230

L 55, 194
Lacy, Gen., 34, 35, 36, 38
Ladoga, Lake, 21, 212, 224
Lagskär, 189
Laioyang, Battle of, 139
Lansdou, 26
La Perouse Straits, 137, 142, 145
Lapland, 223

Index

Latvia, 193
Lave, 104, 105
Lawrence, Cmdr. N., 170
Lazarev, Ad. Michael Petrovitch, 94, 97, 100
Leander, 81
Lebanon, 97
Lefort, Ad., 32
Leghorn (Livorno), 45
Leipzig, 211
Lemland, 38
Lemnos, 53
Lena, 138
Lenin, 11, 33, 191, 200
Leningrad (also see Petrograd, St. Petersburg), 12, 17, 21, 152, 209, 210, 212, 221, 224
Leningrad, 203
Lesina (Hvar), 84, 85
Lesna, 58
Leszczinski, Stanislaus, Duke of Lorraine, 37, 42
Levant, 57
Levetzova, 48
Libau, 165, 167, 185, 212, 222
Lichen, Capt., 153
Liddell Hart, Capt. B. H., 177
Lieutenant Burakov, 165
Ligurian coast, 82
Likhavchev, Cmdr., 107
Lillje, 24
Lilljehorn, Ad., 68
Liman, of the Dnieper, 57, 58, 59, 60
Lisanevitch, Lt. P., 188
Lisbon, 44
Lissa (Vis), 84
Lithuania, 193
Livonia, 28
Livorno see Leghorn, 203
Lloyd, Christopher, 65
Lombard, Lt., 58
London, Treaty of, 93
Lorraine, Duchy of, 37
Louis, Rear-Ad. Sir T., 82, 86
Louisiana, 109
Lübeck, 170
Lucas, C., V.C., 104
Lutfi Djelil, 112
Lützow (later *Tallin*), 205, 209, 221

MacArthur, Gen., 123
Mackensen, Gen., 178
Mackenzie, Cmdr., 51
Madagascar, 31, 140, 141, 142, 144, 156
Madras, 118
Magdeburg, 165, 166, 172

Magnificent, 43
Mahmud, Sultan, 91, 96
Mahomet Ali, 91, 93, 94, 97
Makarov, Ad. Stephen Ossipovitch, 73, 113, 114, 115, 116, 126, 127, 128, 129, 130, 131, 132, 133, 163, 208, 227, 229
Malinovsky, Marshal., 11
Malta, 75, 82, 83, 95
Manchukuo, 155
Manchuria, 120, 121, 125, 153, 155
Manila, 151
Marat see *Petropavlovsk*
Marlborough, Duke of, 25
Martin, Capt. T. B., 77
Masséna, 73
Matapan, Cape, 45, 49
Matassevitch, Gen., 133
Matsushima, 151, 153
Matushenko, Seaman, 159
Maxim Gorki, 209, 211
Maximov, Adm., 182, 184
Mediterranean, 23, 30, 41, 42, 43, 44, 45, 52, 55, 56, 61, 63, 65, 75, 81–89, 90, 96, 179, 190, 202, 204, 205, 213, 214, 228
Mediterranean Fleet, 43, 91, 191, 233
Meister, Juerg, 210, 211, 225
Memel, 40, 169
Mentschikov, Prince, 102
Merkurii, 67, 96
Messina, Straits of, 82, 84
Messudieh, 111
Mexico, 108
Miaoulis, Andreas, 97
Midia, 96
Mikasa, 123, 147, 148
Mikula Maklay see *Kapitan 2R Kingsbergen*
Milwaukee (later *Murmansk*), 214
Minorca, 44
Mishukov, Admiral, 38
Missolonghi, 92
Missouri, 123
Mistislav, 73
Mistra, 45
Mitchell, Admiral, 73
Modon, 49
Moldavia, 86, 97, 99
Moltke, 170, 185
Monasterev, 89
Montenegro, 84, 90, 91, 173
Moon Island, 185, 186
Moon Sound, 170, 171, 172, 186, 222
Moore, Sir John, 76, 77, 78
Mordvinov, Ad., 58, 61
Morea, 45, 49, 92
Moskva, River, 225

Moskva, 216
Muklevitch, Chief Commissar, 206, 222
Müller, Capt. von., 118
Münnich, General, 34, 36
Murmansk, 175, 213, 215
Murmansk see *Milwaukee*
Mussolini, Benito, 204, 205
Mustapha, Sultan of Turkey, 87

N 267, 157
Nadezhda, 45, 46
Nakhimov, Vice-Ad. Paul, 94, 100, 101, 102, 103
Napier, Sir Charles, 103
Naples, 81, 82, 84
Napoleon, Emperor, 14, 15, 22, 72–80, 81–89, 90, 91, 102, 109
Napoleon III, 104
Narcross, Buccaneer, 31
Narva, 23, 193, 222
Narva, Battle of, 22
Narvik, 223
Nassau-Siegen, Gen., 59, 60, 61, 68, 69, 71
N.A.T.O., 18, 19, 230, 231, 232, 234, 235, 236, 237, 238
Nauplia, 46, 47
Nauplia, Gulf of, 46, 47
Navarino, 45, 46, 47, 48, 49, 93
Navarino, Battle of, 15, 90–97, 100, 154
Navarin (1), 114, 115, 152
Navarin (2), 160, 161
Ne Tron Menya, 46, 47, 51, 54
Nebogatov, Rear-Ad., 143, 144, 145, 150, 152, 153
Nebolsin, Ad., 182
Nelson, Ad. Lord, 15, 62, 65, 75, 76, 82, 84, 86, 87
Nepenin, Ad., 165, 172, 181, 182
Neva, River, 12, 13, 16, 21, 181, 184, 221, 222
Nevelskoi, Capt. A., 97
New Orleans, Battle of, 63
New York, 108
Nicholas I, Tsar, 15, 89, 95, 96
Nicholas II, Tsar, 131, 146, 153, 156, 159, 177, 180, 181, 183, 197
Nicolaiev, 52, 159, 189, 205
Nicolson, Capt. Sir F., 105
Nikopol, 113
Nile, 55
Nile, Battle of, 81
Nisshin, 147, 149
Nordenfelt, Engineer, 119
Nore, The, 72
Norris, Ad. Sir J., 26, 27, 28
North Cape, 213, 223
North Pole, 127, 214

North Sea, 14, 27, 72, 73, 79, 146, 167, 168, 171, 172, 209, 215
Nossi Bé, 141
Novik (1), 128, 129, 130, 137, 142
Novik (2), 161, 169, 170, 171
Novorossisk, 174, 178, 190, 191, 192, 216, 217, 218
Nürnberg, 211
Nyenschantz, 21
Nystadt, 25
Nystadt, Treaty of, 28

Oboro, 123
Odensholm, 165
Odessa, 18, 61, 101, 114, 157, 158, 174, 195, 216
Okhotnik, 185
Oksford 26,
Oktiabrskaia Revoltia see *Gangut*
Oland, island, 210
Old Bahamas Passage, 43
Oleg, 151, 163, 167, 169, 194
Oranienbaum, 64, 198, 221
Ordzhonikidze, 13, 229
Orel, 146, 152
Orel, 195
Orkneys, 130
Orlan, 196
Orlov, Count, 45, 46, 47, 48, 49, 50, 53, 54, 55, 57, 61, 91
Osel, 170, 185, 186, 222
Osliabia, 145, 149
Oslofiord, 67
Osmanieh, 115
Ostend, 128
Otchakov, 32, 35, 36, 57, 58, 59, 60, 61, 71
Otchakov (later *Kagul*, later *General Kornilov*), 159, 196

Pacific Fleet, 15, 18, 105, 156, 163, 179, 213, 225, 226
    First Pacific Squadron, 122, 125, 126, 138, 139, 141, 142, 147
    Second Pacific Squadron, 125, 139, 143, 144, 147, 153, 154, 156
    Third Pacific Squadron, 143, 147, 153, 154
Paderewski, President of Poland, 193
Pahlen, Count, 76
Pakenham, Capt. W., 135
Palermo, 82
Palestine, 97
Pallada (1), 105, 124, 138, 141, 142
Pallada (2), 163, 167
Pamiat Azova (1), 95
Pamiat Azova (2) (later *Dvina*), 159, 183, 194

Index

Pamiat Merkuria (later Komintern), 193, 203
Panama Canal, 214, 223
Panteleimon see Kniaz Potemkin Tavricheski
Paris, 103
Paris, Treaty of, 106, 110
Pariskaia Kommuna see Sevastopol
Paros, 49, 54
Patras, 93
Paul I, Tsar, 14, 15, 72, 73, 74, 75, 83
Paul Jones, John, 59, 60, 61
Pearl Harbour, 123, 125, 147
Peipus, Lake, 21
Peking, 238
Pelari, 53, 54
Penang, 118, 179
Perekop, 36
Peresviet (later Sagami), 129, 131, 136, 141, 142, 179
Persian Gulf, 224
Peter I (the Great), Tsar, 13, 14, 20, 21, 22, 24, 25, 26, 27, 28, 29, 30, 32, 33, 34, 37, 38, 42, 51
Peter II, Tsar, 37
Peter III, Tsar, 41
Petr Kochka, 139
Petr Veliki, 109
Petrograd (see also St. Petersburg, Leningrad), 168, 172, 175, 181, 184, 186, 194, 198, 199
Petropavlovsk, 105
Petropavlovsk (1), 128, 129, 130, 131, 132
Petropavlovsk (2) (later Marat), 160, 171, 184, 193, 194, 197, 198, 199, 201, 203, 209, 211, 221
Philosoph, M., 44
Pilki, 196
Pinnes, Cape, 88
Pitarevsky, Lt., 115
Pitt, the Younger, William, 57, 63
Plevna, 112
Pobieda, 129, 131, 132, 141, 142
Pocock, Ad., 43
Pole, Sir Charles, 76
Polish Succession, War of, 37
Poltava, 22, 25, 33
Poltava (1) (later Tango, later Tchesma), 129, 130, 141, 142, 179
Poltava (2), 160, 179
Pommern, 169
Poniatowski, Stanislaus, 42
Popov, Ad., 110
Popovka, 110
Poros, 97
Port Arthur, 117-34, 135-45, 147, 152, 155, 163, 175, 179, 209
Port Dickson, 214

Port Mahon, 44
Port Said, 179
Porto Rafti, 49
Portsmouth, 13, 44
Portsmouth, Treaty of, 155
Pospechni, 192
Potemkin, 59, 61
Potemkin see Kniaz Potemkin Tavricheski
Poti, 175, 217, 218
Povalishin, Ad., 67
Prahovo, 220, 221
Pressburg, Treaty of, 84
Preussen, 210
Price, Rear-Ad. D., 105
Prins Gustaf, 64
Prinz Adalbert, 169, 170
Prinz Eugen, 205, 213
Procida, 82
Profintern see Svietlana
Putiatin, Rear-Ad., 105
Putoshkin, Rear-Ad., 82, 88
Putrid Sea, 32, 35

Quebec, 43

Rafail (later Avni-Illah), 87, 88, 96, 99
Ragusa (Dubrovnik), 84, 85
Rapallo, 200
Raskolnikov, Naval Officer, 187, 197
Rasputin, 180
Rasvozov, Rear-Ad., 184, 187
Real Mustapha, 50
Rechitelni, 128, 137
Respublika (see Imperator Pavel I)
Retvisan (1), 73
Retvisan (2), 124, 128, 129, 136, 141, 142
Reval (Tallin), 22, 23, 26, 27, 69, 70, 76, 168, 183, 193, 210
Rheinland, 189
Richmond, 43
Riga, 22, 28, 168, 169, 222
Riga, Gulf of, 168, 170, 171, 172, 173, 185, 186
Riou, Edward, 65
Ritchmond, 26
Rochensalm, 68
Rodney, Ad., 43
Rodzianko, President of Duma, 181
Rögersvik, 77
Rome, 16, 82
Roon, 169
Rossia, 137, 163
Rostislav (1), 51, 64
Rostislav, 176
Rostov, 32
Royal Sovereign (late Archangelsk), 214

Index

Rozhdestvo Christovo, 62
Rozhestvensky, Vice-Ad., 113, 125, 137, 139, 140, 141, 142, 143, 144, 145, 147, 148, 150, 153, 154, 156, 163
Ruffo, Cardinal, 82
Rügen, 76, 167
Rurik (1), 119, 120, 137, 138
Rurik (2), 162, 167, 168, 169, 173, 194
Ruschuk, 220
Russian Revolution, 16, 151, 153, 155, 162, 172, 180–96, 197, 199, 201, 203, 226
Russo-Japanese War, 15, 16, 18, 117–34, 135–45, 156, 160, 161, 162, 163, 164, 176, 178
Russo-Swedish Wars:
1699–1721, 20–31, 33, 34
1739–43, 38–39
Russo-Turkish wars:
1736–9, 34–36
1768–74, 42–56
1787–91, 62–63, 81
1806–7, 86–88
1828–9, 95–97
1877–78, 107–16, 125

Sablin, Vice-Ad., N. P., 189, 190, 191, 192
Sagami see *Peresviet*
Said Ali, 87
Said Bey, 62
Saigon, 137
Saint Cast, 43
Saint Malo, 43
St. Pavel, 54
Saint Petersburg (see also Petrograd, Leningrad), 15, 21, 22, 38, 39, 61, 64, 66, 69, 70, 76, 79, 84, 107, 117, 121, 122, 125, 126, 129, 142, 164, 168, 177
Sainte Marie, 141
Saken, Capt., 59
Sakhalin, 137, 155, 200
Salonika, 49, 86
Samothrace, 87
Sampson, Ad., 128
San Francisco, 105, 108, 138
Santa Maura, 81
Santiago, 70, 128
Sarajevo, 174
Saratov, 46, 47
Sardinia, 72, 101
Sarikamish, 176
Saritch, Cape, 175
Sasebo, 122, 123
Sassnitz, 170
Saukko, 211
Saumerez, Sir J., 76, 78, 79
Saunders, Adm., 43

Sazanami, 123, 128
Scapa Flow, 130
Scharnhorst, 213
Scheer, Ad., 171
Schlesien, 96, 210
Schleswig-Holstein, 210
Schmidt, Lt., 159
Schmidt, Vice-Ad. Erhardt, 170, 185
Sebastiani, M., 86
Seifez, 112, 113
Selim III, Sultan, 61, 87
Semenov, Cmdr. Vladimir, 127, 130, 146
Seniavin, Vice-Ad. Alexis, 55, 56, 61, 84, 85, 86, 87, 88, 89, 90, 93
Serbia, 173
Serditi, 129
Serpent Island, 60
Seskari, 65
Sevastopol, 15, 18, 56, 59, 62, 101, 102, 103, 105, 107, 157, 159, 174, 178, 183, 189, 190, 192, 193, 195, 215, 216, 217, 218
Sevastopol (1), 129, 133, 136, 142, 163
Sevastopol (2) (later *Pariskaia Kommuna*), 160, 197, 198, 199, 202, 203, 215, 216, 218
Seven Years' War, 39, 43
Seydlitz, 205
Shah, 115
Shamyl, rebel leader, 101
Shanghai, 153, 137
Shantung, Battle of, 135
Shikishima, 147, 149
Shimonoseki, 120
Shinano Maru, 146, 147
Shinonome, 123, 218
Shirakumo, 123
Siberia, 72, 97, 122, 126, 226, 204, 214, 219, 199
Sibirski-Strelok (later *Konstruktor*), 225
Sibiryakov, 214
Silistria, 100
Singapore, 144, 123, 223
Sinob, 158
Sinope, 15, 98, 99
Sinope, Battle of, 98, 99, 100, 104, 177
Sinope, 114, 115
Sirène, 94
Sissoi Veliki, 152
Sitka, 105
Sivash, 35
Sivutch, 170
Skagerrak, 76, 79
Shaw, 44
Skoryi, 80, 88
Skrydlov, Vice-Ad., 132

251

Index

Slade, Capt. Adolphus, 99, 111
Slava, 162, 170, 173, 181, 185, 186
Smeeton, Vice-Ad., 234
Snappup, 67
Sobrasitelni, 218
Sokolovsky, Marshal, V. D., 235, 236
Someri Island, 211
Souchon, Ad., 174
Spanish-American War, 128
Spanish Armada, 45, 52
Spanish Civil War, 17, 204
Spanish Succession, War of, 25, 29
Sparre, Ad., 28
Spartak see *Kapitan 2R Kingsbergen*
Spee, Ad. Graf von, 179
Sphaktena, 93
Spindler, Ad., 202
Spiridov, Ad., 43, 44, 45, 46, 47, 48, 50, 57
Spithead, 44, 72, 228
Stalin, 12, 13, 17, 19, 195, 199, 203, 204, 205, 209, 226, 228
Stalingrad (formerly Tsaritzin, now Volgograd), 191, 217
Stark, Vice-Ad., 122, 128
Stchaslivi, 196
Stchasny, Rear-Ad., 187, 188, 189
Stchelinski, Capt., 115
Steevens, G. W., 108
Stereguchi, 128
Stockholm, 23, 26, 27, 69, 71, 77
Stockholm, 24, 38
Stoiki, 210
Stolp Bank, 167
Straford, 26
Stralsund, 76
Strashni, 170
Stremitelny, 158, 159
Stroiny, 185
Suez Canal, 140
Sukkum Kale, 114
Sulina, 114, 115
Suvarov, Gen., 58, 59, 73, 81
Suvarov, 148, 149, 150, 151, 152
Suvla, 73
Sveaborg, 65, 66, 77, 104, 105
Sverdlov, 203, 228, 229
Sverskund, 69, 70, 71
Sviatoslav, 46, 47, 53, 54
Svietlana (later *Profintern*), 203
Svistova, 220
Svobodnaya Rossia see *Imperatritza Ekaterina II*
Sylvia Basin, 147

Taganrog, 32, 33, 55, 56
Tagus, River, 88

Tahir Pasha, 93
Taif, 99
Takachiho, 123
Takasago, 130
Talbot, 94
Tallin see *Lützow*
Tangier, 140, 141
Tango see *Poltava*
Tannenberg, 210
Tannenberg, 166
Tartary, Gulf of, 97
Tashkent, 203, 216
Tchervonaia Ukraina see *Admiral Nakhimov*
Tchesma, Battle of, 60
Tchesma Bay, 50, 52, 55
Tchesma (1), 114, 115
Tchesma (2) see *Poltava*
Tchestakov, Lt., 112
Tchitchagov, C. in C., 65, 67, 68, 70
Tchitchagov (jun.), 74
Tendra, 62
Tenedos, 86, 87
Tereschenko, historian, 89
Theodosia, 159, 174, 218
Thetis, 170
Thrace, 96
Tiger, 101
Tikmeniev, Capt., 192
Tilsit, 88
Tilsit, Treaty of, 76
Tirpitz, 211, 213, 223, 224, 228
Tito, Marshal, 91
Tobago, 30
Tobruk, 92, 216
Todleben, Fort, 200
Togo, Vice-Ad. H., 122, 123, 125, 129, 130, 132, 134, 35, 136, 145, 147, 148, 149, 150, 151, 152
Tokiwa, 130, 148, 149
Tonnante, 104, 105
Torgau, 40
Torpedoist, 115
Toulon, 82
Trafalgar, Battle of, 62, 84, 86, 87, 88
Trana, 24
Trans-Siberian Railway, 125, 139, 171, 175
Trebizond, 88, 178
Trelleborg, 170
Trent, 108
Trevenen, James, 59, 65
Tri Sviatitelia, 158, 176
Trieste, 85, 90
Tripoli, 63
Triumph, 12, 13
Trotsky, 191, 197, 200, 206
Tsarevitch (1), 112

252

Tsarevitch (2) (later *Grajdanin*), 124, 129, 136, 162, 173, 181, 183, 186
Tsingtao, 120, 136, 137
Tsugaru Strait, 138, 145
Tsushima, 107, 137, 146, 151, 154
Tsushima, 137
Tsushima, Battle of, 146–55, 156, 160, 162, 175
Tsushima, Straits of, 144, 146, 147
Tuapse, 217
Tukhachevsky, Marshal, 199, 207
Tulcea, 114
Tulen, 196
Tunis, 62
Tverdyi, 88

U 26, 167
Ukhtomsky, Rear Ad. Prince, 131, 132, 136
Ukraine, 57, 189, 190, 195, 212
Ulm, 70
Umea, 78
Undine, 170
United Nations, 233
Unkiar Silessi, Treaty of, 97
Upottery, 111
Ushakov, Vice-Ad., 59, 61, 62, 75, 81, 83
Usugomo, 123, 128
Utfall, Ad., 38
Utka, 196

V 99, 170
V 100, 170, 172
Vakulinchuk, Seaman, 157
Vancouver, 105
Variag, 124, 142, 179
Varna, 59, 62, 63, 102
Veliki Kniaz Constantine, 113, 114, 115
Venerable, 72
Venice, 81
Venus, 67
Vepr (later *Bartrak*), 202
Verden, 26
Verderevsky, Rear-Ad., 184
Verestchagin, 131
Vermicular, 59
Versailles, Treaty of, 201
Verulam, 194
Vesta, 116
Viborg (Viipuri), 22, 28, 70
Viborg, Battle of, 70
Victory, 76 ,78, 79
Vienna, 225
Vietminh, 232
Viktoria, 26
Viktorov, Ad., 204

Vildmanstrand, 38
Vilkitzy Strait, 214
Villeneuve, Vice-Ad., 84
Viren, Rear-Ad., 139
Visby, 77
Vitgeft, Rear-Ad., 132, 133, 136
Vitiaz, 127
Vittoria, 194
Vittorio Veneto, 205
Vladimir, 102, 113
Vladimir Monomakh, 152
Vladislav, 64
Vladivostock, 105, 107, 121, 132, 133, 134, 135–45, 146–55, 163, 179, 215
Vlieter, 73
Voinovitch, Ad., 60, 61, 62
Volga, River, 21, 34, 201, 217, 225
Volya see *Imperator Alexander III*
Voronezh, 21, 32, 33
Vsevelod, 77

Waliszewski, 30
Wallachia, 86, 97, 99
Wambola see *Kapitan 2R Kingsbergen*
Warrior, 162
Warsaw, 195, 196, 199
Washington, Treaty of, 16, 201
Wattrang, Ad., 23, 24
Weichs, Field Marshal von, 221
Werden, Charles van, 21
West Indies, 30, 31, 43
White Sea Fleet, 38, 39, 43, 66, 67, 80, 179
William V of Holland, 73
Wilson, H. W., 151
Winchelsea, 55
Wittelsbach, 166
Wolfe, Gen., 43
Wrangel, Baron, 195, 196, 199, 200, 202

Xenia, 112

Yakumo, 148, 150
Yalta, 218
Yamato, 162
Yarmouth, 74
Yashima, 132
Yatsushiro, Capt., 148
Yellow Sea, 124
Yellow Sea, Battle of, 135
Yenissei, 126
Yessen, Ad., 132, 138
York, Duke of, 73
Yoshino, 130, 132
Ypsilanti, Prince Alexander, 91
Yudenitch, Gen., 194, 195
Yunnan, 120

253

Zabiaka, 171
Zante, 81
Zatzarennyi, Lt., 114, 115
Zavetny, 190
Zeebrugge, 128
Zerel, 186

Zieb, Rear-Ad., 219, 220, 221
Zonguldak, 175, 176
Zorki, 196
Zurich, 73, 74
Zvonki, 196

DATE DUE